The
Kundalini
Phenomenon

The Kundalini Phenomenon

The Need for Insight and Spiritual Authenticity

Kate Thomas

NEW MEDIA BOOKS

2000

First published in Great Britain by
New Media Books in 2000

New Media Books

For all enquiries please e-mail
newmediabooks@hotmail.com

ISBN 0 9526881 1 5

Printed in Great Britain by
Redwood Books, Trowbridge, Wiltshire

Cover image: 19th century depiction of Shakti

Contents

Content

Preface

The phenomenon of *kundalini* was first introduced to a readership in the West by the Tantric scholar Sir John Woodroffe
(d. 1936), a British official and barrister who served in the Indian
court system as a judge. Writing under the name of Arthur Avalon,
Woodroffe produced in *The Serpent Power* an influential study of
Kundalini yoga, translating the texts of two Tantric treatises for
this purpose: the *Shat-Cakra-Nirupana* and the *Paduka-Pancaka*,
along with his own extensive introduction.

Woodroffe's book was first published in London in 1919, and
intended as a serious scholarly work, but was soon to arouse an
experimental interest amongst an enthusiastic general readership
of theosophists, esotericists, occultists, and would-be Western yogis.
Much later the book came under the scrutiny of the Swiss
psychologist Carl Gustav Jung, who linked the concepts of the
chakra system and the dramatic symptoms of *kundalini* with his
own psychoanalytic theory on what he termed the process of
individuation.

In 1932, Jung presented a seminar on Kundalini yoga for the
Psychological Club in Zurich, an event seen by his followers as
a milestone in the understanding of Eastern thought on human
psychology and the transformative power of inner states of consciousness. The seminar drew the attention of psychologists in
Europe and the USA, and interest in the subject of *kundalini*
from that time onwards has steadily increased, escalating rapidly
with the growth of the New Age movement and the search for
a readily available form of spiritual experience, and resulting in
a veritable plethora of questionable books on how to arouse the
kundalini force. Regrettably, for some experimenters there is also
the serious issue of disturbing psychological and physiological side-
effects that all-too-frequently arise as a consequence of the regu-

lar use of these recommended "arousal" practices. The symptoms, almost invariably severe, inevitably require treatment from an uncomprehending medical profession, and often culminate in hospitalization, thus further confusing the situation.

Although well known in the East by yogis and practitioners of various disciplines, the *kundalini* phenomenon is intrinsically still little understood, as soon becomes evident when any attempt is made to co-ordinate the widely differing accounts of *kundalini* experience in contemporary literature (including translated texts from antique archives and the records of contemporary yogis) with the findings of recent research. These findings, as yet, do not go far enough, for they ignore the significant distinguishing factors of *kundalini* experience clearly discernible in the very few published autobiographical records of Westerners, such as, for example, that of Irina Tweedie (d. 1999) whose highly detailed but seriously misleading *Daughter of Fire* (1986) incorporates a powerful (albeit partial) *kundalini* experience and much else of a purportedly mystical nature, including the "heart" awakening spoken of by Sufis and Christian contemplatives. Another such record, with marked similarities of experience yet at the same time major methodological differences and effects (the most apparent divergence being in the *kundalini* experience itself), is my own, recorded in full, with all the events and experiences that preceded it, in the three volumes of my autobiography, namely *Signals from Eternity* (1984), *Beloved Executioner* (1986), and *The Destiny Challenge* (1992), and detailing a process which took place in its entirety in the West – in Cambridge, England, the place of my birth. [Further material on the actual *kundalini* experience, along with an extensive commentary, will be found in *Kundalini and Conscious Evolution* (forthcoming).]

These latter records cast much light on *kundalini* as a specific organic evolutionary process, not to be compared with the mechanistic "break-in" into the human energy system open to anyone who cares to practise certain techniques. More usefully, in my own case, the account is not handicapped by cultural attitudes appropriate to an earlier century and a now outmoded way of life. These are present-day experiences, presented in modern English by someone reared in the West and stable in temperament – unlike the psychotics, psychic dabblers, or sensationalists so often favoured by researchers. *Kundalini* is worthy of further research, along lines rather different to those used to date, not least to rectify misinformation and prevent more tragic mishaps, but also to validate the existence of this volatile energy, and to accurately discern its true significance for the human race.

Kundalini is the Sanskrit name given to the evolutionary energy said to lie dormant in the area of the base of the spine in all human beings. When "awakened," at some crucial point in the life of an adequately prepared individual, it proves to be the link between the mundane physical consciousness of the person concerned and a higher range of consciousness encompassing other dimensions. This consciousness eventually expands to a totality of knowledge and experience equal to that of the greatest saints of recorded history, and climaxes with the ultimate evolutionary consummation, *conscious* Union with God, or one's Source.

The early stages of this process often bestow certain abilities generally regarded as "miraculous," such as an interior perception of things not normally cognizant, and the power to heal. Because of these (and other more sensational) attributes, and the desire to possess them by power seekers and pseudo-teachers of all races, it was long ago discovered that *kundalini* could be forced into premature awakening by untoward means (e.g., Tantric sexual practices), an activity leaving its negative mark on many cultures, particularly those of India and Tibet, the disastrous effects of which are increasingly operative in our present-day society. A more precise knowledge is now needed to make possible the counter-action of these effects, and also to enable recognition of the effects themselves.

An indication of some aspects of the foregoing is given by Dr. Stanislav Grof in *Realms of the Human Unconscious: Observations from LSD Research* (1979) in which Grof notes that the experiences of many transpersonal LSD sessions bear "striking resemblance" to phenomena recorded in various schools of Kundalini yoga, where they are acknowledged as signs of *kundalini* activation and of the opening of individual *chakras* (p. 202). These LSD induced experiences can range from obvious somatic symptoms of *kundalini* to transpersonal experiences equally attributable to this energy and described by Grof as *Consciousness of the Universal Mind*, and *The Supracosmic and Metacosmic Void*, which allegedly parallel the most profound and complex mystical experiences known to man. Grof further comments that the differing techniques used in Kundalini yoga and LSD psychotherapy similarly induce "instant and enormous" releases of energy, "profound and dramatic experiences," and "impressive results in a relatively short time" (p. 203). At the same time he concedes that these techniques involve risk and can prove dangerous to the participant if not "practiced under careful supervision and responsible guidance." The above observations, without exception, equally apply to holotropic breathwork, currently promoted by Grof as an alternative to the now-banned LSD experimentation.

In view of the extreme and sometimes psychologically unbalancing effects of all such activations, this leaves the question of what comprises responsible guidance, and what calibre of knowledge is required to conduct these practices? Further, should these activations in fact be conducted at all, by whatever means, in whatever circumstances, for whatever purposes? Last, but not least, what is their long-term effect on individual growth and human evolution?

With these questions in mind I have researched a wide variety of books on *kundalini*, and have utilized a selection by persons considered authorities on this subject for critical review. This treatment, together with autobiographical material containing firsthand accounts of this process, will hopefully enable serious researchers to approach this controversial subject in a more comprehensive manner than in the past.

Kate Thomas

October 1999

Introduction

In late August of 1995 in England, UK, a conference entitled "Beyond the Brain: New Avenues in Consciousness Research" was held in the world-famous precincts of St. John's College, Cambridge. This conference was hosted conjointly by the Scientific and Medical Network of Great Britain, and the Institute of Noetic Sciences, USA, along with two smaller organizations. Among the many eminent speakers in the field of mind and consciousness research were such names as Dr. Stanislav Grof, Professor Willis Harman, Professor Ervin Laszlo (advisor to the Director-General of UNESCO), Professor Charles Tart and Professor Brian Josephson, to mention but a few. The conference was acclaimed as an event of significance by the organizers, and highlighted the fact of a growing academic interest in the subject of altered states of consciousness (ASCs) and the possible evolutionary meaningfulness of such states. It signalled also an acceptance, hitherto withheld by mainstream science, that consciousness constitutes a valid field of enquiry – one which may eventually authenticate the premise of an organic developmental process at work within humankind – a process designed to extend man's consciousness beyond the limits of the physical world and into finer, more complex dimensions.

The many books authored by the various speakers at the conference contain the most recent research-based conclusions of scientists, physicists, transpersonal psychologists and others, on the matter of possible spiritual evolution for our species, and the means by which it can be achieved. A close reading of certain of these books will yield the interesting fact that it is widely accepted by researchers that transcendental experiences induced by psychotropic drugs such as mescaline, psilocybin, LSD, and empathogens, etc., are akin to the experiences described by mystics through the ages, an opinion consolidated by more recent experiments conducted with the use of hyperventilation. These latter experiments produce virtually identical syndromes to those experienced with the use of psychedelics, and are likewise acclaimed as indistinguishable from authentic mystical experience. Dr. Stanislav Grof, for instance, has stated that with a variant technique commercially promoted as Holotropic Breathwork™, it is now undeniably possible to gain "not only access to one's biological, psychological, social, racial, and spiritual history and the past, present, and future of the entire phenomenal world, but access to many other levels and domains of reality described by the great mystical traditions of the world."[1] Leaving aside the validity or otherwise of this statement, kinship of experience is certainly a plausible possibility in the instances of a number of obscure saints canonized by the Catholic Church, whose experiences were doubtless exacerbated by severe fasts and other forms of extreme austerities which artificially reduced the carbon dioxide levels within the blood, thus producing biochemical changes and affecting the cerebral mechanism in much the same way as hallucinogens and hyperventilation. This assumption falls down, however, when examining cases of a different order,[2] and is seriously open to question with regard to certain states recorded in the annals of traditional Sufism and Vedanta.[3]

It is in areas of differentiation such as these that this type of research strategy comes to grief. Too many deductions are made from a false premise – that the entire spectrum of spiritual experience formerly confined to authentic saints and mystics is now open to virtually everyone under suitable research conditions. The loss of the use of LSD for these purposes (such use is at present illegal, but is regrettably under consideration by health authorities in the UK and the USA for limited controlled research purposes) is compensated by the employment of a variety of other techniques, some equally powerful, and producing an ever widening range of results. What should carefully be considered, however, is whether these results are of any real deductive value in consciousness research, and if they bring us any closer to understanding the mechanics of a finer level of human development. Do these experiments in fact prove their point beyond all dispute?

An acknowledgement of this dilemma is found in the work of

Jenny Wade, who pinpoints the very mixed value of all techniques, religious and secular, in *Changes of Mind: A Holonomic Theory of the Evolution of Consciousness* (1996) – including "meditation; yoga; the martial arts and other forms of physical training; sensory deprivation or overloading through motion, sound, gazing, and the like; trance; ingestion of psychotropic drugs; and altered breathing, to name a few" (pp. 177–178).

Dr. Wade clearly recognizes the limitations imposed upon artificially induced ASCs by the presence of the mundane ego. She continues: "An outgrowth of all such techniques is the experiencing of nonordinary states of awareness. Since the ability to experience an altered state is available to virtually everyone operating at any level of consciousness, the significance attached to an ego-transcending motivation is of paramount importance in distinguishing the Transcendent stage from any others that include altered states, and from the altered states themselves. Not only is ego-transcendence the crucial stage delimiter, it also underscores the potential for the misuse or idealization of nonordinary states at earlier (egoic) stages. The desire for ego-transcendence drives some form of disciplined practice, of which altered states and personal benefit are only a by-product, not an end."

"Furthermore," avers Wade, "the emphasis on motivation presupposes qualitative differences in the altered states possible, depending on the practitioner's level of development manifest during mundane consciousness *regardless of the phenomenology of the altered state*" (p. 178).

The significance of this observation appears to have escaped the attention of most researchers, who persist in excluding the premise that there are two completely different processes at work here (within the mystic and within the research laboratory), both of which require further investigation and very much more precise information; moreover that these profound and major differences are being needlessly confused through an unnecessary ignorance on the part of researchers, certain of whom in recent years have declined to give even passing attention to important data on states of consciousness that arise as a *natural* effect of inner development. However well documented these states, they are ignored, perhaps because they cannot be replicated within the laboratory. Vital data is inherent within, and derived from, these states, and yields a consistent and overall grasp of an all-encompassing universal scheme which follows its own rules – a recognition of which would indisputably displace various theoretical assumptions and nullify certain avenues of popular experimentation, to say nothing of negating the entrepreneurial self-development industry as evidenced within the New Age movement.

Break-in techniques dependent on drugs or on Holotropic Breathwork™ (the technique of hyperventilation commercially expanded and utilized by Stanislav Grof),[4] may evoke the desired experiences, and sometimes a very wide variety of experiences, but they cannot by their nature evoke a lasting spiritual orientation in the experiencer, nor do they engender spiritual growth or an overall comprehension of what is experienced, as scores upon scores of drug-based and breathwork related experiments bear witness. It is already clear that the methods presently in use can *never* resolve the question of authentic mystical experience versus the counterfeit. Other factors are necessary, and ones that researchers, however competent, may not be in a position to provide.

This issue is further complicated by the fact that many researchers are themselves still grappling with spiritual concepts – such as the reality of an omniscient intelligence, and find it embarrassing to involve themselves with insights and assertions which radically contradict the accepted norm promoted by fellow researchers and scientists of repute, many of whom are atheists and agnostics. Those less conservative may opt to listen to the professional psychics and *avant-garde* "spiritual teachers" into whose field they have ventured, and tend to give credence to the more sensationalist individuals backed by so-called "Colleges" of Psychic Science and prestigious New Age Centres – or to those "channelling" in trance who, sincere though they may be, are as likely to produce erroneously based information as researchers themselves.

The sad fact is, that unless one has personally experienced a very wide range of other-dimensional states *without* an accompanying mental illness, and *without* the use of psychedelics or other intrusions into the psyche, one cannot assess with any degree of accuracy the functions of the higher reaches of the mind. It is also a fact that the majority of psychics, including "channels" or mediums, do not themselves experience such higher range states, and thus make incomplete assertions that are not incompatible with research findings and are therefore more readily acceptable to researchers. A further consideration is that they are similarly in the same business of "anyone can do it with a little training."

This attitude is increasingly complemented by New Age workshop leaders who teach that "self-development" is one of the simplest tasks in the world, necessitating only a few weekend courses and an introduction to an assortment of "break-in" techniques, plus the inevitable affirmations, visualizations, and meditations.

Other complications are presented by researchers with inadequate background knowledge who investigate the many instances in the West of *kundalini* and *chakra* experience, the former being the soaring, volatile energy assumed to reside at the base of the spine, and the latter, latent vortices of energy allegedly linked to the nervous system which, when fuelled by an awakened *kundalini*, whirl into activity and induce all manner of supersensory experience of a psychic, occult, or mystical nature. Also, in all too many cases, an accompanying disruptive effect on the everyday life and wellbeing of the subject concerned.

Interest in these phenomena has gained such exposure that chakras are currently listed in the Glossary of the Health Education Authority's publication, *HEA guide to Complementary Medicine and Therapies*,[5] and the subject has recently been broached in the tabloid press, when a two-page article on "*chakra*-balancing" was presented to the general public. (*Daily Mail*, Monday, June 23rd 1997, pp. 47–8). Unfortunately, the material from which the information in the article was derived is seriously suspect – a newly published book by "*chakra* expert" Anodea Judith, *Eastern Body, Western Mind*. When techniques for the activation or "balancing" of *chakras* (whatever this latter term implies) are encouraged for the use of mass readerships, this clearly makes the whole issue of sufficient consequence for sober evaluation (as distinct from the attempts to deliberately raise the *kundalini* force in volunteers – a situation existent in various Kundalini Research Institutes).

[*Chakras* unfortunately cannot be "balanced" in the casual fashion decreed by self-styled "experts," but can certainly be stirred into activity by undue attention in the form of recommended Eastern breathing exercises, yoga, and *chakra*-focused meditation.

People who experiment in these areas are playing with fire, as any *"chakra* expert" should know.]

Nevertheless, the product of this body of research, despite commercial distortions, has brought to the forefront of public awareness the existence of a range of experience attainable to man which is far superior to his own limited consciousness. It also validates to some degree the historical and mythological records which acknowledge the visionary abilities possessed by a few in each generation, abilities which were dismissed retrospectively in the age of scientific materialism as being either of suspect psychiatric origin, or wholly imaginary.

In this context, and in the efforts of individuals to reclaim these documented abilities, much interest surrounds the use of peyote and similar narcotics found in accounts of shamanistic practices, both past and present, particularly those of South American origin – with attention focused primarily upon the shaman's use of spells, the shamanic "journey," and the evocation of supernatural forces. There is an equal interest in the many repetitive and often frenetic syndromes conducive to shamanic entrancement (as carefully documented by Mircea Eliade,[6] and others), all of which can generate an accompanying "speaking in tongues" and attunement to a non-physical mode of experiencing in which certain powers are demonstrable. Trance dances and purportedly shamanistic rituals are much in vogue at present within the New Age movement, and largely as a consequence of the credence given to current research findings on the above – a credence which dwells on the ease with which such states can be induced, whether by rhythmic drumming, the ingestion of hallucinogenic substances, sweatlodge ceremonies, or manipulation of the breathing processes.

Some prominent researchers (Professor Charles Tart in particular) appear convinced that the altered states of consciousness derived from hypnosis, intensive and prolonged meditation, self-induced trance, and specific techniques of hyperventilation, constitute a greatly increased accessibility in the twentieth century to speedier methods of personal growth. These methods (attributed by many to a higher agency despite their obvious but undwelt-upon dangers) are rapidly infiltrating Western culture as a whole – a process considered by numerous persons as the prelude to a significant, world-wide spiritual quickening in the new millennium.

These assumptions give added fuel to New Age declarations on planetary evolution, and the part purportedly played by various individuals and groupings in providing a co-operative spur for this much publicized operation. The outcome is the establishment of a so-far unassailable position for New Age teachers who, like the Sophists of old, wield their unproven status authoritatively, if unknowledgably, and thereby wrongfully imprint thousands of searching minds, including the minds of academics, with false information on seminal matters of vital consequence which they actively present as facts. Because so much experimentation has been conducted on these lines at the Esalen Institute in the USA, certain aspects of which have been further promoted under the auspices of the Findhorn Foundation in Scotland, UK, and elsewhere, close affiliation between well-known researchers and popular New Age exponents has occurred, and interchanged ideas and viewpoints are a matter of course. Unhappily, each party confirms the other in erroneous conclusions, and consolidates the escalating body of misinformation which threatens to block all possibility of real progress.

What is not given credence, indeed no attention at all in popular literature or professional research, is the *mode of life* which produces natural and spontaneous abilities far superior to "trance" or other artificially induced states, and which are the by-product of a further, and finer development of the human entity – a maturation which enables *comprehension* of the underlying purpose of life, and similarly of the mechanics of spiritual evolution.

It is noteworthy that despite intensive research programmes covering well over two decades, Professor Charles Tart himself has stated, in his Introduction to the Second Edition (December 1971) of *Altered States of Consciousness*: "Research in the past four years has not provided any radically new perspectives on altered states" (p. 9). In his Introduction to the Third Edition of the same book, dated February 1990, Tart says, ". . . this continuing timeliness of the original collection meant that there had not been much fundamental progress in some areas if articles twenty years old (or older) were still that useful! The need for research on the nature, uses and abuses of ASCs is as strong today as it ever was"[7] (p. 12).

These men and women appear to be following the wrong track, and are seemingly too busy promoting their own ideas to see what lies beneath their noses. They pursue by incorrect and inadequate means what is already a *fait accompli* – already known, though not to them. Their experimentation with hallucinogens (currently illegal) and with hyperventilation (suspended or banned in the form of Holotropic Breathwork™ in one major UK New Age centre through official intervention by the Scottish Charities Office)[8] is of a similar order to vivisection, which uses a damaging (to the participant) approach to the requirement in ignorance of both the origin of the problem, and the long-term consequences of the chosen *modus operandi*.

Scientific research has already evidenced that disease can originate from within the interior (or psychological and/or subliminal) processes of the individual and *can also be cured* in some cases by a change of orientation. Perhaps it is time for researchers into human potential for spiritual development to apply the same rules.

Notes

1. S. Grof, *The Adventure of Self-Discovery* (Albany, New York: State University of New York Press, 1988), p. 39.
2. See for example, W. Donkin, *The Wayfarers: Meher Baba with the God-Intoxicated* (Myrtle Beach, SC: Sheriar Press, Inc., 1988). See also R. Abdulla, *Ramjoo's Diaries 1922–1929: A Personal Account of Meher Baba's Early Work by Ramjoo Abdulla* (Walnut Creek, CA: Sufism Reoriented, 1979), pp. 412–523, which will repay close attention from anyone interested in Sufi states of consciousness.
3. See Meher Baba, *God Speaks: The Theme of Creation and Its Purpose* (second edn., New York: Dodd, Mead & Company, 1973), a significant, yet still largely overlooked work (first published in 1955), that combines the technical terminology of both Sufism and Vedanta in charting the evolutionary and metaphysical nature of consciousness. The author was described by the Tibetologist Dr. W. Y. Evens-Wentz in terms of: "No other Teacher in our own time or in any known past time has so minutely analysed consciousness as Meher Baba has in *God Speaks*. . . ." For an introduction to the life and teachings of Meher Baba which

avoids the devotional stereotypes and includes a summary of *God Speaks*, see K. Shepherd, *Meher Baba, an Iranian Liberal* (Cambridge: Anthropographia Publications, 1988).

4. For a critique of Holotropic Breathwork™, see K. Shepherd, *Minds and Sociocultures Vol. One* (Cambridge: Philosophical Press, 1995), pp. 66–84, 945–951.

5. A. Woodham, *HEA guide to Complementary Medicine and Therapies* (London: Health Education Authority, 1994), p. 170.

6. M. Eliade (trans. W. R. Trask), *Shamanism: Archaic Techniques of Ecstasy* (Princeton University Press, 1974). See also M. Harner, *The Way of the Shaman* (third edn., San Francisco: Harper Collins, 1990), which is far more misleading.

7. C. T. Tart, ed., *Altered States of Consciousness* (third edn., San Francisco: Harper Collins, 1990).

8. See S. Castro, *Hypocrisy and Dissent within the Findhorn Foundation: Towards a Sociology of a New Age Community* (Forres, Scotland: New Media Books, 1996), pp. 79–106. See also S. Castro, "New Age Therapy—higher consciousness or delusion?" *The Therapist* (Worthing, 1995) 2 (4): pp. 14–16.

Chapter One

Potential Hazards to Spiritual Growth: 1

So much is said in the present decade on the subject of "spiritual growth," "self-development," and the "awakening of *kundalini*" (the evolutionary force in humankind), that sincere enquirers become confused and eventually confounded by the spectrum of supposed possibilities presented them in both book and lecture form. Various respected establishments, including universities, promote "consciousness studies" and research on "out-of-the-body" experiences, near-death states, and the phenomenon of precognitive dreams. Serious consideration is also being given to certain types of psychism and the cerebral insights of meditation. Yet despite the increasing evidence that mankind is an unfinished product with latent possibilities for further, extensive, non-physical development, little is available of an explanatory nature on the *reality* of such evolution, the laws by which it is determined, or the requirements for the individual.

This book is intended to clarify some of the issues involved, and is proffered from a personal experience of the type of states of consciousness currently under research, and also of states that are less well-known and therefore less well-authenticated. To define a state of consciousness outside our normal physical experience is a difficult undertaking, and to posit a gradation of differing states which pertain to levels of being and interior growth is even more problematic. My reason for attempting to do so arises from observing, over a period of many years, the tragedy of misinformed but genuine people who become hopelessly side-tracked and often damaged beyond repair by unsubstantiated New Age doctrines, older forms of so-called "esoteric" teachings, and the use of in-adequately researched "breakthrough" techniques purported to

1

expand the mind, or at the least induce altered states of consciousness (ASCs) presumed to be "spiritual."

A second reason is the factor of my own experience, and to qualify this I must refer to my published autobiography, at present in three volumes (see bibliography), which details the wide spectrum of other-dimensional experience that, unsought, and not being the product of technique, traditional discipline, or meditation, has intermittently permeated my life. This range of experience included an activation seemingly within the spine, and known to many researchers as a *kundalini* awakening, a classification that as yet takes little or no note of the truly vast differences between various forms of activation, the originating causes, and the overall meaningfulness of these events. This volcanic condition attuned my consciousness to another dimension for fourteen days and nights, without loss of awareness of my mundane existence, or the ability to relate to events coherently, and returned me at the conclusion to my normal everyday self, and the sane, rational, physically healthy state which was mine at the commencement. There were no adverse after-effects.

It was this experience that brought into full consciousness the reality of the force of *kundalini* and its essential place in evolutionary development. This vital subtle energy is the link between human life and an altogether finer dimension of existence – one that is normally screened out by the mind, and cannot be attained to in all its fullness without first completing specific requirements of interior growth. This growth, as I was made starkly aware, can be seriously damaged in its earliest stages by the indiscriminate use of allegedly spiritual practices, a fact that needs to be made more widely known.

In view of the foregoing, I have enlarged upon some of these hazards in the interests of all serious enquirers, pointing out areas of danger best avoided by those who may care to consider the validity of these observations.

In releasing information concerning the very wide range and increasing complexity of this mode of experience outside the context of a detailed autobiography, I wish to stress that I do not seek to make any elitist claim. It is my uttermost conviction born of the insights retrieved from such experience, that what happened to me is part of a universal process, one that cannot intrinsically be forced prematurely, but which nevertheless is open to all humankind, individually, at a specific stage of evolutionary growth. I am furthermore convinced that the knowledge of this process has existed, in its entirety, throughout the ages within graduating circles of mystics, and was known to the earliest cultures on this planet now lost to us historically.

There are many degenerated remnants of this ancient knowledge abroad in the world of today, some still in use by largely outmoded religions which have lost the key to former wisdom and become mechanistic (Tibetan Buddhism is a case in point). Other facets, equally obscure, have been passed down to us in grossly distorted form by Western esotericists and occultists. As clinical psychologist Richard Noll observes in his article *The Presence of Spirits in Magic and Madness*: "Ritual or ceremonial magic is a Western occult tradition which utilizes visions to contact and manipulate 'spirits' for divinatory and psychokinetic purposes and empowerment. Although its roots extend far back into pagan antiquity, it reached its ascendancy in classical, medieval, and Renaissance Europe, only to virtually disappear for several centuries. The present popularity of ritual magic can be traced to its rebirth in the French occult revival of the mid-1800s and to the founding of the Hermetic Order of the Golden Dawn in Britain in the 1880s" (see S. Nicholson, ed., *Shamanism*, 1990, p. 57). These remnants have also infiltrated the New Age movement and are now being utilized, piecemeal, by workshop leaders and commercial entrepreneurs as techniques or guidance for what is promoted as "self-development." ["Channelling," "affirmations," and "creative visualization" are but three contemporary examples of previously termed "occult" practices.]

This situation is greatly complicated by the profusion of books available on subjects concerned with the "Higher Self," which it is generally claimed can quite easily be contacted and is infallible in its wisdom and ability to direct our lives and developmental processes. The sweeping statements presented as facts by so many New Age teachers are very attractive to persons seeking a deeper meaning in their lives, and they trustingly place themselves in the hands of "spiritually" minded course leaders and therapists, also self-designated "researchers" with PhD's, and others equally if even less legitimately assertive who glibly profess knowledge of our evolutionary meaningfulness.

This knowledge, in its totality, was once kept secret, and for

3

very sound reasons – one being that without experiential preparation people cannot understand the developmental process, and another, that such knowledge is open to serious misuse. Evolutionary progression from total unconsciousness of our source and likewise of our destination, to total realization of the human condition and the certainty of its ultimate transcendence, is a complex matter hinted at in various ancient and medieval mystical texts. Yet the comprehension of this process, and the *modus operandi* required to achieve completion of the human entity, is a sacred science, known only to the few in each generation who attain to it. This science is an *intact* knowledge, already complete. *It is not dependent upon academic research*, and is not open to innovation. It is operative in certain prepared levels of humankind in every millennium, but always from "above to below," meaning that it is operative only *through those that have such knowledge* and have already completed their own evolution. These teachers alone can safely adapt the constituents for the relevant time and culture and individuals. Their tuition is not merely formal, but extends to, and is experienced in, all areas of the self, including the mundane personality, and the everyday life.

The complexities involved in evolutionary development towards the spiritual state are such that the inadequate and misinformed efforts of today's "teachers" who have not attained to such overall knowledge (most of whom are primarily concerned with the commercial aspects of their careers) are more harmful to the aspiring student than anything else. Unless one knows what one is doing in the name of "growth," and the actual long-term results of the exercises, visualizations, meditations, subliminal programming and powerful techniques that are currently in fashion, one should leave them alone, and certainly not sell them in workshops and courses.

The rules applying to education as a whole and to teacher-training in particular, are not applicable to the science of evolutionary development, save in writing about it. The former relies on all things pertaining to the intellect, i.e., memory, formal training, assembled research, etc., whereas the latter requires the use of an active organ of spontaneous comprehension and perception only attainable through a specific type of human effort, and capable of an accurate and immediate discernment (when necessary) of the psychological blocks in others, the state of the

4

individual subconscious (and its content), levels of development, degrees of aspiration, present possibilities for those concerned, primary requirements, and much else.

The faculty I have referred to is not "natural" to humankind, and should not be confused with psychism. The average human being is not born with it; it is not part of our equipment. This organ of comprehensive perception belongs to a higher aspect of our being, and cannot be reached, or utilized, until we have first created a centre of gravity within ourselves, which must then be nurtured, developed, honed, and the resultant nucleus finally attuned in order to connect with this higher aspect.

To form such a centre in the personality self is likewise not a natural ability. We cannot do this unaided, without direction or assistance. A skilled instructor is indispensable.

The need for an instructor is a much-argued subject, greatly complicated by the false concepts generated by modern gurus of recent decades who were not what they were purported to be. The trail of human debris left in their wake is no doubt in part the reason why New Age course leaders insist that the role of teacher is outmoded. In their stead, these surrogate "teachers" have formulated their own concepts, largely derived from Jungian psychology admixed with numerous techniques adapted from Eastern religions and Western psychotherapy. These indiscriminately combined concepts are often simplistic in the extreme; yet the generalized use of "techniques" constitutes an even greater problem.

Self-development is the aim and assumed end-product of the use of these techniques, for guidance comes from within, we are told, therefore learn to turn inwards and all else shall be added unto you. Unfortunately, this is only a very partial truth, and a dangerous one, as until a certain level of development is reached, delusion is almost inevitable. What happens here is that the psychic faculties so readily activated by techniques are mistaken for something much more rarefied and refined.

Break-in techniques, such as the use of hallucinogenic drugs, breathwork, *kundalini* exercises, and most forms of meditation – to name but a few – can artificially open up areas of the psyche or the subconscious and produce experiences that may seem akin to those described in authentic developmental documentation. Yet it is folly to ignore the essential safeguards and preparation that

5

authenticity demands. These techniques will lead nowhere in a spiritual sense, though they may well produce problems that will necessitate a specialist unravelling before any genuine development can commence.

There is a disturbing lack of knowledge amongst breathwork exponents on the dangers of inadvertantly triggering the force of *kundalini* in their clients, and the likely consequences. Gunnel Minett, a Rebirthing practitioner, exemplifies this lack in her book, *Breath and Spirit: Rebirthing as a Healing Technique* (1994), particularly in the sections relating to this subject. It is also evident that, like most advocates of Rebirthing, she has little understanding of the far-reaching and long-term repercussions involved in the premature disturbance of certain aspects of the psyche, or of what she is setting into motion in general. If clients repress memories there are reasons for this, not all of them due to shock, or pre-birth traumas, or the wish to "forget" disturbing events. Moreover, there are far safer ways of dealing with these problems than the means afforded by Rebirthing, which continues to remain a controversial "therapy," even amongst liberal psychotherapists (see N. Albery, *How to Feel Reborn?: Varieties of Rebirthing Experience*, 1985).

Holotropic Breathwork™, for example, has caused extreme and prolonged symptoms completely unconnected with therapeutic healing or spiritual growth. Some are outlined in the sociological documentation provided by Stephen Castro (see Introduction, note 8), and others are described by no less an authority on this subject than Stanislav Grof himself. Holotropic Breathwork™, which was initially adapted by Grof from Primal Integration therapy, and bears marked resemblance to the Rebirthing practices of Leonard Orr, is a modification of Yogic Pranayama in its most extreme form, and has not, to date, been clinically researched. Its early use and often horrific effects are minutely recounted in Grof's *Beyond the Brain: Birth, Death and Transcendence in Psychotherapy* (1985), and include terrifying visions of demons and all manner of nauseating scatological details. The technique, considered to have therapeutic advantages (despite the distraught and continuous screaming that frequently accompanies it), has latterly been trademarked by Dr. Grof for commercial purposes, and experiential courses are promoted in various venues in the USA and Europe. People who attend these courses unfortunately do not realize to what risks they expose themselves. Despite the re-assurances of facilitators (invariably enthusiasts and not infre-quently entrepreneurs), and also of Dr. Grof, there is no knowl-edge at all of the fundamental dangers inherent in these prac-tices in relation to the possibilities of authentic spiritual growth. To utilize such powerful techniques for the purposes of therapy, or mere experimentation, is a veritable Pandora's box from which literally anything might emerge, transpersonal, primordial or demonic, and which either cannot be controlled at all, or control-led only at the cost of further damage to the inner potential of the individual.

Grof cites in *The Adventure of Self-Discovery* (1988) that there "exist many individuals in whom even dramatic hyperventilation carried over a long period of time does not lead to a classical hyperventilation syndrome, but to progressive relaxation, intense sexual feelings, or even mystical experiences" (p. 172). This he considers positive, but he is evidently unaware that the reassur-ing statement: "Specific techniques involving intense breathing or withholding of breath" which are part of "various exercises in Kundalini Yoga, Siddha Yoga, the Tibetan Vajrayana, Sufi prac-tice, Burmese Buddhist and Taoist meditation" etc., (p. 170) refers to techniques which were originally intended for specific and extremely limited use with selected pupils under the personal care of an authentic guide – that is, if the adaptations in question were ever valid at all. This possibility does not confirm that such techniques are *safe*. The fact that they are used indiscriminately these days on the general (unselected) public in therapy sessions and at retreat centres, whether the latter are of Buddhist, Taoist, Sufi, or Christian orientation, means simply that the organiza-tions concerned have deteriorated and no longer embody what they originally exemplified. So-called Sufi organizations which distrib-ute *zikrs* and *kundalini* exercises to all and sundry are examples of this deterioration.

People do not realize that before real growth (of an interior nature) can begin, a foundation for such growth must be prepared within the mundane self, or personality. The forms of such initial preparation were once taught to the Western cultures by the Christian Church and by earlier religions, and in Eastern cul-tures by the synagogue, mosque, or temple, or its equivalent. The

7

basic rules, in West and East, are the same: obedience to external law, observance of one's family duties, right conduct, honesty, assistance to those less fortunate than oneself, harmlessness to all men, kindness to all creatures, and acknowledgement of the higher Source that brought us into being. Implicit in this was the injunction not to hate, not to covet, not to steal, not to kill, not to commit adultery – all rulings designed for the wellbeing of the community, and more specifically, as a means to ensure the beginnings of self-control in the individual. How far we have deviated from this, as a race, is evident in our present day civilization. If the above requirements were practised, there would be no necessity to add, "not to use coercive power, and not to manipulate for one's own ends," both tendencies much in evidence in areas of supposedly spiritual tuition at the present time.

The preparation abovementioned, in its original, very literal form, was a kind of mass prescription which, when adhered to, helped raise the individual from the conglomerate and separated that individual from his or her more primitive attributes, gradually evolving in those concerned a durable conscience (the sense of right and wrong that governs a person's thought and actions). This all takes time, it cannot be done quickly, and there are many, many pitfalls, backslidings, and fresh starts. Only when conscience is active and established in the human entity can other possibilities arise, and other forms of preparation ensue, a fact that seldom achieves exposure amongst contemporary gurus.

It is this more complex preparation that requires the attention and expertise of a teacher of a different order to those merely trained formally – one who, for example, can evoke events in which psychological conditioning is exposed. In such events emotions are amplified, observed, and brought under control, and the ability to act consciously (as opposed to passively experiencing), is clearly profiled to the students concerned. Such teachers, who are not readily recognizable and may not necessarily be known as teachers (save to their immediate students), are very few and far between, but they ensure that these processes are usefully integrated into the individual psychology, aligning them to the ultimate eradication of specific, and usually deeply ingrained, behavioural modes of a negative nature. (These processes are not achieved in "workshops," but are introduced into everyday life).

The result is increasing self-knowledge, and a commensurate

8

integrity, without which no lasting realignment can be made. First must come the observation and conscious registration of psychological malfunctioning and/or emotional problems and repressions, for only then can they be dealt with by the person concerned. During this period – of greater or lesser duration in accord with the need and capacity of the student – hidden propensities for jealousy, deceit, irrational resentment, and hostility (fruitful sources of recurring syndromes) and other similar, formerly concealed dispositions are likely to surface for confrontation in unexpected situations. In some persons, blocks of solidified impressions still lurk in the subconscious from the seemingly obliterated past – in particular those pertaining to ruthlessness and the misuse of power, plus sexual excesses and deviations – and these in their turn become clearly evidenced, and are by various means dispersed. Further progress cannot be achieved until this crucial stage is accomplished.

Following the preparation of the mundane self and the resolution of any hindering obstruction, work in earnest commences on the purification of the psyche. It is here that true aspiration arises, and with it a whole new octave of meaningful experience. In aspiration lies the key to our redemption and the eventual completion of the human entity (still as yet a long way off). Nevertheless, this phase marks the beginning of the end of the individual evolutionary process, and is a significant landmark.

One purpose of this book is to define some of the states and stages of this process, and the means by which the process itself becomes operative; to illustrate, to some degree, the route that is open to each one of us at a certain phase of our existence. This presupposes more than one lifespan on this planet, indeed, a series of lives, although reincarnation is so often simplistically explained by partisans and similarly refuted by sceptics. Our beliefs are largely dependent upon the culture in which we are reared, and most of them are based on distortions and must be undone. One of the difficulties at the commencement of this process is the undoing of incorrect imprintation, meaning the accumulated misinformation that everyone gathers at earlier stages of their lives. When false patterns are structured in the mind, a clear understanding of the mechanics of spiritual growth is not possible, with confusion and doubt a likely consequence. Imprintation can be dealt with relatively easily in a willing participant keen to study; but the tracks formed in the mind which precipitate reflex moods and actions in associative situations can create many problems, and will take more time and much effort to overcome.

A most serious hindrance, strongly highlighted in our present culture, results from the ingestion of powerful drugs like LSD and Ecstasy. Drug ingestion can, and does, cause havoc. Many otherwise promising spiritual aspirants have wrecked their chances for this lifetime by LSD sessions, the effect of which, in most cases, prohibits the safe reception of the live stimulus operative in organic developmental work. To safely receive this organic stimulus requires a cerebral system with undamaged cells: and cells are frequently damaged in typically "mind-blowing" LSD experiences. High dosage LSD invariably leaves the recipient prone to psychological complications, not assisted by what are termed "bad trips" producing alarming after-effects.

Drugs in general affect the human system in ways that render impossible the essential regulation of experience demanded by interior processes of evolution, which aim to preserve psychological orientation, not to disrupt it. Drugs do much damage to both the nervous system and the human aura, the effect upon which might be compared to that of a punctured lung. Well-known experimenters like Timothy Leary, Aldous Huxley, and Richard Alpert (Ram Dass), and the many misguided PhDs who assiduously followed in their footsteps (including some of today's researchers and teachers), inevitably damaged themselves extensively and made higher forms of growth impossible, whether known to them or not. Newer drugs such as Ecstasy and Vitamin K [Ketamine, used as a hospital anaesthetic and a veterinary tranquillizer, which in overdose can cause "terrifying hallucinations, heart and kidney damage and can kill" (*Daily Mail*, July 18th 1998)], despite being quaintly termed "recreational chemicals" in New Age sectors (along with LSD and amphetamines), have their own serious dangers, all of which are counter-productive to genuine spiritual growth.

Sadly, the same principle applies to the effects of the indiscriminate and intensive use of hyperventilation, whether Holotropic Breathwork™, Rebirthing, or casually prescribed Yogic Pranayama. Persons who do not possess the developed capacities of genuine instructors, and who persist in the commercial promotion of experimental practices like holotropic breathwork that artifically activate the subconscious and precipitate powerful subliminal experiences into unsuspecting lives, do no service at all to those concerned. Most workshop participants are nowhere near the requisite level of preparedness to deal with psychological projections triggered under stress. The plexuses of impressions so released do not necessarily disappear at the point of experiential "replay" as experimenters like Stanislav Grof assume, but may in due time externalize as physical life events of a similar nature (including illnesses, accidents, and all the varied upheavals of human existence) – though in these cases without the necessary developmental factors to mitigate, transmute, or transform them; without any control as to their velocity, frequency or magnitude; and with absolutely no guarantee that the experiencer will in any way benefit from them.

It is well known to breathworkers that the content of experiential sessions often spills over into the daily life of the participant in the form of acute disturbance and disorientation – and sometimes leads to breakdown, but it is naively and conveniently considered that such crises can be resolved by therapists and counsellors, and that any residual problems are one's own "stuff" (subjective impressions) that must be worked through under the assured protection of one's soul. Unhappily, this comforting notion is not in keeping with the facts, nor with the suffering caused by unleashed forces which neither therapist nor counsellor can switch off once set into motion.

That traumas and other conditions can be alleviated in psychotherapy by reliving long-buried incidents that surface in the mind, is not here denied. But the haphazard and uncontrolled nature of the energies invoked in breathwork courses is another matter, and can court serious consequences. These energies are unlike those dealt with in standard psychotherapy. They may not even originate with the individual who is experiencing them – as with the non-human or animal behaviour frequently exhibited in breathwork sessions. Such "replays" of extreme traumatic events *not* linked to the present life of the experiencer are undergone *solely in the mind* – they are not reclaimed memories of earlier life events too painful to assimilate at the time of occurrence, and are thus not subject to the same controlling factors, i.e., they are

11

outside the allocated experience of that lifespan, and whatever their origins, past incarnatory or otherwise, would not have emerged into the current life process at that juncture unless artificially introduced.

The contention of those in charge of breathwork courses is that these "replays" from earlier lives are brought into consciousness and confronted (and thus nullified) in the same manner as present-life memories, and that in fact these long past events may be the root of present-life traumas, a view that is shared by Regression therapists, and which latter is no doubt a possibility. Yet this side-steps the issue of what *karma* constitutes, and what it is *for*, and ignores entirely the organic oscillation of experience between opposite poles of expression referred to by certain authentic teachers. An example of this is the fact that abused children frequently become child-abusing adults, also that the trauma arising from the suffering inflicted by a drunken parent *does not* unfortunately prevent the sufferer, when adult, from committing the same offence. It is further known that those who have been victims of political and other oppression, when in later positions of power themselves, tend to act similarly to their former oppressors, and so on. Unless something is changed in individual lives by a conscious act of conscience or self-control, there is evidence to suggest that such oscillations will continue. Bringing buried present-life memories into consciousness may well alleviate repression syndromes, but *this will not alter* "karmic law" (to use a popular religious expression seldom gaining any adequate analysis). Something more is required.

There is an insufficient knowledge of these processes, and facilitators are taking upon themselves the equivalent of the roles of highly trained surgeons, minus the stringent qualifications that are essential for such roles, in which they perform but half of an operation and leave the rest to fate. Stanislav Grof himself, in his introductory cassette on the subject of holotropic breathwork, says that this therapy is an *experiment*, and that he, personally, does not know *why* certain syndromes occur or what the possible short or long term consequences may be. In various articles and talks he also makes plain the purely conjectural nature of his findings. Yet he nevertheless presents certificates purporting to qualify his students to safely and knowledgeably conduct their fellow human beings through this grossly over-extended yogic

12

technique.

If past-life experiences reclaimed by the use of holotropic breathwork are "nullified" non-selectively (assuming that this is what is occurring), such untimely intervention can unfortunately *deny* the later possibility of productive spiritual growth, which is normally engendered in the very process of overcoming, in a natural manner, the vicissitudes inherent in these (prematurely) neutralized impressions. They (the impressions) are the fuel – the actual means of healthy progress. Interior development can only arise as a consequence of the mastery of the self in the midst of friction, and this is known to all authentic teaching sources.

A further, and seemingly unconsidered possibility, is that these impressional constituents, once dislodged from the central core of the psyche, if not negated by the mere act of mentally and emotionally reliving them (as claimed by breathwork facilitators and regression therapists), will become part of the impressional present-life, or imminent future-life, store of the experiencer. This must needs externalize into the physical life in some form or another (not necessarily in the scenario projected associatively by the brain during the breathwork session) in the way that all stored life impressions do throughout the lifespan – and will recur in the same manner as all other syndromes of impressions until such time as they achieve resolution – whether the person concerned can cope with them or not.

The Rebirther, Joy Manné, presents a further example of well-intentioned ignorance on the subject she both teaches and practices as a therapist and breathworker. Her work is nevertheless recognized by the Scientific and Medical Network (of which she is a member) who included her as a speaker and "workshop" conductor in their "Mystics and Scientists 21" Conference of April 1998, held at the University of Warwick Conference Park, UK. Titled *The Breath of Life*, the subject is self-evident. According to the brochure, Manné spoke on *Breath as a Language*, and *Buddhist Breathwork and the Nature of Consciousness*. It was not made clear, however, if her involvement was as a "mystic" or as a "scientist."

The format of the "Mystics and Scientists" conference included, for the first time in its twenty-one years, the questionable option of "practical exercises" of a participatory nature, e.g., in Manné's case, indiscriminately applied breathing techniques that, by their very nature, could prove neither mystical nor scientific in demonstration.

Joy Manné took a degree in Psychology, studied Sanskrit and Pali, and wrote her PhD thesis on the debates and case histories in the Pali Canon (the Theravada Buddhist scriptures). Her practice of breathing techniques commenced in 1961 with instruction in Vipassana meditation, and came to fruition in 1984 when she discovered Rebirthing while undergoing therapy. (Rebirthing was originated by Leonard Orr, a "guru" who now prefers to be known as Young Len Orr Raja, an appellation which reflects his belief in his own physical immortality). Following a three year training course in "Spiritual Therapy" (i.e., Rebirthing) with Hans Mensink and Tilke Platteel-Deur in Holland, Manné opened her own school of "personal and spiritual development" in Switzerland (1989–1995). She now has an advertised "international" career as a teacher and lecturer, and has recently produced a detailed workbook, *Soul Therapy* (1997), concerned principally with promoting her own version of breathwork as related to the "Soul Quest," a slogan coined by herself. [It should be noted here that, in opposition to Grof and Orr, Manné now views the use of hyperventilation as a "rape of the soul."]

With regard to the Soul Quest, Manné writes: "As long as there have been humans, Ego has sought Soul. The Soul Quest has had many different names. These days it may be called personal and spiritual development, personal growth, empowerment, humanistic or transpersonal psychology, humanology, or shamanism, among other expressions" (*Soul Therapy*, p. 5). This easy denominator includes Manné's newly created "Soul Therapy."

Just before launching her school, in late 1988 Manné found that the effects of her Rebirthing experiences, which ranged from "powerful regressions to traumatic experiences, to the attainment of ecstatic states of altered consciousness" were causing her problems. She felt that she was fast becoming absorbed into something much bigger than herself and was in danger of being "lost forever." At this point she met a Jungian analyst and decided to enter psychoanalysis, which halted the slide into the unknown (p. 158). Despite this cautionary personal experience of breathwork, Manné nevertheless still worked as a professional Rebirther, and records her alarming session with a man whom she regressed to

14

the age of four, at which time he suffered a highly traumatic experience from which his therapist was unable to speedily retrieve him. Manné recounts: "His regression was so strong that after he relived the escape he did not recognize me but wandered around the room, lost and terrified, calling pitifully, 'Mama, Mama.' Finally, he sat by the foot of the sofa, despairing, cut off from the world, autistic." Manné was horrified by her patient's degree of suffering. She was also very frightened. Suppose he became "lost in this unconsciousness?" Mercifully, he gradually came to recognize her; it took several more sessions, however, "before he integrated his autistic part, and that was not through Rebirthing . . ." Manné was obliged to resort to art therapy and other practices. The effect upon her of this session was "profound," she tells us, "and remains so to this day" (p. 160).

Whatever the shock or trauma, "profound" or cautionary, it did not deter her from her intentions – for Manné proceeded with the founding of her school, amalgamating Rebirthing (in both the traditional and self-modified form) with Jungian theory, Voice Dialogue, Regression techniques, Buddhist breathing practices, and sundry other allegedly therapeutic disciplines, and systematically taught others to establish themselves professionally, using her methods. It is an interesting fact that her pupils were drawn from her clients (p. 123), all of whom had been in need of therapy, and were now deemed ready to be placed in charge of clients them-selves.

One of the principal dangers of breathwork, as already stated, is the inadvertant activation of *kundalini* and the premature awakening of the *chakras*. Manné is fully aware of this possibility, and refers to her second personal session of Rebirthing in which her *chakras* "opened up one by one and the universe was making love with me" (p. 154). No further information is given, but the subject is mentioned again on page 168, where she writes of an Aikido teacher who, during his first Rebirthing session, presented an "overwhelming ecstatic experience – a Kundalini awakening." This so terrified him that he declined further ses-sions, believing the process to be dangerous.

Manné's view is rather different. She considers that breath-workers "are only at the beginning of a most exciting time in their discipline," and says she is "very enthusiastic" about what she has so far discovered. She has "not yet" found a limit to what can be done "when working consciously and intelligently" with the breath (p. 173).

In view of this author's rapidly increasing profile as a discerning teacher, and her acceptance into the realm of science via the auspices of the Scientific and Medical Network, it is perhaps relevant to point out that Manné demonstrates in *Soul Therapy* an extreme lack of functional knowledge of the interior development in which she professes proficiency.

Likewise, on a mundane level, her tracing of human knowledge of the spiritual and its pursuit by twentieth-century Westerners is almost unbelievably naive. Westerners, it seems, showed little interest in these matters until "a few exceptional people" like Aldous Huxley, Milton Erickson, Alan Watts, Fritz Perls and Stanislav Grof publicized their ideas in the 1960s (p. 6). The common knowledge regarding some of these "exceptional people" is factually as follows: the hedonistic "Zen" exponent Alan Watts died of alcoholic poisoning; Huxley indulged in mescaline and LSD and had numerous sexual encounters with other women whilst married (in fact he was encouraged to do so by his first wife Maria, who on innumerable occasions actually selected the women for him); and Perls, also a known womanizer, most unprofessionally publicly mocked one of his partners (Marcia Price) when she threatened suicide during a Gestalt workshop at the Esalen Institute – she afterwards shot herself dead. Perls showed no remorse at this event, and indeed, another suicide occurred when Judith Gold drowned herself in the Esalen baths after a similarly traumatic encounter with Perls in a Gestalt context.

Moreover, according to Manné, if one has asked oneself such questions as "How can I develop self-esteem?" or, "How can I succeed in relationships?" – or, more pointedly, "How can I have a good sex life?" – plus the equally blithe, "How do I become intuitive?" or, "How do I become empowered?" and, even more importantly, "How can I manifest the inner shaman that I truly am in my life?" – this is indicative that the querant has entered the Spiritual Path (or in Manné's terminology, the "Soul Quest"). The statement is qualified by the comment – "if he or she is really interested in discovering the answers" (pp. 19–20).

There is also the repeated implication that one cannot have spiritual development without paying for it in hard cash. We must therefore be prepared to re-evaluate our priorities, for "If we use

16

our money to pay for our development, we will have less to spend elsewhere. Sometimes we have to choose between amusing ourselves and taking a holiday or making further commitments to our Soul Quest and using our time for workshops and trainings." Manné cites the "martyr" type on the "Ego-level" who says, "I don't have enough money to buy myself the things I want and to pay for the workshops that lead to development . . ." (p. 57), and informs her readers that "The Soul Quest demands sacrifices." These sacrifices are, of course, monetary, and do not include a sacrifice by the entrepreneurial therapist-cum-teacher of a lucrative fee for "spiritual" therapy and/or development.

In a similar vein is the nonsensical statement, "Self-esteem is Soul-esteem. Without self-esteem, we do not even begin our Soul Path: we do not feel good enough to do so." Apparently it is necessary to feel sufficiently worthy before such a transformative process can commence (p. 59).

Manné has something to say about the matter of tests on the Spiritual Path (or Soul Quest). Her view is as follows: "Tests can be scary. If the tests are worthwhile and if we are well prepared, they can also be fun. The Soul Path is ever more fun as we acquire the skills to tread it with confidence. Surprisingly, the skills are hardly difficult to acquire! Once we know what they are, and have the appropriate exercises, they are almost easy" (p. 25).

The whole of *Soul Therapy* is of the same shallow level of assumption, and although Dr. Manné has appeared as a speaker at the "Mystics and Scientists" Conference, in the view of the present writer neither her academic status, nor her mystical pretensions, equip her to promote randomly applied breathing techniques to unsuspecting members of the general public, or to encourage others to follow her misleading version of the soul quest.

The theory of Rebirthing is reminiscent of the efforts of practitioners of Kundalini yoga who, in their search for enlightenment, seek by certain means to "release" stored *karma* from the subtle body in order to "burn it up" rapidly and non-experientially, thus freeing themselves from the endless wheel of reincarnation. This is said to be achieved (or partially achieved) by a deliberate, out-of-sequence activation of the unawakened higher *chakras* before the lower *chakras* are functioning – most usually by an initial assault on the *anahata*, or heart, *chakra* – which holds the power

17

to neutralize karmic impressions collected around the lower *chakras*. The scope for deception should be readily apparent. One cannot ignorantly tamper with subliminal processes, even when it is traditional to do so, without some consequences. What happens as the result of the use of break-in techniques is a direct interference in the evolutionary development of a human being – a very wide and complex topic which cannot be adequately summarized in these few lines.

Other dangers to potential development include: conditioning to the techniques of hypnosis (particularly the techniques used in Regression therapy); *all* forms of subliminal programming, however popular (cassette subliminal programming tapes are some of the worst offenders); *all* commercial technical apparatus claimed to stimulate alpha and theta rythms in the brain, and not least, certain forms of unprescribed intensive and prolonged meditation.

In using the word "prescribe," I refer of course to authentic directives, and here one must query *everyone* who purports to teach and dispense advice. Even those who should prove most trust-worthy have been known to lead others astray – including well known and well respected Tibetan Buddhists, Indian Gurus and Western mystics. This is why *bona fide* biographies (or autobiographies) should be obligatory in the rapidly externalizing science of evolutionary metaphysics, complete with explicit details of the qualifying experience of the instructor concerned, as there are no other visible qualifications as yet in this field to act as safeguards against the many self-designated and entirely bogus teachers that abound throughout the world. Adulation and success are not indicative of knowledge; they are more frequently the result of good publicity and commercial enterprise.

People are often deceived by what they believe to be evidence of spiritual expertise at work. It is beyond dispute that many currently used techniques produce effects, and sometimes sensational ones. Those used at New Age Centres such as the Esalen Institute in the USA and the Findhorn Foundation in Scotland, UK, evoke powerful emotional releases in the name of spiritual growth or self-development. These experiences of amplified emotion are often followed by euphoria or a tranquillizing sense of peace. Group bonding processes release inhibitions and engender intense feelings of intimacy and brotherhood – panaceas for locked human emotions, loneliness, and inferiority complexes.

18

Other techniques can activate a psychic faculty that the participants did not know they possessed, and the serenity experienced during group meditations when in these artificially heightened states cause many to think they are in the charge of persons of proficiency. Unhappily, this is rarely, if ever, the situation, and the temporary gains are more than offset by the neurosis left in some unfortunates in the form of disturbances in the subconscious, the over-intensification of sexual energies, and the exposed repressions which continue to regularly surface and cause problems long after these "workshops" are over. Immediate and pronounced effects do not necessarily denote growth, nor even the beginnings of it. They are, in general, simply the by-products of an amplification of the senses by untoward means, and an out-of-sequence intrusion into the realm of the psyche. The New Age psychobabble utilized during these activities is quite impenetrable, and not open to reason once implanted in the mind.

Self-empowerment, self-assertion and self-esteem are workshop icons that, again, are not going anywhere. People are taught to repolarize themselves around attitudes that are the antithesis of those required for interior growth, and are encouraged to attempt to integrate into the personality self the very problems that need careful observation and subsequent elimination or exclusion.

To "love oneself" and include one's faults, however reprehensible, is to strengthen the ego rather than diminish it. The knots of hidden impulses that should rightfully cause shame and the urge to overcome them, instead are validated. (This is a distortion of loving those close to us *despite* their faults – which does not make the fault lovable). These attitudes, if persevered in, will eventually establish the equivalent of a wrongly formed centre of gravity – the very reverse of what is required.

What therefore constitutes a correctly oriented centre of gravity? In this context it is a strengthening and drawing together of those aspects of the psychology that are conducive to further growth – aspects that recognize and comprehend, however dimly, the central aim and will cooperate with it, as opposed to those facets that will ruthlessly sabotage any obstruction to what is currently desired. The former, with time, effort, and effective assistance, will form a nucleus, or core – a functional ego around which the entire life revolves – so that eventually all aspects of that life work towards the same end, and any residual unruly

19

elements become gradually subservient to it, or under control.

"Shamanic" training offers a break-in technique of a different type to those formerly mentioned. Shamanism involves the "deliberate production of trance states" and is currently much in demand in the West. One reason for this is the speed of gratification, or apparent success. As Professor Roger Walsh informs us in *The Spirit of Shamanism* (1990), pp. 3–4: "Disciplines such as meditation or yoga may be powerful but may require weeks or months of practice to induce significant effects. This is not so for shamanism. . . . some people with no prior training may walk into a workshop and, within minutes of listening to shamanic drumming, attain meaningful insights." Such enthusiasm should arouse caution.

The above quote refers specifically to drumming, and shamanic drumming is one of the methods used to induce states of trance. Shamanic work is conducted in trance, and Westerners by the score now seek to become modern shamans via commercial weekend workshops and week- or month-long courses.

Leo Rutherford, self-styled "shaman" and founder of the London-based Eagle's Wing Centre for Contemporary Shamanism has in the past produced a drumming tape in conjunction with Howard Charing, a fellow "shaman," to further the popularization of shamanism in the UK. [Rutherford was formerly a successful businessman and industrialist, and well-known in his more recent capacity as the enterprising promoter of *Playworld*, a weekend non-competitive "therapeutic" party system for adults and highly popular with the New Age Fun and Games circuit.] When Daniel Perret reviewed this tape in the Spring 1997 issue of the glossy New Age magazine-cum-mart, *Kindred Spirit*, he pointed out that not much is said about precautions in the cover notes, "as the emphasis is on the shamanic journey to other worlds." Perret rectified this with the comment that exposure to constant drumming "can sometimes bring forward unexpected and unpleasant experiences. People with poor grounding – that is, with poor body awareness and fragile mental balance should not use this tape without experienced guidance." With concern he adds: "But would they be able to detect this lack of grounding in themselves in the first place?" Perret plainly recognized the dangers of mental immersion in 2 x 40 minutes of "completely regular" drumbeats.

(*Kindred Spirit*, pp. 60–61).

The trance states evoked by shamanic drumming, like the states created by hypnosis, should always be avoided by students of evolutionary metaphysics, as predisposing tracks are laid in the mind that facilitate increasingly deeper levels of trance or more rapid and intensified states of hypnosis at the drop of a hat (metaphorically). Some course leaders consider this admirable and strongly encourage the tendency, apparently unaware that in the more sensitive this can be likened to prising open a carefully closed valve and permitting entry to a deluge of often adverse material (or to possessing entities, not necessarily benign), effects which can rapidly cause disorientation and also intense fear. Very real dangers accompany these states, particularly for the type of person who could otherwise have responded well to a different mode of tuition, and the factor of such dangers should not be ignored.

Hypnosis used for entertainment, for instance, can prove hazardous, even lethal, and can also disturb the mind for a very long period after the event, particularly when false or frightening material is fed into it, as Steve Tooze reports in a double page article in the *Daily Mail.*

"Celebrity hypnotist Paul McKenna is being sued for more than £50,000 by Christopher Gates, 28, who claims he developed schizophrenia after taking part in the TV star's act in March 1994. The High Court will decide whether this claim has any justification. Meanwhile, other tales of death and despair are emerging . . . fuelling calls for a total ban on what for some is an increasingly dubious entertainment."

Also included among the reported casualties of stage hypnotists were Sharron Tabarn, a 24-year-old mother of two who died only hours after taking part in a stage hypnotist's show in 1992 (the hypnotist suggested to her in trance that she had suffered a 10,000-volt shock), and Irene Carbin, 48, who for ten years was haunted by an alarming ordeal at the hands of a stage hypnotist which drove her to the edge of a nervous breakdown. This was a particularly insensitive event for the woman concerned, who was told at the conclusion of an embarrassing session under hypnosis that she had lost a breast, which at the time she fully believed as she sought frantically to locate it. This left in her a terrible fear of losing a breast from cancer. (See *Daily Mail*, October 17th 1996, pp. 46–47).

McKenna (the "celebrity" hypnotist referred to by Tooze) is part of the "Bandler–McKenna–Breen" trio now making a fortune from NLP® (Neuro-Linguistic Programming), another high-powered trademarked enterprise designed to ensnare the unwary, and who are currently promoting various trainings, including in-depth Hypnosis. In the light of these widely advertised "trainings," one could justifiably conclude that the aforementioned Gates lost his case, for in the 1998 Spring Edition of *Kindred Spirit*, two of the trio (McKenna Breen Ltd), notify readers of the launch of a new training as part of the NLP curriculum, namely: *Learning Hypnosis in Depth* (16–20 May 1998, £649 plus VAT). [NLP courses cover quite a range of tutorial offerings and include the New Master Practitioner training (23–31 March 1998, considered a bargain at £999 plus VAT), and "becoming a Guru in your own field in just 8 days" (NLP International). This latter course is "updated for the 21st Century" and reveals "closely guarded secrets" for the first time in the West, with **"unlimited"** fame and fortune as two of its aims – plus an invitation to become a member of the "Guru Club" for life, and to "receive the guidance of the Master for as long as you wish." There are sundry other swiftly taught ranges of proficiency under the NLP logo – all at a price, naturally (pp. 31, 55).]

However, McKenna remains in the news in a less elevated capacity than the one above-advertised, and the *Daily Mail* of July 14th 1998 reports that Paul McKenna faced a £200,000 damages claim in the High Court in London, brought by the traumatized Christopher Gates. Anthony Scrivener, QC, on behalf of Gates, revealed that McKenna has no medical qualifications and no formal hypnotherapy qualification "yet held himself out as an expert." He further revealed that 34-year-old McKenna had commenced his career running in-store entertainment at a shopping centre before becoming a disc jockey, and that his interest in hypnotism began in 1985, when "he realized he had a knack that could be used for entertainment."

As the case proceeded, Scrivener obliged McKenna to admit that a woman had a sexual orgasm under hypnosis during his stage show. "You have done that, haven't you?" said Scrivener: "You put her under hypnosis on television in America [The Howard Stern Show] and made her have an orgasm."

The court was also told how a man in the same show was

convinced he was pregnant after he was hypnotized by McKenna. Scrivener accused the hypnotist of using inappropriate acts which put people under considerable distress, and said the star routinely hypnotized men and told them they had lost their penis. McKenna, in response, said he could not recall anyone being distressed by that routine. He had performed this manipulation many times and it never occurred to him that such manipulation was inappropriate. This dubious routine was also included in the Howard Stern Show. (*Daily Mail*, Wednesday, July 22nd, 1998).

McKenna was later questioned about his website on the Internet, and agreed that some of the claims on it may be inaccurate. He promised to correct them. Scrivener stated that McKenna claimed to have a PhD from a US university. He treated private clients, including some celebrities, and made audiotapes to help people "succeed." Scrivener said that according to McKenna, a member of the Federation of Ethical Stage Hypnotists, hypnosis was "powerful and safe," although not suitable for people suffering from epilepsy or psychiatric disorders. The hypnotist denied negligence and contended that Gates' illness was not caused by hypnosis.

Gates is said to have displayed pronounced and alarming signs of personality change immediately following his inclusion in McKenna's act at the Swan Theatre, High Wycombe, Buckinghamshire. Nine days later he was admitted to hospital, where he stayed for nearly a month, "was taken off medication after six months but had to go back on drugs when paranoid symptoms returned and he exhibited childlike behaviour." Gates, now thirty years old, had no previous mental illness and has been unable to work since the stage show.

Having heard all the evidence, the judge expressed his sympathy with Gates "but nothing else." The *Daily Mail* of Saturday, August 15th, 1998, duly reported: "Giving judgement at the end of a ten-day hearing at the High Court, Mr Justice Toulson turned down 30-year-old Christopher Gates' legally-aided claim for £200,000 damages." The judge said, "I conclude that it is highly improbable that the onset of the plaintiff's schizophrenia had anything to do with his participation in the hypnotism show."

The decision, in a 38-page judgement, "was greeted with delight" by McKenna, who commented "If I had lost, stage hypnosis shows would have come to an end in this country." (Although working

23

mostly in America, McKenna owns a £900,000 home in Kensington, West London, no doubt a tribute to his earning power). He later said: "While I have great sympathy for Mr Gates and his family, the verdict has proved conclusively that hypnosis was not, and could not, have been the cause of his schizophrenia."

Having read the account of what Gates had been subjected to by McKenna at the Swan Theatre, High Wycombe (reported below), I disagree entirely with Mr Justice Toulson and the "scientific evidence" put forward by his advisors. For a stage show to evidence such power of control of one mind over another for a period of two-and-a-quarter hours is indeed terrifying, and in no sense "family entertainment" as described in Toulson's judgement.

According to the *Daily Mail* reports of Wednesday, July 22nd, and Saturday, August 15th, 1998, Gates, who had been to a hypnotist's show five years earlier, began to feel "strange" as soon as the lights dipped and the music began. McKenna warned the audience not to offer to be hypnotized if they were suffering from clinical depression or psychiatric illness. He then asked for volunteers to come on stage "now."

Gates told the court that he regarded the word "now" as a command. He "shot out" of his chair and was the first person on stage, where he became the central pivot of McKenna's act. Amongst other things, he ballet danced, strutted like Mick Jagger, was an interpreter for aliens whilst walking on the moon, "and acted like a contestant on Blind Date" (an inane British TV show presented by former 1960s popstar Cilla Black).

Gates believed that McKenna "had made himself invisible as he swept the stage with a broom and leapt out of the way as it came towards him. He said he really thought the broom was moving by itself and found it 'extemely disturbing.' He also put on 'special' glasses to allow him to see people naked. 'Although it did not work he felt embarrassed and came over hot and flustered', said the judge." Gates also found it embarrassing "when a woman was given glasses and told she too would be able to see other people naked. 'He turned away and crossed his arms in front of himself, but the defendant turned him back to face the audience and removed his hands to stop him covering himself up', said the judge. 'By all accounts the plaintiff appeared to be the star performer of the evening and his apparent attempt to avoid being seen by the lady participant was likely to have been

24

seen by the defendant as good entertainment'" (*Daily Mail*, Saturday, August 15th, 1998).

After a sleepless night, Gates "behaved oddly at work, laughing when a shop steward said there were going to be redundancies. He later became terrified of going upstairs in case he died when he reached the top, and thought that he could stop cars with his eyes. 'The whole experience must have been terrifying', the judge said."

Gates' solicitor, Martin Smith, had "a blunt message for anyone thinking of going to a hypnotism show, 'don't', he said. He claimed his wife Rachel fell into a trance just by watching a hypnotist's video at home" (*ibid*).

[Thanks to the ignorance of Justice Toulson and the ineptitude of his advisors, McKenna has now extended his "act" to streets, shops, parks and public houses. British Channel 4 television transmitted an hour-long programme featuring McKenna on Monday, 30th August 1999, described as follows: "In a one-hour special, the hypnotist unleashes his powers in the street as confused passers-by witness the effects of his mesmerism." McKenna was shown hypnotising disbelieving members of the general public and causing them to act out a wide range of scenarios – mostly sexual or bizarre in content, to a background of (often nervous) laughter from those watching. Had the audience actually registered what they were witnessing, they would have expressed horror that an individual's mind should so thoroughly and speedily be brought under the absolute control of a stranger. As one man said following his own experience of McKenna's powers, "I was aware of what I was doing, but *I could not stop it*" (my italics). In my view, subliminal processes are not to be played with. With the type of sustained hypnosis demonstrated, there must be effects, not necessarily displayed immediately, though in the short term or long term they will manifest in some form quite inevitably. Fortunately for McKenna, the law has decreed that those effects, of whatever nature or severity, are not his responsibility.]

Trance inductions in would-be shamans are equally fraught, yet are as readily sanctioned by certain researchers bent on glorifying the paranormal. But shamanism is much wider in scope than stage hypnosis or the hypnotism used for research purposes, and far more wide ranging in long-term effect. The fact that uni-

25

versity professors and highly qualified researchers choose to sponsor shamanic trance practices is serious enough, but even more serious is the fact that they clearly do not differentiate between the native shaman steeped in his own cultural background with an awareness from birth of elemental forces, and the Western would-be practitioner to whom such concepts are largely alien, yet who wishes to utilize them to his own advantage, and to ends quite other than those of traditional shamans serving their communities.

Spiritualist mediums enter trance habitually, but have proven many times over that Westerners in general have not the ability, nor the inborn acuity, to undertake the work of genuine shamans, having quite different orientations and dispositions.

Sweatlodge ceremonies abound in the promotion of "Shamanism" and carry their own hazards. Nik Purnell, a sweatlodge leader, has urged the formation of a British Council of Elders "to accredit workshop leaders who organize Native American [Indian] ceremonies in the UK." His plea follows the recent death of a friend who collapsed after suffering a cardiac arrest immediately following a sweatlodge ceremony.

This event shocked Purnell into the due awareness of the vulnerability of the human body "to the physical extremes suffered during Native American ceremonies." His suggestion is that "all practitioners who conduct Vision Quest events, such as sweatlodges, should be accredited by a Council of Elders, and that they should all be trained in first aid techniques such as CPR (cardio-pulmonary resuscitation), mouth to mouth resuscitation, and the management of the effects of heat exhaustion. Anyone running an accredited sweatlodge or other Native American workshop would have to display a certificate detailing their qualifications, to reassure participating members of the public" (*Kindred Spirit*, Winter Issue 1996/97, p. 4).

This is all very well, but who will comprise this "Council of Elders," and what will constitute the qualifications – other than training in first aid? Glancing down the lists of Shamanic courses advertised in the same magazine, some of which promote correspondence based courses "leading to certificate or diploma" (invariably at considerable expense to the trainee shaman) one can only conclude that these are entrepreneurial ventures, commercial enterprises with the prime concern of making money, and that the resultant certificates are unlikely to be worth more than the paper they are written on. To the best of my knowledge, authentic, indigenous shamans are the products of inherent abilities and dedicated lives given wholly to the service of their people, whether the recipients can pay for their services or not. They cannot be made in Western weekend courses tutored by persons who have no conception of the inner realities of genuine shamanism, much less the nature (and control) of the energies utilized.

In response to Nik Purnell's plea for Regulation, Leo Rutherford informed the Editors of *Kindred Spirit* that a group of experienced sweatlodge leaders, including himself, as well as practitioners of contemporary shamanism, were meeting together early in 1997 to "look at these issues." In the meantime he recommended some guidelines "for sweatlodge leaders working with beginners." These included (firstly) verbal health checks re various diseases and medication: "Speak with them until you feel it is okay or otherwise for them to participate. If they do participate, you know you have to look out for them. Have someone with at least basic first aid knowledge on hand." Secondly, it was pointed out that "if you chief a lodge, particularly with beginners, the ceremony which you are chiefing is putting people into an altered state of consciousness, and you are therefore bound to take a measure of responsibility for them. . . . to keep them as safe as possible and see they get back adequately to everyday consciousness before they leave." [Please note the word "adequately."] Thirdly, there must be no competitiveness, no sense of bravado (common to Western males) "in staying in the lodge and taking heat. . . . any sense of competitiveness about the number of rounds a person takes is completely against the ethic of a properly conducted sweatlodge ceremony."

Rutherford concludes with the view that, although these rules "may be slightly different from those put out by some native medicine people . . . we are not Native Americans and rules need adjustment to people and place. There should be no lack of safety if everyone keeps to this simple set of guidelines" (*Kindred Spirit*, Spring 1997, pp. 97–98).

Having led sweatlodges for over ten years (as he tells us), Rutherford should therefore know quite a lot about the psychological disorientation induced by hyperventilation, and the physiological stress caused by heat exhaustion, though he places no emphasis on either. Moreover, he makes no mention of other criteria, such as the very high risk of *kundalini* activation in sweatlodge work for those who are sensitive to this syndrome. Nor does he mention that artificially activated altered states of consciousness do not simply confine themselves to the sweatlodge – something has to move within the subliminal processes to produce the altered state in the first place, and can set in motion trends which affect the mind and emotions long after the event.

Bearing in mind that most UK sweatlodge shamans are the products of Western courses, the big question here can be formulated as: Do Western shamans have sufficient ability to deal with matters of heightened consciousness (and related results) without damaging the delicate growth in another human being so prematurely intensified by their ceremonies? So far I have found no evidence of such ability.

And where are the safeguards for weekend "Trance-Dances" that can so readily be duplicated at home, or four-day "Soul Retrieval" courses in which "you will learn new techniques for bringing back split-off parts, with quality tuition in a safe supportive environment." There is no way the Western promoters can ensure such safety. [Sad to relate, nor can many of their North American counterparts, as not all indigenous shamans are authentic.] People who genuinely understand the process of spiritual development, in East or West, do not provide operative, sometimes high-level, shamanic experiences for unselected members of the general public. Nor do they prostitute their knowledge in pursuit of lucrative livelihoods.

Other hazards arise in popular workshops of a different nature. Courses in Tantric sex are snares for the incautious – the practice of recommended techniques can create a continuous, in some cases, insatiable, desire for sexual experience under the guise of spiritual progression. Margo Anand, the Rajneeshi exponent who is busy opening centres promoting "Skydancing" Tantra and training course leaders from all over the world, is herself a testimony to this, as is clearly evidenced in her book, *The Art of Sexual Ecstasy: The Path of Sacred Sexuality for Western Lovers* (1990). There is also the extremely revealing video in which Anand actively participates, *Sacred Sex* (a film by Cynthia Connop, produced by Triple Image Films Pty Ltd and the Australia Film Finance Corporation, 1992), which carries the ambivalent inscription "Fun, Fantasy and Spirituality."

It is stated in the video that Tantrists use the sexual ecstasies of the body as "a direct pathway to enlightenment," and that "total body orgasm is akin to the highest states of religious ecstasy." These concepts are sold to the public as "spiritual sex," although there is absolutely nothing in this video, nor in Anand's book, for that matter, even remotely connected with spirituality, or with the word sacred. The video merely demonstrates that a certain type of hype and the bonding processes utilized by most New Age centres, plus acts of "risk," i.e., daring exhibitionism on the part of course leaders, lead to extremes of "emotional release" and to a total loss of all inhibitions. The group nudity and orgiastic behaviour of the participants would have surely progressed still further had the course tutor not had an eye on the resultant commercially oriented video and the laws of censorship.

On page 3 of her book, Anand states: "High Sex takes the experience of orgasm to a new dimension – a dimension in which genital orgasm is only the beginning. It inspires you to explore the full capacity of orgasm, culminating in ecstatic body-to-body and soul-to-soul communion." This is a big statement to make on such a flimsy basis. Without any previous high-level experience of a mystical nature, indeed, any experience other than the sexually related "ecstasies" proffered in her book, it is difficult to see how she can legitimately conclude, and furthermore teach, that the experience referred to is "soul-to-soul communion" of a transcendental type. Anand posits no range of personal other-dimensional experience with which to justify such assertions. Her course on "sexual ecstasy" is self-concocted, and the aim, she tells us, is to redirect the energy generated by erotic arousal into "a whole range of peak experiences." This, apparently, is open to all, and constitutes a short cut *par excellence* to all things spiritual, at least according to Anand.

On page 51, Anand reveals the basis of her experiments: "In High Sex, deep breathing is what connects us to our sexual centres. The deeper we breathe, the more we come into contact with our sexual energy." Breathwork, in fact, is the keynote to the whole book, and an essential component of all the orgasm and/or ecstasy related exercises described, which also yield other bonuses such as the sexually based "Yin-Yang Game" – which, "if you feel adventurous" can be played with more than one partner. This game is designed to loosen the inhibitions in order to ask for "what you have always wanted, especially in sex" and cultivates the feeling (we are assured) that one deserves the best (p. 258). However, a partner is not essential for the pursuit of these benefits: "Discovering the art of self-pleasuring [masturbation] is essential in High Sex," says Anand (p. 197), who plainly considers it an indispensable feature of her coursework.

Anand, as a practising Tantrist, considers she has found a way to transform sexuality into a "truly spiritual experience," and *en route* to this her students are taught, among other equally suspect practices, to undo past conditioning and any feelings of guilt they may experience in the (highly recommended) area of anal orgasm – and explicit details are given with regard to effecting this. Anand appears unaware that the original taboos on awakening this mode of sexual desire and procuring its satisfaction were not rooted in either conditioning or hygienic considerations, as she assumes, but in something far more serious. Nor is she concerned that her prescriptions are actually creating in normal people appetites and desires they did not have formerly, and which generate yet further sexual *sanskaras* (or impressions), rather than transmuting them. Anal "massage," according to Anand, can produce in men "a deeper, subtler implosive type of orgasm," and is also "the most powerful shortcut . . . to orgasm enhancement" (p. 338). This aberrant statement doubtless explains the addictive quality of some types of homosexual activity.

Yet Anand is not speaking of homosexuality. Her aim and objective, by the use of breathwork and visualization, is to force the sexually based energies into the power centres of the *chakras*, and there create a state of ecstasy attainable at will – both partners "shooting the energy together from the genitals . . . directly to the crown chakra or the third eye chakra" (p. 370), a prodigious feat that is quite impossible in such chronically miseducated circles.

Despite the popularity of Anand's courses and the widespread interest in her Tantric "work" (which has the support of numerous fellow-Tantrists, and many quite eminent PhDs), I personally do not find her directions in keeping with what she purports to promote. For instance, one of the recommended preludes to *chakra*

30

activation (an undertaking supposedly of a spiritual nature) is to adopt "The Piercing Tiger Position," in which the female tantrist "crouches on all fours with buttocks raised" prior to the extended lovemaking that precedes the practice termed "Waves of Bliss." Anand states that the "animalistic quality" of this experience "can be very exciting," and that the "pleasure and sensuality" of the posture can be greatly enhanced by "making sounds like animals in heat" (p. 398). This, and oral lovemaking, eventually leads the participants to the point of "Opening to your Inner Light." The whole practice culminates in the establishing of a continuously operating circuit in which, mouths conjoined, one partner inhales the breath of the other, and in turn exhales into the partner's lungs, thus circulating the same shared breath. Both partners at the same time are "visualising an infinite cycle of energy," which process becomes "extremely ecstatic" (assisted no doubt by decreasing levels of oxygen to the brain). Eventually, says Anand, the woman can have the impression that the man's sexual organ "is reaching all the way to the third eye . . . and that her whole body has become a vulva" (p. 422). Such enticements attract a certain kind of client willing to pay for sensation at the cost of learning priorities.

One of Anand's many misleading statements is to compare her proffered sexual experience with the samadhic experience of the saintly Indian celibate, Ramakrishna of Dakshineswar (d. 1886), whom, she asserts, made reference to this practice when he explained that the male and female had united within him, "and every pore of his skin felt as if it had become a genital organ." If Ramakrishna ever used this latter term as an illustration of the indefinable (for which no reference is given by Anand), it was certainly not intended for use in support of her sexual excesses. Ramakrishna consistently warned his students throughout his life to "shun women and gold," married an equally saintly soul who remained a virgin (as indeed did Ramakrishna) despite her desire for children, and inspired an Order of celibate monks.

Popular courses and books on sexual Tantra leave their legacies in a variety of ways, one of which is the infiltration of tantric methods into the marital aids departments of social counselling. Persons who utilize and adapt methods originally connected with powerful rituals are asking for trouble, though they nevertheless inflict these "enhancements" upon the ignorant and the unwary in the fashionable demand for unlimited orgasms.

They also inflict even more serious problems on vulnerable readerships. With the confidence derived from the massive success of *The Art of Sexual Ecstasy*, Anand produced a second book, *The Art of Sexual Magic*, which furthers her degenerate introduction of suspect Eastern lore into the West. Susan Bridle, the Managing Editor of *What is Enlightenment?* (the magazine founded by Andrew Cohen, a controversial contemporary Western guru), comments: "It was [Anand's] second book, *The Art of Sexual Magic*, that raised the most questions for me. In it she combines sexual techniques with creative visualization for the purpose of manifesting personal desires. She has developed a unique method of projecting a visualized object of desire into the "astral network" at the moment of orgasm. . . . Throughout the book she includes examples of how to use this technique to acquire, among other things, a new job, a new home, or even a new lover. According to Anand, her system of sexual magic is a means to access higher states of consciousness and to bring more of the spiritual dimension into her work; she often describes it as a spiritual practice. Yet as I read her book, while I found it educational and innovative, I couldn't help but wonder again and again, What does all this really have to do with the spiritual path?" ("You Have To Do It All," *What is Enlightenment?* Issue 13, Spring/Summer 1998, p. 51). The answer, of course, is that it has nothing whatsoever to do with the spiritual path, only with sex, sensuality, sensation, and occult manipulation for materialistic or personal ends. It is, in other words, a form of primitive witchcraft.

Yet the dubious book in question is enthusiastically promoted by the highly acclaimed UNESCO sponsored "spiritual" community in Scotland known as the Findhorn Foundation, an offshoot of which, the recently formed Findhorn Bay Community Association, gave Anand's book pride of place on the back cover advertisement of the July 1998 issue of their publicly distributed magazine, *Genesis*. Under the heading HOT SUMMER READING, The Phoenix Community Store (which serves the whole of the Findhorn Foundation Community) described the book as "An advanced course in erotic enchantment and the magic of extended orgasm, with exercises based on ancient Tantric rituals." Beneath this advertisement is displayed another spiritual gem, *The New Good Vibrations Guide to Sex*, containing "Tips and Techniques from America's Favourite Sex Toy Store," and dubbed "The *Joy of Sex* for the electronic age."

That these books should achieve promotion in a Community proclaiming itself "an evolutionary spearhead" and a centre for meditation and inner development is ludicrous in the extreme. It also speaks volumes for the interests of senior staff in official charge of all "educational" programmes within that charity.

Margo Anand was doubtless much influenced by the practices of her former teacher, the deceased "sex guru" and Tantrist, Bhagwan Shree Rajneesh (d. 1990) now known as Osho, who led astray thousands of predominantly young intellectuals (including highly qualified professionals) who naively trusted him and believed in his professed enlightenment.

In *The Promise of Paradise: A Woman's Intimate Story of the Perils of Life with Rajneesh* (1992), the disillusioned Satya Bharti Franklin, a former Rajneeshi, records that at a private meeting of Rajneesh's exclusive circle of female devotees, he instructed them "to 'allow' their sexual energy to be awakened during darshan and to use it for 'the work.' . . ." He also required Vivek, his closest companion, to "instruct the mediums [the specially selected elite circle of female devotees] not to wear anything under their darshan robes at night, allegedly putting his hands under their gowns when the lights went out." Those involved were "warned not to discuss it" (p. 131). Franklin furthermore states: "Bhagwan made no attempt to hide the bizarre nature of the energy darshans . . . Visitors were welcome to attend darshan; the press was welcome. If outsiders saw the energy darshans as group orgies, and Bhagwan as a hypnotist who controlled his disciples through paranormal powers, aided by mesmerising music, flashing lights, and ordained frenzies of undisguised sexuality, it was fine with him" (p. 132). She added, however, that she did not wish her parents and children to know of the darshans, as she could not explain them in terms of the spiritual life for which she had left home.

Satya Bharti Franklin, who describes herself as coming from an "upper-middle-class" background, was lured by the usual promises of rapid and unconditional spiritual enlightenment, and left her three young children in 1972 to become a disciple of Bhagwan Shree Rajneesh. Her children moved in with their father, from whom she was separated, and she departed for India, remaining with Rajneesh either in Poona, or later in Oregon, USA, for the next thirteen years, for most of that period residing within his household and under his personal guidance.

His "teachings," as described by Franklin, were those pertaining to tantric sex, combined with violent *kundalini*-raising exercises and the release of "dynamic" energies. The route to "total celibacy" as promoted by Rajneesh was via the extremities of continuous orgasms and assorted partners without number. (I have nowhere found any report on attaining the celibate objective, though the extremes were there in abundance). Had these disciples extended their reading material to the *Discourses* (first published in 1938–42) of Meher Baba, who died in India in 1969, they would have found a radically alternative view on this matter – that sexual excesses lead only to yet more sexual excesses, and that the way to enlightenment is via the renunciation of all extremes, particularly those of the flesh. Much less exciting, no doubt.

Franklin writes of one of her lovers, an Italian "swami": "We danced on the tables in the ashram canteen at lunchtime and made love at night sitting on the stone walls outside various Koregaon Park houses, our long robes a perfect camouflage. During work hours, he lured me into private cubicles in the public shower room, bringing me to orgasm after orgasm till I was so weak I could barely stand up" (p. 126). All this, and very, very, much more, approved, or even suggested, by the supposedly enlightened Rajneesh, whose followers assumed they were "wearing out" their karmic impressions with increasing rapidity by the act of "spending them up" whilst in Rajneesh's care, and under his directives.

The same writer describes a revealing protest from a disgruntled devotee regarding the level of noise at night through the "rapturous bouts of lovemaking" by fellow-residents, Franklin writes: "With Bhagwan urging everyone day after day to be totally free in sex ('Let the neighbors hear you!! Scream! Shout! Make it a joyous celebration!'), few of us were making any attempt to be quiet. The Lao Tzu roof, where many of us had bamboo huts, was constantly filled with the sounds of lovemaking" (p. 148).

Franklin later helped prepare the way for the removal of Rajneesh to Oregon, USA, but once installed in the thriving new "spiritual" community of the Rajneeshpuram ashram, she found

34

herself becoming increasingly upset by the behaviour of ashram children, who reminded her of her own, and who, like everyone else in the ashram, were continually exposed to every type and expression of human sexuality. Franklin commented on the "unusual" nature of Bhagwan's theories on sex education – that he considered children from an early age should "watch their parents and other adults making love." He also encouraged child masturbation, and girls of twelve had access to condoms if they wished to use them. The effects of a continual climate of permissiveness were glaringly apparent, as Franklin graphically recalls. She records the behaviour of a six-year-old ashram girl who "delighted in grabbing men's genitals through their robes" (p. 107), and of another small girl who offered oral sex to every man she saw in the public showers. Despite being "privately appalled" by what she witnessed, she yet tried to rationalize these activities.

With regard to Rajneesh's recorded comments on the desirability of parental sexual initiation of their offspring, Franklin tells us that this, to her, was even more disturbing than his "shocking" praise of Hitler years formerly, and admits that she had "judiciously altered" his words as she edited his books for publication, feeling he could not really have meant what he said (p. 107). It is apparent that she, and doubtless very many others, deliberately "screened out" what they did not wish to challenge. Direct query or confrontation would inevitably mean they must leave, thus giving up a lifestyle that would be totally unacceptable anywhere else.

Franklin repeatedly smothered her moments of doubt, throwing herself wholeheartedly into the hectic life of the commune – though she nevertheless states, in relation to the problems resulting from rampant promiscuity (such as unwanted babies and subsequent abortions, the latter openly tolerated by Rajneesh), that hundreds of young female devotees were "subtly coerced into being sterilized . . . the emphasis shifting to vasectomies after one of the teenage girls almost died" (p. 115). She later revealed that in the first year at the Oregon ranch, a single swami infected forty women with gonorrhea before being traced as the source of infection (p. 228). She does not say how many men these women, in their turn, infected. Undoubtedly the instruction given at this time by Rajneesh requiring that all his disciples should use condoms and rubber gloves during their sexual activities, was an attempt to control VD as much as AIDS – for which this preventive move was initiated. The side-effects and results of the practice of tantra were dire indeed, and as far as is known, did not include spiritual enlightenment.

Rajneesh's attitudes and behaviour are well authenticated, having been fully confirmed by many disciples who after his death wrote books or gave accounts to counsellors or interested authors. Jean Ritchie records in *The Secret World of Cults* (1991): "The reality . . . was that Rajneesh's ashram became a free love Mecca. Money and sanyasins poured in, and Rajneesh understandably collected many enemies among the Hindu community in Poona, as rumours of orgies, rape, nudity and violence spread. 'Encounter groups' often included punching, screaming, kicking or sex, frequently between partners who had never met before. The room used for these groups was padded and windowless, to minimize damage, but there were still reports of broken bones and sanyasins being punched black and blue by others who were 'releasing their frustrations.' There were rumours of unexplained deaths, and by 1979 Rajneesh was forced to ban fighting."

A news release stated that the violence was stopped when Rajneesh indicated it had "fulfilled its function within the overall context of the ashram as an evolving spiritual commune." Ritchie continues: "There was no attempt to curb the sexual behaviour of his followers, and a documentary filmed in secret at one of the tantra meditations and screened by the BBC substantiated the allegations of orgies and debauchery. Rajneesh himself was promiscuous . . . There was always a stream of girls willing to share his bed: most of his female sanyasins regarded sex with Rajneesh as the pinnacle of their ambitions, the closest they would get to true enlightenment" (pp. 128–129).

Rajneesh condoned in his devotees the smuggling of drugs and currency, and also prostitution, to which many female ashram inmates turned to raise their fees whilst in India. These "fees" and all other donations were all put to instant use. By the time Rajneesh had established himself in Oregon he owned a huge fleet of Rolls Royce automobiles, plus "four aircraft, a bus fleet – and an enormous armoury." More circumspectly, he kept an armed private "Peace Force" of dedicated followers, and in addition paid for "outside" security contracts. According to Ritchie, "Rajneesh's Utopia was little more than an armed labour camp . . . There were allegations of violence meted out to anyone who did not do as he or she was told" (p. 131).

Ritchie further comments: "His predilection for pretty young sanyasins was unabated, and no girl ever refused the honour of an 'energy-giving' session with the Bhagwan. Although drugs were supposed to be banned, he was known to take nitrous oxide to help him meditate, and regular doses of valium" (p. 131).

After bitter quarrels and serious trouble within the ashram, Rajneesh attempted to flee America, and was arrested as his private plane landed to refuel in the middle of the night at an International airport in Carolina. Ritchie reports: "The guru was taken to jail in handcuffs. It . . . suited the authorities not to hold him for long: the last thing they wanted was an imprisoned martyr as the figurehead of the religion. Rajneesh plea-bargained and was able to leave America after paying 400,000 dollars in fines and costs, with a ten-year suspended prison sentence, five years' probation and an agreement to leave the USA within five days and not return without written permission from the Attorney General" (p. 132). The charges made against Rajneesh were for violation of visa regulations, but these were not the real root of the problems surrounding him. His second-in-command, an Indian woman he had re-named Ma Anand Sheela (of whose lethal activities he denied all knowledge), was charged with corruption and the attempted murder (by poisoning) of numerous individuals. She was sentenced to twenty years imprisonment, later substantially reduced for good behaviour. According to all reports, the authorities clearly believed she "fronted" Rajneesh himself.

Ritchie suggested that the early death of Rajneesh at the age of fifty-nine in 1990 might well have been due to AIDS: "The general debility and lack of resistance to infection from which he suffered are consistent with him having AIDS, and his promiscuous lifestyle makes it a distinct possibility. Other followers have been known to have died from AIDS – two male sanyasins died in 1983, and two of the women close to the top were diagnosed as HIV positive" (p. 133). All this relates to a man who proclaimed himself a spiritual Master of the highest order; who equated himself with Christ and the Buddha, and was accepted as such by thousands upon thousands of Western devotees who gave to him all they possessed – a man who ruined the lives of countless young people that under his aegis descended to the level of drugs and debauchery.

A significant number of the largely dispersed followers of Rajneesh have since made attempts to regroup themselves and project afresh the teachings and practices of this charismatic Yogi under the banner of a new name, Osho, and his numerous books are now in the process of being repackaged and recirculated to an unsuspecting and uninformed readership. Two of these were reprinted and repromoted in 1995 by Element Books, of Salisbury, England, a major publisher and distributor of ostensibly spiritually oriented literature whose policy is "to make available knowledge and information to aid humanity in a time of major transition," and further: "We are always interested to hear from authors who have an original contribution to make based on quality and integrity" (*The Writer's Handbook 1997*) – a company that is nevertheless quite undeterred by the late sex guru's well attested vice and appalling reputation. In their Element Book Club Magazine *New Perspectives* (Issue 1, April 1996), an advertisement for the said books states unequivocally: "Osho brings light into our darkness . . . Heralded as the greatest spiritual teacher of our century, Osho's ashram in India became a mecca with men and women from the West seeking spiritual guidance. These two books will deepen your understanding of your inner nature and help you along the spiritual path."

The factor of proven reprehensibility (backed by a significant quantity of sociological documentation) is similarly ignored by the Review Editor of the official journal of the Scientific and Medical Network, UK, the organization which hosted the earlier-mentioned August 1995 conference in St. John's College, Cambridge, England, *Beyond the Brain: New Avenues in Consciousness Research*. (The Network also hosts the annual "Mystics and Scientists" conferences in Winchester, England). Under the Philosophy/Religion review section of the journal, titled *Books in Brief*, we read of the abovementioned books: "The first book serves as an introduction to the teaching of Osho, whose image is gradually being refurbished (remember Bhagwan Shree Rajneesh?)." The review concludes with this advice: "Whatever the newspapers have told you about Osho is worth disregarding when you come to read any of his books, which bristle with insight and wisdom." It would thus appear that within the SMN rhetoric is given more credence than sociological fact, and that a major pollutant of our society will shortly achieve exoneration in the minds of certain academics, and no doubt with time will become elevated once more to the status of Enlightenment. Indeed, such a revered figure as the Dalai Lama is already implicated in this, as is evident from the following:

In the Spring 1995 No. 3 issue of *Purnima* (the advertising vehicle of Osho Purnima Distribution, Basildon, Essex), the Dalai Lama, Nobel Peace Prize winner and leading light of the 1993 Parliament of the World's Religions held in Chicago, USA (6000 participants), is quoted in a "New book by Osho" advertisement as stating: "Osho is an enlightened master who is working with all possibilities to help humanity overcome a difficult phase in developing consciousness" – HH Dalai Lama.

This quote, for which no reference is given and which remains in circulation in other advertisements at the present date (August 1999), was obviously written during the lifetime of Osho Rajneesh, and sadly, does not say much for the Dalai Lama's own, widely assumed, state of enlightenment.

In a similar vein of irresponsibility, the Lama Karmapa, Head of the Kagyupa Tibetan Buddhist sect, asserted boldly in a further *Purnima* book advertisement: "He [Osho] is the greatest incarnation after Buddha in India" (*Kindred Spirit*, Issue 41, Winter 1997–1998, p. 79). Osho could not have been given a higher accolade, nor greater approval.

Young academics are hugely influenced by reviews appearing in journals of the erudite type published by the Scientific and Medical Network, and will inevitably respond to other advertised material bearing a (reputedly) respectable name, particularly if endorsed by such as the Dalai Lama. Osho Multiversity in Holland, which has offshoots now in London and other major cities, is fully aware of this and provides courses and workshops originated or sanctioned by Osho himself. A caption to one such advertisement reads: "Eat, drink and be merry, together with a lot of beautiful people. Celebrate like the tantrics, and get enlightenment on the side!" The celebration can hurt, and enlightenment is nowhere recorded as a side-product.

The disenchanted Franklin provides, on a cautionary note, the information that following the death of Rajneesh in January 1990, large numbers of his current and former disciples continued, rather less conspicuously, to promote the spread of his ideas in their roles as therapists and leaders of the human potential movement, although rarely acknowledging their past and present allegiance publicly. The evidence of this is unfortunately only too apparent. *Kundalini* exercises and intensive *pranayama* practices reappear continually under a variety of less readily recognizable names, which make them no less dangerous.

An organization blatantly undeterred by coercive criminal activities in the realm of sex, drugs and violence, is the earlier mentioned UNESCO commended Findhorn Foundation in Scotland, UK, the leading "spiritual" centre at the forefront of the New Age movement, which has consistently displayed an abundance of Osho literature and Tarot decks in their on-site shop despite protests from concerned individuals. [The determined inclusion of these materials (apart from the obvious commercial considerations) is justified by the assertion that people have the right to "freedom of choice." Unfortunately, people are not given all the facts, which have only of late become widely available to the general public as former disciples and devotees of Rajneesh yield up the information they themselves previously suppressed.] The Director and Management of this organization furthermore went to considerable lengths to engage a Rajneeshi as Director of Education for Foundation-run Cluny Hill College, Forres, in 1995, bringing him all the way from the USA for this purpose. More recently they have also publicized in their official guest brochure an Osho Mystic Rose Meditation course described as a three week "life-transforming process" (June/July 1997) at an adjacent associate New Age centre, Minton House, in Findhorn. This latter is owned by Judith Meynell, a Findhorn Foundation Community member, whose promotional activities are advertised as "Within the Findhorn Foundation Community" and are featured alongside the courses proffered by Newbold House, Forres, a similar subsidiary to the Findhorn Foundation.

[Meynell's prime focus is her link with the London Sufi Centre, for whom she hosts courses which include the Retreats so lavishly praised by *Harpers & Queen* magazine (Minton "is a magical place to meditate"). These functions are almost invariably led by Westerners with Sufi designates denoting specific grades of spiritual expertise once only associated with genuine adepts, and who belong to the "Sufi Order in the West" founded by Hazrat Inayat Khan (d. 1927), and currently headed by his son Pir Vilayat Inayat Khan (b. 1916). These are the "Sufis" who disseminate exercises for *kundalini* and *chakra* awakening to any who care to pay the fee.]

The Minton-based Osho course is part of a "World Wide event happening simultaneously in 200 locations" – a resurrective attempt, doubtless, to imprint another generation with Rajneesh's tantric concepts and his own catastrophic technique of *kundalini* activation.

What is one to make of this adamant refusal to acknowledge the known facts concerning Osho Rajneesh and the harm he has caused to vast numbers of people? Where does responsibility cease and heedlessness begin? Integrity is sacrificed at the altar of commercialism and nobody seems to care, or is even prepared to consider what is done in the name of spiritual growth, least of all Findhorn Foundation management and staff. [To be fair, one cannot really expect much from an organization that, in their official guest brochure, proffers as the sole listed qualification of a long-term member and senior workshop leader in core education (who is married and has a child) the information that he is "very handsome, dead sexy and extra-ordinarily modest!" See *Findhorn Foundation Core Programmes Brochure 1999*, p. 15.]

To return briefly to the much advocated Tantric "disciplines" of Margo Anand, one of the few Rajneeshis who freely admit their indebtedness to their former teacher, Osho Rajneesh. Anand's reprojection of potent breathwork, visualization, multiple orgasms and erotic sex, purportedly triggers "powerful experiences of bliss," and "the wisdom of all-encompassing consciousness" (*The Art of Sexual Ecstasy*, p. 405). Far more certainly, the reprojection brings into effect all the factors relevant to *pranayama* and other forms of breathwork, complete with their hazards. The same can be said of the Orgasmic Upward Draw taught by the Taoist, Mantak Chia, which "enables both sexes to take the intensely aroused sexual energy out of the genitals and spread it throughout the rest of the body." A plus factor for males who practise this technique is the bonus experience of "whole-body orgasms," and multiple at that.

In view of the sensationalist mass market media used for

advertising the books and courses that tutor the means of attaining these advantages, it seems probable that many participants will "get lost" at this level – and perhaps have even embarked upon these operations for the wrong reasons in the first place, and not surprisingly in view of the advertising material. People attracted by such material are unlikely, in general, to be thinking in terms of higher forms of bliss.

Would-be practitioners of Tantra appear convinced that spiritual enlightenment can be achieved through "ancient erotic mysteries," including those pertaining to "extended lovemaking, semen retention and meditative sex." There is in fact no link between physical sexual activities and higher range other-dimensional states, as those who have actually experienced such states can bear witness. The danger here, as with the "streaming" practices of Wilhelm Reich (virtually identical with Anand's "Waves of Bliss"), is of bringing energies into operation that do not belong to the realm of sexual experience and should lay dormant until other qualities are developed within the psyche. The misuse of these energies in sexual excesses generates plexuses of impressions that act as barriers to spiritual evolution and render impossible the receipt of higher ranges of experience, of which the "ecstasies" of Ms. Anand, and others, are but the distorted subtle counterfeits. (The "subtle world" is a subject scarcely possible to elucidate in the contemporary climate). Once a taste is acquired for the amplified sensations of unbridled eroticism, there is no going back, and the result is the opposite pole to spiritual enlightenment.

The Tantric system is ultimately a sensory means of untoward entry into the psyche and induces a semi-physical mode of transcendentalism. It is a break-in technique into subtle forms of bliss that reflect much higher states not reachable by the methods employed by Tantrists. It is also illicit, as these practices constitute a "dead end" developmentally. Without the basic and traditional qualities rejected outright by Rajneesh in *Tantra Spirituality & Sex* (1983), undisciplined and unprepared people cannot hope to achieve a valid (that is, transformative and lasting) form of illumination, much less enlightenment, whether by means of Tantric sex or of anything else. There are no short cuts on the spiritual path. One can "get beyond the mind," it is true, but one has to come back, and the ground-base of the everyday self remains as unregenerate as before. It is this self that brings one back again and again into incarnation. Until it is dealt with, and in the right manner, there can be no release.

In the abovementioned book, Rajneesh argues the validity of sexual Tantra on the basis of the erotic *maithun* stone sculptures on the walls of the Khajuraho and Konarak temples in India. He does not mention that these temples, like the *Kama Sutra* they illustrate, are representative of a cultural decline. [According to Dr. N. N. Bhattacharyya: "the sculptural extravagance of Khajuraho, Konarak and other temples was mainly the reflection of the abnormal sexual desires of the dominant class whose munificence was responsible for their construction. . . . The impossible copulative poses and techniques of these sexual acts were meant to excite perverse imaginations." See N. N. Bhattacharyya, *History of the Tantric Religion* (1992), p. 373.]

The sexual aspects of Tantra are a debasement of a once functional non-sexual system, the residues of which were adapted for speedy results by corrupt and usurping yogis who had lost the key to former knowledge and resorted to left-hand practices, of which sexual Tantra was one of the most prominent. Degenerate yogis sought to emulate or achieve, by any means possible, the abilities and powers of those whose roles they had appropriated. The subtle "ecstasies" or "bliss" of sexual Tantra were falsely considered as states of enlightenment, and still are to this day by Tantrist practitioners. The essence of this matter is approached more fully in Chapter 3 of the present text.

Sincere and aspirational people are their own best insurance. The quality of their lives will in time yield spontaneous experiences of a spiritual nature, and will safely and surely lead them into the proximity of an authentic teacher when (and if) appropriate. Aspiration is lacking in the New Age, whose exponents are unable to comprehend that authentic teachers do not use "techniques" and "workshops," which are crude fare for the exploited. In contrast, there is everything to be gained by inner striving and silent prayer, plus the traditional virtues of upright conduct, honesty, and humility. It is inner motivation, and the observance of duty (and parental duty in particular) in a proper spirit, that counts. In this decade and the one preceding, the recognition has been lost that duty well done is of consequence; moreover, that such scruple creates an interior energy, and one that in the average human being initially provides the sole propulsive fuel for spiritual growth.

There are two further points to which I would like to draw attention before closing this chapter. Both are concerned with the practice of meditation:

(1) People are usually unaware that meditation is a discipline originally intended for selected pupils under the care of an authentic teacher at a specific stage of their development, and that it was never intended for general use, or continuous use, or for anyone simply wishing to practice it, as is customary today in retreat centres and monasteries (the latter usually of a Buddhist orientation). The discipline of meditation causes changes in the cerebral mechanism, and prolonged and intensive practise can activate, sometimes acutely, the subtle centres that in most persons should remain safely closed. These exercises produce specific and repeatable results, but without the supervisory expertise of a conscious teacher who has completed his or her evolution, such exercises are out of context and will inevitably, and invariably, generate lop-sided growth.

Formally educated Tibetan Buddhist monks who become Geshes and Lamas are often learned in scriptural texts, but this should be distinguished from enlightenment. It is claimed that many of these monks have attained enlightenment or *Nirvana* through learning and meditation. According to Professor Charles Tart in *States of Consciousness* (1983), p. 237, what they experience *in the highest state possible*, way beyond that of Effortless Insight, is – *Total Cessation of Consciousness*, a daunting description implying non-existence and absolute emptiness. Yet is this really the *Nirvana* that was experienced by Gautama Buddha and other fully enlightened beings? Or is this a state reached by those who have not yet achieved the development that unveils the evolutionary organ of instantaneous *comprehension* – an organ essential for the translation of total unconsciousness into total consciousness? In other words, beyond an observed and seemingly *unconscious* Void lies a *Unified Total Reality* in which consciousness, far from being negated, becomes an holistic Totality.

Only the most highly evolved entities can attain to mastery of these states, and some who have gone even further can transmit an increased consciousness to others. The lack of advanced faculties can lead the intensive meditator only to the empty room of Nothingness (a total cessation of consciousness), or to consciousness of the Void, or consciousness of *un*consciousness, or, *beyond* this, and described by only a very few, the experience of pure bliss existent without any attributes – which is not the end of the journey as is generally supposed, but merely the anterior gateway to modes of spiritual existence unsuspected by humankind. Supreme Bliss is an attribute of Divinity; Supreme Bliss plus *Total Comprehension* equals Evolutionary Completion, the full-flowering of human consciousness *consciously* fused with the Divine.

(2) Secondly, what is done in this generation in the name of spiritual tuition and personal growth is nothing short of barbaric, and speaks volumes for the ignorance of the persons who place themselves in charge of these operations. The former Buddhist monk, Jack Kornfield, who obtained a doctorate in clinical psychology, refers uncritically to this situation in *Spiritual Emergency* (pp. 160–161, 180–184) in reference to the meditation retreats separately taught by himself, Professor Roger Walsh and Ram Dass (Richard Alpert), the latter being a former Harvard professor turned hippie who featured prominently in the earliest LSD experimentation. Ram Dass was himself in therapy for many years as a patient, and earlier spent six years along with Timothy Leary and a circle of influential PhDs continuously sampling psilocybin and LSD. Alpert and Leary were both expelled from Harvard University for their subsequent hallucinogenic-oriented behaviour; they pioneered and furthered the drug addictive counter-culture that wrecked the lives of literally thousands of university students. With their drug taking, excessive promiscuity, and wholesale rejection of traditional values, Leary and Alpert set the norm for decades to come – the end result of which is the degenerate drug culture we have today that continues to escalate on a worldwide scale.

When LSD and other consciousness-altering drugs were made illegal, Ram Dass and many like him turned to mind-expanding meditation and to the techniques of Eastern religions, and in an incredibly short time certain of them (in this instance, Kornfield, Walsh, and Dass) felt proficient enough to lead "spiritual" retreats. These retreats ran for varying periods of time, and were sometimes of three months duration and more. Intensive and prolonged meditation was practised by anyone who cared to apply, with the consequence that retreatants frequently produced extreme reactions, not unlike those associated with successive intakes of LSD. Among these reactions, as Jack Kornfield records, were auditory and visual hallucinations, obsession, sleeplessness and various kinds of paranoia and fear. Some meditators had to be given tranquillisers, occasionally in the form of a forcible injection; several were hospitalized, and a few had serious nervous breakdowns.

It is explained by Kornfield that known psychotics, previously hospitalized for mental illnesses, were allowed inclusion in the retreats, and these were the persons who caused the most problems. Many other retreatants were unstable and suffered assorted forms of imbalance, exacerbating certain syndromes attributed (by the course tutors) to *kundalini* activations or to general neurosis. None of these people would have been included in any developmental discipline by a knowledgeable and responsible teacher, but there seems little awareness amongst *these* teachers (or those who taught them) that to activate *kundalini at all* (an undoubted possibility with sustained meditation), in any manner, in unprepared people, let alone damaged people, is never a good thing; that you place them at serious risk by so doing, and that even if they are "grounded" enough to go home at the end of the course, there is likely to be hidden damage of a nature not readily put right. The comments made by Jack Kornfield on the opening of *chakras* (*Spiritual Emergency*, pp. 158–159) are nonsensical, and reveal an acute ignorance in this field. How then, can such "teachers" genuinely rectify anything that goes wrong?

Meditation is not a therapy for all ills, nor is it a fashionable pastime – it is an instrument of development that, combined with other requirements, will further interior growth in selected individuals, and these individuals must first have some form of preparation. (In all developmental work, selectivity is essential in the best interests of all concerned). Yet without that indispensable combination or prescription, the continuous practise of Buddhist-oriented forms of meditation can prove a trap – one which, at the least, may generate as many fixed or conditioned modes of thought and behaviour as anything else. Other symptoms of that trap can be even worse.

Many course leaders speak glibly and apparently knowledgeably to their listeners, and some write beautifully worded and affecting articles and books on spiritual growth. Whatever their intentions may be, their positive attributes are all too frequently spoiled by over-casual attitudes and a non-judgementalism which is carried to an extreme.

Non-judgementalism taken too far gives free licence to all kinds of evil and ultimately renders conscience inoperative. Anything and everything pertaining to human behaviour is considered valid, simply because it exists. There is no longer any "right" or "wrong," no yardstick by which humankind can measure deficiencies. Likewise anything and everything that produces interior experiences (of whatever nature) and other results, is assumed to be equally valid, because these methods are perpetuated by various religions like Buddhism and Shamanism and are therefore considered to be legitimate. No consideration is ever given to the possibility that the religion concerned has suffered distortion in the process of time – has gone into decline and lost original tenets, i.e., is now outmoded. To the contrary, modern teachers imagine they can increase the developmental effects of these religions by amalgamating and adapting assorted techniques from a variety of sources.

Nor is it deliberated that the world in general, and the "New Age" in particular, is in the state it is in today because people have made the wrong choices – have misused their freewill and brought about situations that were not part of the original evolutionary blueprint – have "created their own reality" selfishly, cruelly and egotistically, and the end product of that "reality" will ultimately have to be faced and undone, with all that this implies.

These self-designated "teachers" are no doubt delightful, friendly and intelligent people, intellectually conversant with what they promote. Yet whether they are spiritually competent to have charge of thousands of searching minds is highly questionable. Personally, I do not think they have any business to do so, but I am not a PhD and have no qualification for making such comment outside my own life's experience. It is the extent of that experience, however, that may justify the comment.

Chapter Two

Potential Hazards to Spiritual Growth: 2

The biggest problem confronting today's researchers into the realms of the transpersonal, and in particular those researchers concerned with the possibilities of evolutionary development of a spiritual nature, is *counterfeit* experience. By this I mean (a) experimentally induced experience that so closely resembles the experiences on record of saints and mystics that the former can readily be confused with the latter; (b) experiences produced by individually or group applied techniques of breathwork which are similarly open to confusion, or (c) experiences arising from the frequent use of visualization combined with shamanic techniques, drugs, or some form of magical ritual. The use of prolonged and regular meditation comes into a different category, but this still presents a major source of cerebral experience, particularly in relation to the "awakening" of the evolutionary force of *kundalini*.

These experiences, however valid or profound, are not of themselves indicative of spiritual development. In general, the majority of persons who have these experiences are not going anywhere developmentally (because of insufficient preparation), and the content of their experiences is rarely sufficiently informative to be useful for consciousness research purposes. Random experiences cannot of themselves adequately chart the non-physical world. Only a very wide range of non-laboratory experiences (and not those induced by "techniques") could achieve that end.

It is generally assumed that the possession of an intuitive form of psychism is a significator of inner development and therefore denotes a degree of growth, which is not necessarily the case. A problem here is the lack of sound information on the subject of "inner development" – one that is not helped by pseudo teachers and commercially oriented "spiritual" enterprises. Even those personages known historically as sages and saints, with few exceptions, may not have achieved the ultimate states attributed to them by the layman. There are gradations of development, each level of which has access to certain perceptions of truth, and only very rarely including an holistic comprehension of the mechanics of spiritual evolution. One must also remember that suppressive regimes like the Catholic Inquisition stamped out all suspicions of doctrinal "heresy," and the records that have been passed down to us were in many cases written by those who well knew the penalties for stepping out of line, whatever their insights.

Counterfeit experiences can be defined as experiences unlinked to genuine interior growth, which exhibit the semblance of *authentic* experience but without the qualitative and transformational factors that are their hallmark. They are the result of forced or artificial modes of entry into the psyche, or soul, induced before proper preparation for such experience has been made in the human self. Inadequate preparation inevitably produces distortion; the receptive nucleus required to translate and interpret the content of interior realms is in most instances as yet insufficiently evolved for the task, indeed, may not even have begun to form.

"Break-in" practices invariably masquerade as legitimate, and *initially* evoke similar or even identical signs to those appearing in persons in whom correctly oriented growth has commenced, misleading both observer and observed alike. Yet the former interprets what is seen or experienced from the basis of an inadequate or nonexistent structure, and a commensurate inability to accurately comprehend and evaluate. In this way false bases of understanding are laid, which once established in the public mind (and the minds of researchers) are very difficult to alter. Those who knowingly commercially promote these intrusive and wholly inappropriate methods must in time confront what they have done, as they directly damage the work of interior evolution, creating in others what amount to serious obstructions.

The distorted development that occurs as a result of random, out-of-sequence activation (as in the premature use of intensive meditation or the techniques of amplified visualization) engenders similarly counterfeit experiences and must be undone very thoroughly before any genuine growth is possible. This form of pseudo development comprises a foundation which cannot be built upon, nor adapted, and is thus an impediment to what is sought.

This premise will be fiercely opposed in our contemporary society as more and more researchers, frequently highly qualified academics, subscribe to the reverse view and formulate sincere but erroneous theories regarding transcendental experience and all things esoteric, theories which are likely to be collated in research documentation and become accepted as valid representations of truth.

At this point one might usefully pause to consider what constitutes the division between one form of development and another, and whether this division is of an overall significance. New Age course leaders like to tell us that *all* routes are valid – that all developmental efforts in whatever direction will lead to the Godhead or Higher Self. But is this really true? And if not, where do they lead? The determining factor is frequently the use of the will, and nowhere is this more clearly attested than in the matter of witchcraft and magical ritual.

Practitioners of the above form various groupings under the overall rubric of the Western Mystery Tradition, whose adherents range from those practising simple "white" witchcraft to the far more dubious theatrical ritualists influenced by former 19th century secret societies like the Hermetic Order of the Golden Dawn (founded in 1887), the offshoots of which still vigorously exist. In the past, during the long period of their banning, these esoteric and magical groupings grew accustomed to concealing their activities, and in general they find it useful to do so now. Secrecy is the best protection from prying eyes and those who query centuries old practices on moral grounds. But times are changing – there are now few moral judgements and people can do as they please in all walks of life without censure, thus more and more once suppressed information becomes available. We know, for instance, that many groupings now use visualization for their purposes rather than ritual, but some factions use both. The power of a focused mind driven by a strong ego with as yet unpurified emotions is formidable, as many have discovered to their detriment.

Yet, as Kevin Tingay writes in his book review on this subject in *The Christian Parapsychologist*: "For those tempted to seek hidden wisdom in occult orders, *Revelations of the Golden Dawn*

50

by R. A. Gilbert provides a salutary warning. Drawing on archive material, Mr. Gilbert catalogues a sad history of spiritual seekers being led astray by their own egoism. The Order of the Golden Dawn drew into its ranks many creative people at the end of the last century, but it was a house built upon the sand of human weakness and despite the best efforts of its more spiritually minded initiates its fall was probably inevitable" (Vol. 13, No.1, March 1998, p. 38).

Magical ritual, whether neopagan or "hermetic" in orientation, attracts strong wills and imaginative minds, and also, it appears, an increasing number of professionals – one Witchcraft coven in Inverness, Scotland, for instance, was reported by the media to have a doctor, a policeman, and a solicitor among the members. (*Reporting Scotland*, Grampian Television, 9th February 1998). The more potent practitioners possess powers of clairvoyance and certain forms of seership, and can demonstrate very adequately that there are unseen forces in both man and his environment that can be tapped and directed – abilities ignorantly confused now and in earlier eras with a superior development.

Ritual magic has lately become the subject of sociological study. T. M. Luhrmann's book, *Persuasions of the Witch's Craft: Ritual Magic in Contemporary England* (1992) was grant subsidised by several academic sources, and Christ's College, Cambridge, elected Luhrmann to a Research Fellowship. In order to conduct her research, Luhrmann joined several wiccan and ritualistic groupings and made friends with the members. On page 4 of her book she states, "In England several thousand people – possibly far more – practise magic as a serious activity, and as members of organised groups. . . . Their magic involves a ritual practice based upon ideas about strange forces and the powers of the mind. These are people who don long robes and perform rituals in which they invoke old gods to alter their present reality."

More disturbing is the snippet included on the reverse page of the same book and taken from a mail order catalogue produced in the USA, where magical practices are (assumedly) much more widespread:

"WAX IMAGE DOLLS . . . Cure sickness, capture love, heal and hate with image dolls . . . By making an image you can *work magic on that person perpetually*. 6" male or female dolls supplied ready to be personalised. . . . Natural wax colour. Some

51

shamans keep shelf-fulls of dolls to *control all their acquaint-ances*" (my italics).

It should perhaps be pointed out that certain magazines pro-duced in England have for some years printed similar advert-isements. *Prediction* is one of them. Advertisers have even offered to "cast spells" and generate "curses" for a fee. Witchcraft is also advertised in upmarket New Age magazines like *Kindred Spirit* – such as "*Children of Artemis*: Witchcraft & Wicca. Impartial help and advice for newcomers seeking genuine Witchcraft and Wiccan groups or contacts" (*Kindred Spirit*, Issue 42, Spring 1998, p. 65).

Many people do not overtly take seriously the fact of ritual magic, though there undoubtedly exists a subliminal fear of the supernatural that becomes evident in the face of certain events. In *Persuasions of the Witch's Craft*, Luhrmann describes a magi-cal ritual conducted by a branch of the Western Mysteries tra-dition – a ceremony which had occultly alarming consequences that could have proven much worse. This event took place in May 1983 at Greystone, a converted manor house in Wiltshire, UK, and was "the culmination of a series of seven annual rituals." Luhrmann herself was not present, being regarded as "too much of a novice" for inclusion, but the incident concerned was talked of for weeks afterwards and discussed with Luhrmann by many of the forty-odd participants. The intent of the ritual was to "bring the underworld forces into earthly cooperation." Luhrmann comments, "This may seem vague: what it meant is that before the week-end, participants read about a dark goddess, about hell, and meditated on how to transform that destructive energy into happier forms" (p. 140). A very tall order, one would think. The ritual, however, did not proceed as planned. Something went seriously awry, and participants hastily vacated the room in which it was held and rushed outside in states of upset and confusion.

According to a female eye-witness who was involved in the ceremony, "two high-level magicians, considered by the others to be adepts" set in motion the ritual as on former occasions, but with one exception. This time, a new factor was introduced. Instead of the presiding magician (Gareth Knight) facing his female partner with a ritual officer on either side, he placed his wife in the centre of the foursome, which apparently "blocked the flow of energy" and disrupted whatever had commenced to operate.

The eye-witness recounts that, suddenly, she "got a strong contact [a disembodied entity] ... I told it, go back, go back, we're not ready yet. And it got furious ... At one point, Knight leant around his wife and said, 'Are you all right, Augusta?' Something in me snapped. You don't use Christian names in a magical ceremony ... I let this thing loose, and it walloped Knight. He rocked slightly. Then it picked me up and strode down the corridor with me until it left." Luhrmann again takes up the story and records a participant's collapse. When she later discussed the above event with Augusta (in the tearoom of the British Museum), she considered, regardless of the cause, that the woman concerned had suffered "a vivid experience of thwarted spiritual possession during the ritual" (p. 140).

What Luhrmann does not appear to recognize, or perhaps does not like to say, is that the human element remains operative in the arena of occult practices despite the presence of powerful, trained minds; and that the "backswing" of the individual formidable wills involved, if interfered with, or denied, can afflict appalling damage on other participants. Such damage is capable of outworking on more than one level, i.e., in acute emotional agitation, nervous debility, illness, accident, and physical injury. Also in less known ways via disembodied entities partially under the control of magicians.

Further on in her book, Luhrmann makes reference to "magical technology," and notes that visualization is "the means by which the magic works." She further observes that proficiency in bringing about desired effects is directly dependent upon the ability to visualize (p. 191).

These magical skills are readily available in theory, and are taught publicly in fee-charging workshops in many places, including central London, UK. In their Autumn programme of 1991, The College of Psychic Studies under the Presidency of Brenda Marshall advertised Lectures and Workshops by Dolores Ashcroft-Nowicki, author of a *Ritual Magic Workbook* (1986), a work described as: "A practical course of self initiation, a carefully conceived 12 month training programme for anyone wishing to take up ceremonial magic."

Ashcroft-Nowicki is presented by the College as "one of the best known and most respected of contemporary British occultists. She is the Principal of the Servants of the Light, the leading school of occult and magical science and she lectures worldwide." Workshop 1 was titled *Ritual Magic in the Modern World*, and proclaimed as "An intensive one-day workshop for those who would like to know more about practical magic and ritual." Workshop 2, *The Seven Powers of the Body*, took the matter further, advising of "A workshop on the use of the main chakras in magical training."

There followed an astounding statement on the objective of this one-day tutorial, the aim being no less than *Opening the seven psychic centres under your firm control. Using the five senses on four levels*; a statement impossible of verification amongst those attending, and in the view of the present writer, equally impossible of achievement on any level at all. Novices, and even "adepts" of magical ritual, can do nothing of this nature *"under your firm control,"* as Dolores Ashcroft-Nowicki, Gareth Knight, and others, must well know by their own experience. Anyone who had actually "opened" the seven centres in question would not dabble in ritual magic, nor would feel the need to commercially teach such achievement to anyone who chose to pay the fee. This does not, unfortunately, alter the effects of magical ritual, nor the abilities of magicians and occultists who have succeeded, by their practises, in tapping the powers of the two lowest *chakras*.

Since the repeal of the Witchcraft Act in 1951, a number of practitioners of ritual magic and their various groupings have tentatively emerged into public view, and mainly in the last ten years through the New Age movement and feminist factions. Much of their activity has been both advertised and described as "white" magic or "natural" magic, appelatives which immediately allay any lingering fears from our superstitious past. Even "black" magic, or what was once termed as such, finds a sanctioned place on the outermost fringes of New Age Witchcraft, for the self-designated "Great Beast" and black magician, Aleister Crowley, has found respectability in the eyes of the inadequately informed, or merely perverse. His less unsavoury methods achieved a certain popularity amongst those magically inclined because they operate as effectively for "white" purposes as for the more questionable kind. The dabbling in manipulative processes is basically the same for either type of magic. It is the end design that differs, and here "black" and "white" diverge. Yet "white" practitioners also justify the use of ritual invocation, evocation, the conjuration of spirits, and the willed direction of energies to bring about desired effects.

Leaving aside the violation of natural law (laws governing the planet), of which such activities could be deemed an interference, it is argued by exponents of magic that what they are doing is beneficial to all concerned, including the environment, which they seek to bring "into balance." That natural law is out of balance is clearly evident, and in some countries more so than others. Mankind has meddled too much with the environment, has endangered entire species of living creatures and made many extinct, and the growing recognition of similar dangers for *homo sapiens*, i.e., ourselves, creates a widespread urgency not known before in recorded history. The solution, however, is not to be found in magical practices.

A hidden hazard in these practices lies in the use of the developed will – a will trained in concentration and visualization, and honed and focused to magical intent, which can in some cases actually bring about the ends sought – or at the least, those relating to specific individuals, and sometimes to entire groups. It is not generally realized *how* such manipulative interventions achieve fulfilment – as "magic" (both black and white) works in some instances and not in others, depending on the abilities of the operators.

In the case of subversive attack on an organized group, the group may simply disintegrate by sudden closure and dispersal of membership, but ritualized attacks on single individuals can produce more potent results and include serious injury, illness and death.

[It is pertinent to note here that recognition has been made of the dangers of negative prayer. Dr. Larry Dossey of Sante Fe, New Mexico, author of *Prayer is Good Medicine: How to Reap the Healing Benefits of Prayer*, in writing to Canon Michael Perry, the Editor of *The Christan Parapsychologist* (Volume 12, No. 6, June 1997, p. 181) makes this request:

"I wonder whether you, or any of your readers, have any material you can share with me about any *harmful* effects of prayer? I am investigating how people use prayer to manipulate, control, and harm others. What about curses? I would be interested in obtaining any information you might put me on to. My interest in this issue was stimulated by a poll in the USA published in *Life* magazine (March 1994) in which 5% of those surveyed said they had prayed for harm for others. That's just the 1 in 20 who will admit it." Dr. Dossey's research on 'negative' prayer was later published in his book, *Be Careful What You Pray For: You Just Might Get It.*]

A similar process, wholly unrecognized, is at work when individuals attempt to "create their own reality" (or to "co-create with God") by means of visualizations and affirmations, or initiate what amount to ritualistic spells for their own ends. Some people with illicitly developed abilities (whether known to them or not) can doubtless achieve this – but they are not in fact "creating" anything, merely disarranging what is already there, with ultimate consequences that can prove disastrous. In other words, their power extends only as far as their ability to manipulate. They cannot "create" non-existent exigencies, only activate those that exist potentially, in latent form, the manifestation of which could take varying modes of expression (in terms of events), less under their control. Immature psychologies do not comprehend how destructive such sought after events can prove for them, particularly when the foremost desires of the operator are great monetary wealth, sexual conquests, endless leisure, and doing at all times what they please.

It is rarely perceived by manipulators that even "bad" *karma*, i.e., the negative swingback from many types of past wrongdoing, can be usefully, indeed valuably, utilized in a learning process which, among other things, evokes a heartcry of repentance and regret from the transgressor, a factor not taken into account by those busy "creating" their own realities, nor by magically oriented minds concerned solely with their own desires and inclinations. The work of an authentic teacher who realigns the content of a pupil's *karma* for that pupil's benefit is wholly unlinked to such methods. The occult manipulations of magicians and witches are "break-ins" to another's *karma*, enforced intrusions even further from the work of a teacher than a hatchet is from a laser beam. Moreover, the amplified will required for this illicit manner of intervention, when off duty and involved in mundane life, remains as before – a powerful tool developed for ritualistic use, enshrined in a fallible human psychology complete with (in most cases) largely unpurified emotions. This factor constitutes poten-

56

tially *the greatest hazard of all* in certain contingencies *because the use of that will may be unpremeditated*. When emotions are stirred in suddenly arising situations, and irritation, anger, jealousy, rage, and even hatred (all basic human emotions) hold sway, the developed will merely intensifies the poisonous fuel of the mood prevailing. The will of a "white" witch or magician does not adhere to the supposedly altruistic mode for which it was created. Negative emotion is amplified as readily as "positive intent," indeed, is an automatic reflex creating a potent backlash, and sometimes worse, for those involved. Voodoo, after all, operates on the same principle.

Magicians may state that they have full control of all their faculties, including their emotions – inferring a degree of development normally associated with the spiritually evolved. It is indeed possible to establish a close-to-absolute control over the mind and the emotions – an iron will primed by disciplined exercises or intensive concentration and/or meditation can almost achieve this. Yet here we have the cart before the horse – control is established *before* the essential process of purification. It is an "artificial" control; one which has no basis in spiritual development. The emotions are generally forced aside, severely repressed, or otherwise inhibited, but not transmuted – they still exist in the condition they were in when the operative mind excluded them. The root of control is ego-oriented, and concerned with personal aims, or what the ego thinks best for everyone else, including the planet. It leaves out the potent "X" factor of what lies within the subconscious processes, which cannot be ruled by the same criteria. The subliminal content is not open to discipline, nor even to discernment or assessment. Only those who have arrived at a differently focused orientation can reach these processes, both perceptively and transformatively, and these highly motivated individuals do not use ritual, nor do they rely upon props and trappings. They live by laws, and the perception of, and cooperation with, those laws, that render "white" magic or any other kind of magic both nonsensical and superfluous. These laws supersede the laws pertaining to humankind; they operate at a level that undeveloped humanity cannot reach in the unregenerate state. From this level of being the powerseekers and manipulators are likewise debarred by their own lack of spiritual evolution. To attain to that level requires a surrender of the will to a finer and more complex mode of being – the faculties commensurate with which, when perfected, reveal a stratum of existence infinitely superior to our own and not known to the general mass of the population.

This is not to say that the aims of white magicians and Goddess-inspired ritualists are wrong. Concern for the environment and for the preservation of all life is an estimable concern. What is questioned here is the manipulation of natural power by means of ritual magic. For this to be effective, a potent will (or wills) must operate, which brings us back to the matter of will and its place in evolutionary development. The fact is that human will must become subservient to a higher law, and the primary steps towards this are self control and the observation of duty – without denying the natural emotions or locking them up. This means one must take into account the *effects* of the imposition of one's will upon others, and upon nature itself. Energies have been bound up for centuries by magicians who have thereby blocked the actualization of whatever those energies were for. In using elemental energies to add force to magical rituals, the magician incurs a price upon his (or her) head and creates a formidable impediment to his possibilities of growth – a price which he, and those like him, are invariably loathe to acknowledge.

The reader might here ask by what means such power is activated, as the thoughts and emotions of the average human being, even when focused or released in anger, cannot bring about such effects. The answer lies in the premature arousal of the evolutionary force of *kundalini*, which brings raw power into the hands of the unready and, even worse, the unregenerate. The energy of *kundalini* was frequently and deliberately tapped in former schools of magic, and for this purpose. The activation of this energy is still unremittingly striven for today by those undertaking yogic and other disciplines ostensibly with the aim of spiritual Enlightenment. Such disciplines, which include techniques of intensive meditation, are designed to "raise the fire" in the shortest time possible. Many books are written on this subject, which give every encouragement to start the process of activation, with advice (and occasionally cautions) on how to cope with some of the possible consequences. These consequences, which include nervous breakdown, acute psychological disorientation, and insanity, to name but a few, regrettably cannot be remedied by those who so glibly write about this process. Nor can these consequences be rectified by "black" or "white" occultists, or by unenlightened Lamas, pseudo-masters, or self-designated Sufis of Western origin with exotic Middle-Eastern names, or even by therapists, though all of the above promote these activities in various forms.

Exercises and techniques have been used by humankind throughout the ages in the attempt to acquire visionary and precognitive skills and the power to shape events. Many contemporary side-effects of *kundalini* arousal are considered, quite erroneously in most cases, to demonstrate spiritual growth; but such growth, with the relevant attributes and faculties, does not result from an indiscriminately awakened *kundalini*, and can only be made with correct orientation of the participant and under the direct control of an authentic teacher, for only then can these high-level forces of interior evolution be contained with safety and achieve their function, which is the full flowering of cosmic consciousness within the human entity. Authentic teachers, in my experience, work in sophisticated ways and do not issue written directives on this process to their pupils.

On the matter of teachers, Swami Sivananda Radha (Sylvia Hellman, d. 1995) is described on the jackets of her books as "one of the foremost spiritual teachers in North America today," and "one of the foremost authorities on Kundalini Yoga and Yoga psychology." She was furthermore "the first Western woman to be initiated into the sacred order of Sanyas and to become a Swami."

Swami Radha founded the Yasodhara Ashram (1963) – a Yoga retreat and study centre in Canada, and likewise the Association for the Development of Human Potential (1971) in the United States. She also founded many different urban centres, known as Radha Houses, in North America, Britain, and Europe. Commenting on her major work (regarded by many as a classic), *Kundalini Yoga for the West* (1993), Dr. R. Frager of the Association for Transpersonal Psychology expressed the view that this was "the most psychologically detailed and sophisticated book available on the chakras and yoga practice."

It is within this book that Swami Radha states: "For those who have laid the foundation by learning self-mastery, the

Kundalini Energy, when understood, can be controlled at will. The foundation must be built slowly and carefully so that this ability to control can be developed" (p. 4). Her book is a step by step series of exercises designed to tap this energy in her students, including those students outside her contact, who practise by proxy from her book. It was obviously considered by Swami Radha that the *kundalini* energy could be safely activated if her instructions were followed with exactitude. The end product, the "awakening of Kundalini," would then be "not a frightening, but a blissful experience" (p. 261).

The preparation for this experience as advocated by Swami Radha, consists of a series of largely psychological exercises alongside explicit instructions on Yoga *asanas*. There is a swift progression to breathing practices. The preparatory exercises are primarily observational, and designed to produce greater understanding of the personal psychology and motivation. Yet the overall teaching appears based solely on the control of the mind, and the assumption is inherent that the mind controls the emotions, and the emotions themselves can therefore be dealt with by exercises of a mental nature. There is no mention of the knots of *sanskaras* (impressions) of entirely emotional composition that may be pressing for expression in the form of externalising events, and with which most students have to grapple – emotional events which simply cannot be resolved by the recommended methods even with direct supervision. It would require an exceptionally high level of mental control to neutralize such impressions, assuming this were possible, and certainly a preparatory student could not, under any circumstances, be expected to achieve it.

Many exercises are given which must inevitably have potent effects over a period of time. There are precise instructions for *pranayama*, including alternative nostril *pranayama*, and *bhastrika pranayama* (bellows breath), plus *kundalini pranayama*. There are also directions for concentration on the *chakras*, and the deliberate activation of the energy of *kundalini*. These exercises are a strange mixture of traditional Yoga and contemporary psychotherapy. I do not doubt that they are effective, though not necessarily in the way the author describes. The Divine Light Invocation utilized by the Swami's guru is much in evidence, and links her work (and her students) with the umbrella organisation he founded.

Swami Radha, a Canadian immigrant of German birth, was sent back to the West from India by her guru, Swami Sivananda (d. 1963), to promote and spread a knowledge of Yoga. As a consequence, she has unleashed upon the unsuspecting public a book of practices which, in East or West, can prove a recipe for disaster, particularly in the more sensitive and aspirational types who are likely to attempt this "Do It Yourself" course. For example, advice is given on the benefits of *mantra*, a procedure with the capacity to unlock potentially dangerous forces within the mind (a fact that Swami Radha does not mention). She merely tells us: "Prolonged Mantra chanting, which means a couple of hours a day for some months, will bring the effect of directing and pinpointing the vibrations in the body" (p. 127). The practice of *mantra* is so potent in fact that eventually it manifests during sleep, causing one to awaken "not with a dream but with a Mantra," thus proving it a powerful tool indeed.

The anachronistic nature of Radha's yogic teaching is not surprising when one reads of her teacher, whose view of spiritual advancement and how to achieve it is highly debatable. Swami Sivananda – who founded (in 1936) the Divine Life Society in Rishikesh, India – himself wrote what is probably the most detailed treatise on the controversial subject of Kundalini Yoga, and included in his text a translation of the *Yoga-Kundalini Upanishad*. Published in India by The Divine Life Society, *Kundalini Yoga* by Swami Sivananda had run into nine editions by 1991 (32,000 copies in print).

In Sivananda's translation of the *Yoga-Kundalini Upanishad*, the Swami gives no hint of criticism or warning regarding the advocacy by this dubious text of the cutting of the *frenum lingui* (the fold of membrane beneath the tongue) so that "by daily drawing it up [the now free-moving tongue] for six months, it comes as far as the middle of the eyebrows and obliquely up to the opening of the ears." The purpose of such mutilation is to eventually enable penetration by the tongue of the *Brahmarandhra* (the "hole of Brahman"), a "hollow place in the crown of the head known as *anterior fontanelle*" (*Kundalini Yoga*, pp. 183–184, 50). Sivananda's further endorsement of the above tongue-lengthening procedure can be found on pages 111 and 193 of the same work, where he makes reference to the *Khechari Mudra*.

Under the heading "Who is a Guru?" Sivananda answers: "Guru

61

is one who has full Self-illumination and who removes the veil of ignorance in deluded Jivas" (p. 17). Some gurus, one fears, contribute to the veil of ignorance – they do not remove it.

Swami Radha was ostensibly a spiritually oriented person of considerable intelligence who promoted the qualities of sincerity, honesty and integrity in her students, which is not the invariable case today with modern gurus. Yet these attributes, undoubtedly possessed by herself in abundance, plus an extensive knowledge of Yoga *sutras* and complex scriptural texts, do not qualify her to activate the force of *kundalini* in others, nor justify what she was doing, which was grafting into the West the doctrines and disciplines of the East, regardless of the vast differences in the current Western culture and that of the monks in the enclosed communities of ancient India for whom these doctrines and disciplines were designed. These (suspect) practices are culturally outmoded and not suited to the present day. They are being used as yet another form of break-in technique by the unready. Swami Radha may have had some knowledge, but this is not the same as expertise. She sought to create attributes and abilities in unselected and unprepared people by means of concentrative yogic practices, which can cause incalculable harm and is one of the surest ways of effecting lopsided development. *Unless* the personality self is first brought into alignment (which cannot be achieved with a DIY manual), such practices as concentration, meditation, *pranayama*, are merely developing one part of the self and leaving the other parts behind. *All* aspects must be dealt with before going further if genuine self-development is sought. It is furthermore useless to separate oneself from life to become a renunciate unless *first* the lessons of life have been thoroughly learned and absorbed; and it is *madness* to cultivate *kundalini* before the ego has been brought under the fullest control, or dispersed – by which time one will know from deep intuitive experience that it is courting disaster to attempt to activate this energy at all. The desire to do so will not be existent.

If Swami Radha had actually experienced in the fullest sense the activation she taught in very expensive courses [for instance, the "Ten Days of Yoga" cost 635 US dollars, and the three-month "Yoga Development Course" based on the "Kundalini System of Higher Consciousness" a further US$4,500, according to the 1996 brochure published shortly after her death; see A. Rawlinson, *The*

Book of Enlightened Masters, p. 485], she would have known that there is no way this searing, other-dimensional experience can be "not a frightening, but a blissful experience" on its first *full* upraising in the unmonitored human system. Nor could she actively promote the solo Do-It-Yourself disciplines explicitly detailed in her book – she would know full well the risk to which she was exposing hapless students with nowhere to turn in an emergency save to an uncomprehending medical profession.

To achieve stillness, and silence of the senses, is for some persons extremely valuable, but it is not Enlightenment. To transcend the body and lose all awareness of it in states of bliss, is not Enlightenment. There is a Reality beyond these states which is infinitely greater than anything experienced within the boundaries of the mind, and which cannot be reached solely by one's own efforts, nor acquired from a book, no matter with how many exercises. In developmental work, exercises and disciplines, though helpful at times, are not the main criterion. The criterion lies in proper preparation, and this is to be found in mundane, everyday life, and the way that we live it; the thoughts we allow to dwell in our minds, our level of integrity, our degree of aspiration, and our compassionate response to all creatures (including humans) – or our lack of it. The widely held belief that people cannot develop if they are "householders" and have children, and must therefore wait until later in life when there is time for retreat disciplines, is completely erroneous. It is in the provision for, and care of, our children, our old people, and our infirm, that the basis of true development lies. All higher forms of growth arise from this foundation, and are not dependent on breath control or yogic disciplines. A yogic belief is that one cannot develop without retreating from life and undergoing strenuous processes. In contrast, the natural mode of development is a gradual increase of interior one-pointedness; a focus upon a conscious entity infinitely wiser than oneself, an inner contemplative state, or state of intermittently uprising prayer that becomes, in due time, continuous – all of which can be accomplished in everyday life, however hectic, and will engender perceptive abilities as surely as any amount of yogic or related practice, and in perfect safety. My own life is proof that many years of mundane domesticity and a total lack of exposure to religious disciplines does not debar one from spiritual experiences, nor from a full and conscious experience of

63

kundalini upraisal. This being so, what is the necessity for Kundalini Yoga? When the time is right, and the system prepared, activation will happen inevitably.

[The factor of a living teacher is, of course, at some point essential. In my own case, the introduction of this factor into my life over a twenty-month period did not in any sense over-ride the above considerations – rather they were reinforced. (See *Beloved Executioner*).]

Within her publicly distributed course material, Swami Radha acknowledges that the warnings surrounding the practice of Kundalini Yoga are well-founded, and that an experienced teacher is necessary. Yet in the same paragraph (p. 154) she says that there is no need to be fearful "if scrupulous attention is paid to *following each step in this book*" (my italics).

On the matter of "siddhis" or psychic powers, Radha considers that these are not attained "without the necessary exercises to bring about certain physical-emotional-mental conditions" which apparently require around "3 or 4 years" of intensive practice to procure (p. 197). This implies that her pupils started off as raw beginners despite their exposure to formidable disciplines, and that even she herself had to follow this route to attain her (assumed) powers of perception. The compulsive desire to gain powers distracted many yogis, and allowed much exploitation through exercises, notably *pranayama*.

It is the Yogic view that the practice of *pranayama* of a certain type leads to emotional control and purification. A claim is that *pranayama* also burns up extraneous *karma* and establishes command over the nervous system and of the mind itself, at the same time giving the power and ability to do many seemingly miraculous things, some of which are referred to by Swami Radha in her text. One of these is the art of becoming invisible, another is the ability to project one's own image wherever one pleases. A footnote gives the information that advanced exercises for the attainment of the powers of the *chakras* can only be given after due preparation and through "personal instruction." It is clearly an option on offer. This supposed safeguard with reference to "powers" is quite unconvincing. I totally disagree with the presentation as a whole.

At the end of her book, Swami Radha suggests, in capital letters: "MAYBE NOW YOU WILL LOOK FOR YOUR GURU!"

(p. 326), a surprising suggestion after the practise of so many powerful Yogas. On page 318 she provides some comments on gurus, which unhappily do not inspire great confidence in view of the seriousness of the undertakings in question. Moreover, in my personal experience, one does not "choose" a teacher, the teacher chooses *you*. Perhaps this difference in viewpoint is explained by the quote itself: "The criticism by followers can undermine the Guru. Too much admiration will do the same, but only to a Guru who still has much ego left, who does not have sufficient discrimination, perhaps not even the intellectual understanding of what it means to be a Guru. *The Guru can make a mistake but, like a good parent, without intent.*"

I can only say heaven help those students foolish enough to attempt to raise the titanic force of *kundalini* under such auspices.

Ajit Mookerjee, in his book *Kundalini: The Arousal of the Inner Energy* (third edn., 1986) has this to say on the subject: "The passage of the awakened Kundalini through the various chakras is the subject of a unique branch of tantric esoteric knowledge whose goal is the merging of the Kundalini energy with cosmic consciousness . . . A deeper understanding of the awakening of this cosmic energy can only be felt when one decides to become actively involved in it" (Preface, p. 7). Further on he says: "Long training and preparatory disciplines are undertaken for the arousal of Kundalini, but there is no fixed rule, and practices vary considerably." He then proceeds to give some information on such practices to interested aspirants: "Taking up the posture he finds most suitable, the aspirant initiates the process by which Kundalini is aroused through 'sense withdrawal' . . . concentrating all his attention on a single point . . . until normal mental activity is totally suspended" (p. 19). A few lines on, Mookerjee states: "It is through the science of breathing that the body's subtle centres are vitalised." The reader will note that the process is self-initiated, and there is no cautionary advice.

On page 59 we learn that: "Among the most important tantric practices undertaken to awaken Kundalini are those of Dakshina marga, the 'right-hand' path, and Vama marga, the 'left-hand' path." The followers of the left-hand path, we are told, practice, among other things, the "ritual of collective sexual union performed in a circle" which is known as *chakra-puja*. This is explained as a transformative process – the end result of non-avoidance of the "desires and passions" which might otherwise prove obstructive, and which by tantric means are made tools of liberation – or so it is misleadingly alleged. On the last page of his book, Mookerjee observes in reference to people in the West that many aspirants are fearful of self-taught *kundalini*-yoga, and that whereas a "competent guru" will assist one's progress systematically, "responsibility must finally come back to oneself. One must learn to work with and control the inner energies."

Having personally experienced a major *kundalini* upraising, my view, unpopular though it may be, is that there is categorically no way that any ordinary human being can control this highly volatile subtle force, and the people who claim that they can do so have not experienced a genuine upraising of this evolutionary thunderbolt. This force, or energy, in its progression through the *chakra* points at full velocity, cannot be safely worked with, or controlled, save by a Teacher who has already completed his or her own evolution, for only such entities have the power, the knowledge, the authority, and the expertise to release such force in others, and they do not do so until the time is appropriate. A solitary aspirant working from a book is in great danger, and this is *not* the way the system operates. As Ramakrishna stated on this matter: ". . . the mother bird doesn't break the shell until the chick inside the egg is matured. The egg is hatched in the fullness of time." (*The Gospel of Sri Ramakrishna*, fifth edn. 1969, p. 310). Forced activation can lead only to catastrophe.

It is currently considered, if not understood, that the literally hundreds of assorted *kundalini* "awakenings" of a partial nature referred to by Dr. Lee Sannella and Dr. Stanislav Grof in the course of their respective researches – the symptoms of which cause enormous and prolonged distress to so many people – are frequently the products of past activations in former lives. Even less understood is that the greater majority of these were illicit, i.e., out of sequence – effected before adequate orientation was established, and the consequence of break-in techniques whether Yogic, Tantric, Sufic, Buddhist, or otherwise.

In this context there is a form of "upraising" which takes place in the subtle body (a finer non-physical body that intermeshes with the physical body – known to Sufis as the *jism-i latif*, and to Hindus as the *sukshma sharir*) before that body has been fully developed. The result is reflected into the astral sheath, which is, in most instances, wholly unpurified and often congested with contaminatory material. With full development of the subtle body, the astral sheath is discarded and disintegrates, there being no further need of it. It is this evolutionary anomaly (the untimely activation of *kundalini*) which accounts for the extreme amplification of sexual desires recorded by many at the onset of this process; the *karma* has not been sufficiently cleared or sublimated, and the culminating "ecstasies" of the experience, when they are present, leave no trace of other-dimensional realities, or their attributes (evolved faculties), in the personality self. The orientation that proceeds in proper sequence sheds the astral sheath *before* the *kundalini* force becomes active. The former can only occur when the full evolution of the subtle vehicle has been completed, along with other processes. Activation under this circumstance is *never* self-initiated, nor can it arise by accident; through course work; or through verbal advice from any source. It is safely "locked" until an authentic teacher deems the time appropriate to "release" it.

When the subtle body is insufficiently developed, neither *mantras* nor disciplines, nor any form of *pranayama*, will remedy this lack, though they will certainly cause complications. To tamper with this embryonic stage of human interior growth invariably and inevitably leads to distorted development which must later, with great difficulty, be rectified. This is the primary reason for the careful screening of applicants in all genuine developmental processes, which automatically exclude all of the commercial "spiritual" enterprises in the category termed "New Age." An authentic teacher can readily discern this immature condition, along with other essential qualifying, or disqualifying, criteria.

The point here is that there is a proper time for the raising of *kundalini*, at the end of the human evolutionary cycle. There is no necessity for disciplines of Tantra Yoga, or indeed, any other Yoga designed to bring about this end by artificial means. The purpose of life is not served by sitting hour upon hour in meditation, or by chanting *mantras* non-stop in a seated position. These, and other disciplines, may once have held a place in an earlier evolutionary operation, and may still be utilized today, under certain circumstances, but only at specific times, in specific

67

situations, with specific people, and for specific purposes. They were never intended to be used continuously, nor were they intended to force an accelerated degree of growth in the unready. This is the product of ignorance, of lost knowledge, of the decline of former cultures and civilizations, during which periods all forms of legitimate authority, whether secular or spiritual, were overthrown. Illicit attempts to duplicate or reconstruct these earlier processes have burdened our present culture with the harmful misconceptions we have today. None are more compromised than the current vogue of raising *kundalini*.

For instance, *A Chakra and Kundalini Workbook* (1995) by Dr. Jonn Mumford (a Westerner known as Swami Anandakapila Saraswati) provides the reader with "Psycho-Spiritual techniques for Health, Rejuvenation, Psychic Powers and Spiritual Realisation." By the use of these techniques one can also "unleash supernatural powers such as photographic memory, self-anaesthesia, and mental calculations . . . Enter states of ecstasy, realisation, and cosmic consciousness," and "Experience sex for consciousness expansion, ESP development, positive thinking," plus other assumed (and somewhat mixed) benefits.

Mumford is a practising Tantrist with a detailed knowledge of traditional Indian Tantra, which he is much concerned with spreading to the West. His text book, basically another "Do-It-Yourself" manual for anyone who cares to experiment, contains directions on Yoga techniques, plus much medical and anatomical information, and includes a section on "Magical Sexuality" complete with rituals and incantations. There are coloured diagrams for exercises in Chakra Dharana (concentration) which aim to focus psychic power, and detailed guidance beneath headings such as "Tantric Erotic Rose meditation" which will "powerfully stimulate the chakras from below to above, raising the psycho-sexual energy" [this latter presumably in reference to *kundalini*] (p. 195).

Mumford gives very graphic directions for "Tantric coupling" and his esoteric teachings are sexually oriented and under such titles as "Physical Stimulation of a Secondary Erogenic Zone to Arrive at the very Edge of the Ecstatic 'U3' Moment" (p. 201), and "Retarding Ejaculation by Tantric Breath Power" (p. 204). The resultant ecstasies equate with the "cranial orgasm" and "whole body orgasm" regarded by Tantrists as forms of Enlightenment. The Swami debunks many traditionally held concepts, among them that of *Saucha*: Purity – "Fools have thought that it means purity of mind. Who can say that one has purity of mind?" (p. 156). Mumford instead relates this term to internal wastes, i.e., faeces, consistent clearance of which (he claims) extends the lifespan and prepares the nervous system "for higher states" (p. 157). With regard to these latter, we have his assertion that: "Sexual activity promotes sensory hyperacuity... Tantric sexual Sadhana induces profound experiences... converting the whole skin into one extensive, massive, genital organ" (p. 132). He also shares with us a Tantric secret, that "a sexually aroused human is hypersuggestible." The use of this "sex magic" (by which means one can program the unconscious, both one's own and one's partner's), is clearly open to abuse, and has been so through the centuries – a point not mentioned by Mumford.

Varami techniques are likewise enlarged upon, and a description is given of a demonstration of this highly dangerous form of martial art as witnessed by Mumford in 1993 in Southern India. Reference is made to the "remarkable concentration" exhibited by practitioners of *Varami* "in focusing energy into a single blow upon a vital zone [of the body]." This involves a *simultaneous* visualization of "a Deva or Devi (god or goddess) sitting within the opponent's vital zone"; a mantric invocation to that deity, evoking its power; and an awareness of an explosion of *prana* (*Chi* or *Ki*) at the point of physical contact with the zone, plus the "split-second withdrawal of the fist, elbow, knee, or foot striking the surface, leaving the shock waves, psychic and physical, to cause havoc" (p. 93).

This is far more extreme than the martial arts with which the average Westerner is familiar, and constitutes a lethal form of magical attack, designed specifically to maim or kill. The importation of this horror into the West cannot be construed as useful, and pinpoints the very real dangers in the widespread dissemination and practise of powerful Yogic disciplines. The *Varami* technique (or *Varmannie*, as it is sometimes known) was taken to the USA as early as the nineteen twenties, and by 1941, according to Mumford, was actively tutored in New York.

Dr. Mumford's most obvious achievements are depicted on pages 128–129 of his book, where he demonstrates a Hindu torture ritual while in trance with "the traditional piercing of the tongue to open Swadhisthana chakra." In this ritual a skewer is "thrust through the tongue into a lemon." On page 130 there is a photograph of a student licking a "white hot steel bar, impervious to fire, beyond fear, and immune to pain." These achievements, attained through an alleged acquired control of the autonomic system, do not in any sense indicate spiritual growth. (Many such rituals involving the piercing of various parts of the body, including the tongue, have recently been exposed on British television as the physiological tricks of the trade used by numerous false gurus in India, with intent to fool the credulous that the guru possesses superhuman powers).

Mumford's book will undoubtedly produce extensive effects on those who follow his recommendations, which amount to a course in Tantric Yoga. These exercises are powerful break-in techniques which activate the *kundalini* force and stimulate the *chakras*, but they do not, and cannot by their very nature, instigate correctly oriented inner development, and are therefore useless in the context of interior evolution.

The same must be said of other material proffered by the Swami and advertised in the end pages of *A Chakra and Kundalini Workbook*. This includes his *Ecstasy Through Tantra* (formerly published under the title *Sexual Occultism*), a book revealing "special techniques of sex . . . that have been the secret of various magical orders – both Eastern and Western – only recently available to the non-initiate." The text provides explicit information on copulation postures for *kundalini* arousal, and is described as the best single guide to "sexual yoga and sex magic" obtainable. Also on offer is a cassette tape titled *Autoerotic Mysticism* (by Dr. Jonn Mumford) which latter will teach you "how to get in touch with yourself using massage," and will further "deep understanding of your sexual nature . . . through focused auto-erotic activity." Hardly the stuff of spiritual enlightenment.

Another Yoga based book, *Chakras: Roots of Power* (1991), was written by Werner Bohm, born 1896, and a company director, who, after his discovery of the works of Rudolf Steiner and Dr. von Veltheim-Ostrau, became convinced of the need for a book on the *chakras*, which he duly wrote. We are informed on the cover that the book "discusses how we can learn to work with kundalini energy. The chakras are our roots of power – our energy centres – and we can learn how to tap that energy, center it, and cope

70

with the stress filled world that we all now live in." The content, however, gives absolutely no indication of the states engendered by awakened *chakras*, and apart from some emphasis on moral requirements, and the "essential" practice of meditation, takes its readership no further than interpretation of the symbols in ancient texts relating to each *chakra* centre. This, plus Bohm's own Bible-oriented viewpoint which is set against the Theosophical background provided by Steiner, who was once heart and soul in the Theosophical movement until he broke away to found Anthroposophy. Bohm is also strongly influenced by Arthur Avalon (Sir John Woodroffe), whose work *The Serpent Power* is referred to several times in his text, which includes Woodroffe's original *chakra* illustrations.

Bohm rightly notes that there "has to be inner change (without detriment to external obligations)" if further development is to be successful. His stress on moral purification is rare in books of this kind, but he also makes statements which negate his book's validity, such as: "A teacher is able to tell from the colors of the [*chakra*] petals how far the students have progressed and what they may be doing wrong" (p. 36). This is not the way an authentic teacher discerns these matters.

Despite his emphasis on meditation, Bohm makes the statement that "Every time we meditate, there is a danger that demonic forces will ascend from the agitated depths of the psyche or from subhuman elementary levels" (p. 100). He moreover observes that human aspirations "are tainted with evil. Moral evil was ingested by mankind in the distant past, but we were not originally evil. The tragedy was brought about by the power of the Adversary, opposer of the creation of mankind . . . ." (p. 113). Bohm's work is therefore an uneasy marriage between Gnostic Christianity and Yoga, with a smattering of Theosophy thrown in. Dr. von Veltheim-Ostrau, in the Foreword, rashly comments: ". . . Bohm's book appeals to me as being the first successful attempt to present the nature and functions of the chakras to Western minds in a form that can be accepted and assimilated" (p. viii). A misleading statement, to say the least.

A workbook of a rather different kind is *Working with your Chakras* (1993) by leading medium, healer, counsellor and workshop leader, Ruth White. The book is described on the cover as "a highly practical and approachable guide to the chakras" which brings "esoteric chakra knowledge into a Western perspective." In the Foreword, written by Professor Eric Gomes of Belgium, we are told that: "The information given will enable the reader to have direct experience of the chakras and of the energy flow in the body" (p. xl), a statement I would challenge, having read the book. In my view, what Ruth White is doing under the guidance of her channelled entity "Gildas," is attempting to clear the vital or etheric body (sometimes known to healers as the aura) of impurities, most of which derive from emotional immaturity, and psychological malfunctioning. This may be useful work, but it is *not* "working with your chakras." The ingenuous news that "Many channelled sources and gifted clairvoyant observers now speak of newly awakening chakras which are becoming part of the major system" (p. 4) is also not convincing, particularly when such "observers" collectively consider that one of the freshly discovered *chakras* is the "unconditional love centre" – a favourite term with New Age adherents, who appear to believe that they manifest this quality all the time.

White considers somewhat simplistically that all personal evolution is progressive (p. 187), which sadly is not the case. There is a process of *de*volution that runs counter to evolution; a process that can be slid into with tragic ease when unready "aspirants" backfire on serious undertakings, or when initially good intentions turn sour. Another problem is that people frequently *do not learn* from past experience but repeat the same errors (and the same crimes) until their burgeoning impressions become crystallized. No progress is then possible without specialist help, perhaps of a type that channelled mediumship cannot offer.

On page 185 of *Working with your Chakras*, White refers to the content of the lower astral planes, purportedly full of "thought forms and entities," some of which may be encountered "in nightmares, on bad drug trips, when inebriated or during some types of psychotic episode." She then makes a highly debatable statement in relation to the above and to the numerous visualization and other exercises given in her book: "When chakra energies are being wisely explored and managed there is no danger of being caught up in these unpleasant areas during meditation and visualization – but if you have any fears around this possibility speak to a spiritual counsellor or meditation teacher." White clearly assumes that "spiritual counsellors" and New Age

72

teachers of meditation have sufficient knowledge and also the ability to deal with any unfortunate eventualities. This simply cannot be guaranteed, and least of all with unstable types, or with a casual readership attempting to put these exercises into practice.

Chakra awakening, in my personal experience, does not occur until the *kundalini* current becomes active and commences to rise in the subtle system. It is this event that stimulates the *chakras* into activity. The word *kundalini* is not mentioned by White, but assuming that the exercises given for the "central energy column," i.e. to "clear it," or to "increase awareness of its energy flow," etc., relate to *kundalini* under a modern pseudonym, then White's text is yet another DIY manual for the upraising of this force, and as such, gives a false assurance of safety to her students, in this instance, the general public.

The abovementioned authors are all intent upon raising *kundalini* and teaching others to do so. Most are acknowledged as teachers, and some as experts; yet they do not know, or appear to know, that what they are doing is harmful to the very process they purport to represent.

It is a sad fact that far too many people are cashing in on the importation from East to West of snippets of once-sacred knowledge, and far too many people assume a familiarity with subjects of which they have no experience and very little understanding. There is nothing easier these days than setting oneself up as a teacher or "expert" on spiritual matters. Who is to counter these claims? The trusting and vulnerable do not query acclaimed "teachers," and the gullible have no desire to do so, but all are nonetheless at risk. What is the general public (or interested New Age seeker who is part of that public) to make of the following advertisement for a "Chakra Balancing Kit" which appeared in the brochure of The Tao of Books, Rickinghall, Diss, UK, early in 1996: "This kit is designed to help you to balance the seven energy centres of your being, through energetic diagnosis, colour and sound. The kit includes a healing meditation tape, a pendulum for chakra measurement, a chakra colour wheel for chakra balancing, and a chakra information booklet." The price of the kit is £19.95. The claims made for this paraphernalia are absurd; it is simply a money-spinner for the unscrupulous.

In the same brochure appears an advertisement for a music

73

cassette made by the "world-renowned gongmaster," Don Conreaux. The advert states: "Experience the cosmic state of consciousness where Soul Force merges with Spirit. Gong travel on your own path of tone, from planet to planet, through the solar system." The means used for the induction of this experience are "ancient bronze gong, conch, singing bowl, and bell . . ." and "Liner notes tell which chakra is activated by each five-minute piece." The blurb continues, "Listen to this in a quiet place, preferably with headphones, and feel the energising pulse travel up your spine. Don Conreaux will be performing at this year's Mind, Body, Spirit festival."

"Performing" is the word, but no amount of gong playing, potent and powerful though such instrumentation may be, will induce in random listeners the state of cosmic consciousness claimed on behalf of this individual. It is just not possible. Any state procured by this means, in this context, is inevitably counterfeit. The science of sound has been known through the ages, and has certainly been used to activate and increase certain conditions of awareness in genuine students in authentic situations; but as with meditation, only at certain times, and under carefully controlled conditions. Such practices cannot be legitimately touted through the mass media, and to do so is an irresponsible act.

Equally offensive are the advertisements for Self-Help tapes for subliminal programming. Claims are made with no indication of possible long-term negative consequences, and with no knowledge at all of the plexuses of impressions which lie awaiting activation just beneath the surface of consciousness. These tapes are heralded as *A New Breakthrough in Brain/Mind Research to create who and what you want to be*, and prospective purchasers are informed that "Thanks to new technology and contemporary awareness of how the mind works, change no longer has to be difficult."

The "programming" is accomplished by author/researcher Dick Sutphen, who was "the first to create and market hypnosis tapes in 1976, and subliminal videos in 1982." The technique used induces a "unique new kind of 21st-Century Brain/Mind Programming"; and certain tapes utilize combined techniques designed to engender "an altered state and effectively program your mind."

Even more potent are tapes combining seven "ultra-powerful" techniques to "program the conscious, subconscious and super-

74

conscious mind for change." The claim for superconscious achievement is particularly dubious, and is not made any more convincing by the client-instruction: *"Listen with headphones to get the full mind-blowing effect."*

Regrettably, despite "medical interest," this hype serves only to assure the less gullible reader that "awareness of how the mind works" is not an attribute of this type of "research," which is wholly commercially geared, being available to anyone who can pay for it (however vulnerable or unstable), and providing no back-up supervision for those likely to get into difficulties. Imagine what *Video Hypnosis*, with *Four Times the Programming Power* will do to the mentally sick (or even the healthy) when they select such subjects as "Past-Life Regression," "Incredible Self-Confidence," and "Sensational Sex" in the solitude or isolation of their own homes, especially when amplified with Audio Cassettes which infiltrate the mind with "How to Decide Exactly What You Want," "Letting Go of Guilt," and "Power and Success." To advertise "Chakra Balancing and Energising" by means of subliminal suggestion is to add insult to injury. Such things are quite impossible, as Dick Sutphen himself must know. Or, more likely, he does not pretend to know. It is just a good commercial proposition in today's New Age climate of Do-It-Yourself development.

Likewise the material publicized in the Autumn 1996 New World Music *Myth and Magic* brochure, in which Sutphen makes further forays into pseudo-mysticism. In *Temple of Light*, a CD presentation, we are promised "A mind-movie meditation like nothing you've ever experienced. For 65 minutes, you become the central character on a journey of self-discovery, with soul searching questions that you'll answer in your mind. *You will also experience a chakra initiation* [my italics] and be offered the opportunity to have all your questions answered within." This latter statement is an outright lie, and an utterly shameless manipulation of undiscerning minds reassured by Sutphen's advertised role as a serious researcher.

Despite his stated knowledge of "brainwashing" (the behind-the-scenes military discovery of "how to reprogramme your enemy"), Sutphen does not appear to know that although one can change a conditioned pattern in the mind by superimposing another via subliminal processes, this is not the end of the story. Any impressional impulse entering the subconscious by means of such processes displaces the content (which is entirely impressional), making possible the extrusion, sooner or later, of other patterns that may not otherwise have arisen in this lifetime, not all benign to the programmed individual. These programmed states as inducted by Sutphen can only endure for a limited period – they are not transformative. They are then superseded by the force of events and the emotions that arise with them. To interfere with these natural (and organized) processes, however chaotic they may appear to superficial observation, is like flinging a lighted match on dry tinder. The only safe way to "change" is to make the necessary personal efforts to do so. Cassette tapes and videos are, sadly, not the answer.

Kundalini-raising is now big business. Such is the interest in Western New Age and occult circles that book publications, seminars, weekend courses, lectures and classes are all booming, and constitute an enticing financial proposition for the entrepreneur. Persons with little or no knowledge of the actual experience acquire what they need for tutoring purposes from books, which are frequently written by authors who, more often than not, have obtained their own "knowledge" in much the same way. Thus irresponsible recommendations to a general readership interested in "personal and spiritual growth" (some of them sufficiently seriously to diligently follow text-book directions) are increasingly generated, and exhortations such as the following on energy centres and *chakras* encourage practices which are known to produce very powerful effects. Eddie Shapiro (author and workshop leader) suggests: "Let us take our minds to where they [the *chakras*] are located and repeat the name of the centre and then try to visualize the symbol. Let us try to awaken these centres. We start at the base [of the spine] and move upwards, pausing between each one" (E. Shapiro, *Inner Conscious Relaxation: A Renaissance in Consciousness*, 1991, p. 93).

What follows is a detailed programme designed to stimulate the energy in the *chakras*, using visualization and breathing exercises. Unhappily the text does not give the impression that the writer is aware of what he is setting into motion. A similar procedure is followed by his partner, Debbie Shapiro in *The Bodymind Workbook: Exploring How the Mind and the Body Work Together*. Again, the recommendation is to "explore" the *chakras* in the interests of understanding both body and mind, with the "X" factor of higher consciousness thrown in. Shapiro tells us: "Generally the higher chakras remain closed or functioning in only a minimal way. It takes conscious awareness and perseverance for them to begin to open, enabling us to reach higher states of consciousness. Exploring the chakras takes us on to a deeper level of development" (p. 43).

The Shapiros conduct their courses on the New Age circuit, including Gaunt's House in Wimborne, Dorset (owned by Sir Richard Glyn), a popular venue where many commercial tuitional ventures of similar standard are regular features. No responsibility is taken for what is here set into motion. No warnings are given and no follow-up supervision. The reason for this latter is not difficult to discern – for writers of such books lack genuine knowledge, and have no possibility at all of controlling the force of *kundalini* once activated.

The level of comprehension on the part of New Age teachers of this subject is well encapsulated by a report in *Rainbow Bridge*, the internal newsletter of the Findhorn Foundation, the largest and best known New Age Centre in the UK. The report is presented by the Foundation's Health and Wholeness Department and is taken from the recorded minutes of the Crisis Awareness group meeting of August 21st 1990. This group was brought into being to assist those with problems connected with spiritual development in general (primarily the effects of technique-induced *kundalini* activation), and the disorientation resultant from the therapy known as Holotropic Breathwork™ in particular, this latter being widely practised within the Foundation at the time.

Two of the three persons present were Courtenay Young, senior consultant therapist at the Findhorn Foundation, and Cornelia Juliane (now Cornelia Fellner Featherstone) a German medical doctor in charge of the Foundation's Holistic Health programme. The group's assessment of the matter in question is stated thus: *"We tried to define it to take some of the mystery away which often increases fear and misconceptions. 'Kundalini rising' describes a somatic expression of an emotional process. This is well known as psychosomatic symptoms. It is a useful label if it helps the person to own their process and to reduce the stress around unusual physical symptoms. It is not helpful when it is used as a jargon to cover up stress, to hang in there without seeking help, etc. Also*

77

in a 'kundalini rising' situation it is facilitating the process, making it more graceful, when there are treatments on the physical level in addition to support for 'going through it' with emotional or spiritual assistance. If the symptoms persist for any length of time it is necessary to have them checked out medically."

It is evident from the foregoing that to experience a violent *kundalini* upraising as a result of excessive breathwork "therapy" (or anything else) is not a good idea at the Findhorn Foundation, as there is nobody in charge who can assist you, nor any comprehension at all of the process being undergone (and this remains as relevant at the time of writing [1999] as in 1990, according to all reports). You can touch insanity in this establishment (as some have done to my knowledge) and still be told that your soul is cleansing itself and all is in order and just as it should be.

Perhaps the above paragraph provides the reason for the unusual disclaimer in the 1997 brochure advertising Findhorn Foundation courses, which states clearly and simply, under the heading "PLEASE NOTE":

We do not accept liability for:

Participants' medical or psychiatric conditions which may be existing *or which may arise during, or subsequent to*, participation in one of our programmes" [my italics]. (*Welcome to the Findhorn Foundation: Programmes and Workshops for April – October 1997*, p. 39).

A prominent Fellow of the Findhorn Foundation, William Bloom, PhD, who regularly conducts courses for this New Age organization, epitomizes the standard of knowledge proffered in his entrepreneurial advertisements for workshops given both at Findhorn and in London at Alternatives, St. James's Church, Piccadilly – of which he is the founder-Director. Under the heading *Spiritual Freedom, Healing and Fulfilment*, Bloom (also a long-term member of the Scientific and Medical Network), makes the statement: "Yes! You can transform your life at this weekend initiation. Learn the simple and practical steps which will enable you to experience the consciousness and healing power previously thought only available to gurus, saints and mystics. This is a revolutionary new approach which is accessible to anyone and easy to learn. It works with new techniques developed from energy medicine and modern psychology. It is genuinely for everyone!"

78

(Advertisement: *Kindred Spirit*, Issue 42, Spring 1998, p. 42).

Note the key words *consciousness, healing power, gurus, saints,* and *mystics* – and the assertion that high-level attributes are now readily attainable in *one weekend* by *anyone* and *everyone* (for a fee, of course), and additionally that Bloom's 1-year Open Mystery School Course is currently bookable – and you have a phenomenon that casts shame on Dr. Bloom's academic status, and brings into disrepute the averred serious aims of the Scientific and Medical Network.

[Bloom has recently developed his weekend course into a process called *Body-Soul Harmonics*. Referred to as "new strategies" in his full page advertisement, the techniques used (as "developed by Dr. William Bloom over 25 years") are comprised of a "blend" of "classic techniques from meditation" and the "latest insights of psychology and science." Once learnt, declares Bloom, "the dramatic and wonderful results can be used by *anyone* at *anytime* – and furthermore, you can generate a "*total* experience of love, healing and connection *whenever you choose*" (my italics). Full training for those who wish to "teach or coach" the techniques is currently being organized. "Some scholarships available. Visa/Mastercard accepted." See *Kindred Spirit*, Issue 44, Autumn 1998, p. 2.]

What is actually being sold here? Certainly not what is claimed. Anyone making such claims betrays a total ignorance of spiritual principles, or is simply concerned with making money in a lucrative, uncritical market where authenticity is not a requirement, and honesty in advertising is non-existent. [For further information on the questionable New Age activities of William Bloom, including his dabbling in the field of ritual magic and the conjuration of spirits, see K. Shepherd, *Minds and Sociocultures Vol. One*, pp. 930–931, 933–938. See also S. Castro, *Hypocrisy and Dissent within the Findhorn Foundation*, pp. 99–101, 104.]

Chapter Three

Dysfunctional States of Consciousness

There are manifestly huge areas of misconception with regard to spiritual development, a matter of increasing significance and concern as more and more Westerners turn to Eastern doctrines, in large part due to the decline of the Christian Church.

This escalating situation is hardly surprising. It is fed by books and courses in which Eastern techniques are publicized, advocated, and/or inaugurated, in the belief that the seemingly intact religions of the East are valid vehicles for inner growth, and that the practices of Tibetan or Zen Buddhism, for example, will produce the development so earnestly sought by Western aspirants. The expanding publicity given to Kundalini Yoga is a case in point. Kundalini itself, it seems, is about to become the subject of serious investigative research. Yet despite numerous references to this primary force in scholarly texts and New Age literature, and even entire works devoted to the *kundalini* experience, it is a phenomenon that still remains obscure.

Material pertaining to *kundalini* falls broadly into three categories:
1. The translation of ancient and medieval texts by scholars (some of whom are considered authorities on the subject), and the elaboration and interpretation of those diverse texts by various persons who purport to understand them. The sectarian nature of such texts may be considered a limitation, as is the aberrant nature of some of them.
2. Assembled research documentation of individual experience believed to derive from *kundalini* activation
    (a) via the use of LSD and other drugs or breath-related exercises, or

(b) through the practice of Eastern techniques of meditation and yoga.

3. Statements on *kundalini* made by persons accepted as spiritually knowledgeable in Eastern and New Age literature, or in the form of biographical or autobiographical accounts.

Having myself read most of the currently available documentation, and having also experienced a substantial *kundalini* activation, I regret to state that there is an alarming discrepancy between texts and assumptions, and the actual experience. This is made more complex by the differing types of experience collectively described as *kundalini*, and the vital factor of originating causes. It might therefore ultimately serve a useful purpose to clarify these discrepancies and the discernible reasons for their existence, for unless these misconceptions are rectified, more and more people will be placed at risk in their efforts to achieve spiritual states by investigative methods.

First, scriptural texts may not be what people would like to believe. They may be the products of orally transmitted traditions open to distortion, or the work of yogis who used artificial modes of induction to engender certain abilities, in the absence of a legitimately acquired knowledge. Secondly, the accounts of *kundalini* experiences currently in circulation are not necessarily what their authors, or commenting academics, consider them to be. The majority of recorded "awakenings" are dysfunctional, i.e., although the condition described may be genuine, it does not lead to spiritual completion because the essential apparatus for such completion is insufficiently evolved for the purpose. The experience is therefore non-functional; it cannot proceed to fulfilment.

One of the prime movers behind the current enthusiasm for *kundalini* activation was Gopi Krishna, who died in 1984 at the age of eighty-one, and who left behind him a highly detailed autobiography describing minutely his personal experience of a prolonged and dramatic *kundalini* awakening.

This experience brought total havoc into his life and the lives of his family, and caused him many years of acute mental anguish and an extremity of nervous and physical depletion graphically recorded alongside extensive experience of a transpersonal nature. As a consequence of this latter, Gopi Krishna deduced that the "lost" science of *kundalini* should achieve resurrection, and that it was his task in life to ensure this restitution by making known his experience to the world of science in every way possible.

In the Editor's Foreword to Gopi Krishna's book *Living with Kundalini* (1993), Leslie Shepard informs us: ". . . it is useless to follow teachers without real experience, who are only concerned with building their own reputations and cults. You will need to listen to someone with total experience of kundalini in both its negative and positive aspects, who knows its place in the evolution of the human race." In his view this teacher was Gopi Krishna.

Shepard, who worked as editor of the *Encyclopedia of Occultism and Parapsychology* (1991), studied the stories of "hundreds of mystics, psychics and other remarkable individuals," and considered that the Pandit's experiences "provide guidance for the human race as a whole." He tells us that Gopi Krishna persistently sought scientific validation of the phenomenon he had experienced, viewing it as a sign of the evolutionary progression in store for all human beings. Unfortunately, as Shepard laments, parapsychologists and researchers were not at that time sufficiently interested to "conduct research on the Pandit," and the opportunity for this type of investigation on a living exemplar was therefore lost.

In the light of his own conviction, Shepard wholeheartedly supports Gopi Krishna's contention that the *kundalini* experience is the rightful heritage of humankind, and avers that through the writings of the Pandit we now know the way to achieve this, and all that is necessary is the study of his work, and practise of his recommendations.

So once again we have a mass prescription, toned down slightly by Gopi Krishna's own qualifying assertion with regard to the scientific experimentation he so strongly advocated and desired – that the "heroic" enterprise (of voluntary activation of the *kundalini* force for the purposes of research) should only be open to the highest type of human being in order to attain the most significant results. Even so, "the experiment is to be made by them on their own precious flesh and at the present moment even at the risk of their lives and sanity" (p. 381). He stresses that the results of these experiments will "surely be successful" in a small number of cases, and certainly sufficient for the purposes of research demonstration; but conversely these successful activations may also "... lead ultimately to permanent injury, either mental or physical, or even death" (p. 382). These latter afflictions were presumably considered a worthy martyrdom in view of the resultant experimentally acquired knowledge. It would thus seem that despite Gopi Krishna's indisputable experience (which endured on and off for forty-seven years), his insight into the universal scheme of things remained somewhat limited.

Krishna's experience, which occurred in the winter of 1937, was the outcome of many years of daily practice involving lengthy periods of intense and one-pointed meditation. He was accustomed "to sit in the same posture for hours at a time without the least discomfort" (*Kundalini: The Evolutionary Energy in Man*, p. 11), a disclosure which gives an indication of his willpower. He had commenced this discipline at the age of seventeen, following his failure to pass the necessary exams to enter university, and the practice was continued throughout the early years of his subsequent livelihood and his marriage.

Each morning at 3 a.m. he rose to meditate for several hours before leaving for his clerical employment in the Public Works Department at Srinagar in India. On the day the momentous event exploded into his consciousness (at the age of thirty-four), he "sat breathing slowly and rhythmically," his attention focused in the top of his head, "contemplating an imaginary lotus in full bloom, radiating light" (*Kundalini*, p. 1). What happened next is the primary subject of his autobiography. Without any warning, he felt "a strange sensation below the base of the spine ..." and then, "Suddenly, with a roar like that of a waterfall, I felt a stream of liquid light entering my brain through the spinal cord ..."

Krishna's description of his experience is of great interest; he graphically records how his consciousness moved beyond the realm of his body into a vast expanse of light – his conscious immersion in that light, and the state of exaltation with which his consciousness was infused. During this period he lost all awareness of his physical form and senses (pp. 12–13).

As he returned to normal consciousness, Gopi Krishna remembered the books on Yoga he had read, and concluded he had experienced an upraising of *kundalini* – an event he naively considered an immense stroke of good fortune – as to elevate the force purportedly bestowed great psychic and mental powers. He tried at once to repeat the experience but felt "so weak and

83

flabbergasted" that he could not collect his thoughts sufficiently well to concentrate. Over the next twenty-four hours he sought again and again to induce the condition he had earlier undergone, eventually succeeding; yet the aftermath, as before, was devastating, the heat in his body almost unbearable, his debilitation and exhaustion extreme, his heart thumping wildly. The process left him uneasy and depressed, and proved the commencement of many months of acute disturbance, both mental and physical, during which time he hovered between his normal state and outright insanity. The Pandit realized he had aroused into activity a force he could neither cope with nor control, and one which was to cause him untold suffering.

The description of his longlasting mental and physical tribulations is utterly harrowing. He lived in a state of terror and depletion so extreme that at times this verged on madness, and the urge to self-violence as a means of release arose in him repeatedly – an alarming state from which he only gradually emerged. Yet six years later, in December 1943, when at last restored to health again, and during the annual winter removal of his office to Jammu (having that year left his wife and family in Srinagar), incredibly unwisely he recommenced his meditations, feeling irresistibly drawn to do so, and quickly achieving what he felt to be positive results. So profound and overwhelming were his visions that he increased the period of meditation by rising earlier than usual for this purpose (he still had to arrive at his workplace on time). The success of his efforts incurred in him a powerful sense of elation which persisted day and night until the next hour of practice. Of this period he records his joy at the "glorious possibility" now within his reach. He was fully cognizant of the fact that he had awakened the *kundalini* force, and considered it an honour that for some reason had been bestowed on him. The state of elation, however, proceeded to escalate, and after a fortnight the ferment in his mind was so potent, and his excitement so acute that he lay sleepless for hours before the time of meditation, athirst to re-experience the bliss that accompanied it. On the last day of this "unique" experience, he had no sleep at all throughout the night, and artlessly reports: "My mind was in a state of excitement and turmoil with joy and exhilaration at this most unexpected and unbelievable stroke of luck" (*Kundalini*, p. 186).

It is this extraordinary attitude exhibited by Gopi Krishna which illustrates, in my view, the reason for all his sufferings. He was unready for the major experience that prolonged and one-pointed meditation had unlocked within his system, and his symptomatic ego inflation tends very much to prove this. It is also apparent that the experience was wholly self-induced and self-sustained, despite his evident wish to believe otherwise. Yet his state of euphoria was not to last, for that same evening, when lying down prior to sleep, the Pandit knew he had "woefully blundered" once again. His head filled with harsh and discordant sounds, and the *kundalini* current objectified in his mind as a raging, leaping fire, well out of control. His fear was intense, and he knew beyond any doubt he had overdone the practise of meditation and had dangerously overstimulated his nervous system.

"Overdone," is to put it mildly. He had enforced upon himself a known discipline designed to produce specific effects, which were duly experienced. Gopi Krishna could not have been unaware of this factor, as his father before him had done the same thing, abandoning his young family to "renounce" the world only twelve years after his marriage to a girl of sixteen – who with admirable fortitude shouldered the burden of rearing their three young children and caring for her disoriented husband. This headstrong gentleman, having removed himself from the onus of daily life, ceased even to speak with his family (*Kundalini*, p. 19). [Why this negligent and wholly irresponsible act should be deemed "spiritual," I am at a loss to understand.] The knowledge of yogic disciplines is confirmed by the disclosure that following his failed exams [see page 83 of the present text], Gopi Krishna resolved to avoid further humiliation by acquiring control of his mind in order to bring his "rebellious self" into subjugation. He thereafter devoted his attention to two objectives: "concentration of mind and cultivation of will," directing all his energies to this self-appointed task. In his efforts to attain self-mastery, he made a point of asserting his will in all things, and found that it was only a short step from these focused activities to Yoga, occultism, and a growing distaste for ordinary life (pp. 19–20).

During this youthful period of acute mental conflict, Gopi Krishna turned away from his earlier intention to achieve worldly success and went to the other extreme. He tells us that his life soon became geared solely to "gaining success in Yoga" despite the fact that such success unavoidably "necessitated the sacrifice of all my earthly prospects" (p. 20). In the light of these statements it seems clear that the Pandit knew quite well what he was doing, and that the *kundalini* activation he had noted in his father, and for which his father was locally honoured and acclaimed, was the desired result. This makes all the more incomprehensible and misleading the following comment by Dr. Frederic Spiegelberg (Professor emeritus of Comparative Religion and Indology, Stanford University, California) in the Introduction to *Kundalini: The Evolutionary Energy in Man*, "We have here, in this wholly unintellectual personality, a classical example of a simple man, uneducated in Yoga, who yet through intense labour and persistent enthusiasm, succeeds in achieving . . . some very high state in Yoga perfection" (p. 6). Dr. Spiegelberg clearly ignored Gopi Krishna's familiarity with the subject.

An extended period of extreme disturbance followed the above episode in Jammu. Having "forced the door" on the *kundalini* process, not once, but twice, Gopi Krishna again reaped the inevitable consequence, one that lasted in its most severe form for another four months. During this time he suffered excruciating internal agony, physical and mental deterioration, an overwhelming lassitude and depression, and an increasing terror of insanity.

These symptoms, to which were added delirium and insomnia, were exacerbated by acute digestive disturbances that made it almost impossible for him to eat. His life was spared, he tells us, only by the devoted attention of his wife, who used the entire family budget and denied herself food and sleep to feed him with freshly cooked nutritious delicacies (which were all his fatigued system could absorb) at hourly intervals of the day and night, until he at length recovered. The Pandit deduced from this that the reason students of Hatha Yoga were obliged to master the art of emptying the stomach and colon "at will" was to guard against the "utterly unpredictable behaviour of the digestive and excretory organs" after the awakening of *kundalini* – he could see no other rationale for these practices (p. 195).

Krishna's physical recovery left him with the heritage of his experience, described by him as a transformation of consciousness. This took the form of a "silvery lustre" pervading his entire field of vision, an effect that continued unabated for the rest of his life. His dreams exhibited the same brilliance and were frequently "premonitory and prophetic," which factor curiously enough filled him with a sense of uneasiness.

In November 1949, Gopi Krishna once more prepared to spend the winter season away from his family when his office moved temporarily to Jammu. This time in his subsequent hours of solitude he "made absolutely no attempt" to meditate, having learned from his past experience (December 1943) to leave well alone; but he allowed himself instead to slip into states of contemplation in which the former activation manifested afresh as a luminous state of consciousness. The consequence was that the tendency towards deep absorption became more marked in him, and "a source of happiness and strength." The luminosity proved increasingly all-encompassing and profound – with the side-effect of a semi-trance condition that he could slip into, and out of, with the greatest of ease. Each time he surfaced from these states, couplets and verse in a wide variety of languages were dropped, fully formed, into his mind (p. 209).

This achievement, co-existent with the sublime nature of his contemplative absorption, created in Gopi Krishna an exaltation and excitement similar to his earlier phase of meditation. Of this he again naively writes: "I could not believe in my good luck; I felt it was too astounding to be true" (p. 209). His literary outpourings in semi-trance intensified, and soon, with growing confidence in his health, he ceased to feel it necessary to resist these impulses and submitted wholeheartedly to the spiritual moods which came upon him. Apart from a few hours of fitful sleep each night, these states now encompassed him almost continuously throughout his waking hours. All through this interlude he remained in Jammu, and his host soon became uneasy having unavoidably noted the "constant perambulations in a state of deep abstraction" of his guest. In the course of the next few weeks, as the Pandit informs us: "unable to resist the fascination of the newly found subliminal existence, I found myself powerless to come out of my contemplative moods" (p. 215). The outcome was that he became unable to continue with his employment, taking a long leave to recover his equilibrium, and thereafter making the decision to retire.

In the meantime, whilst still in Jammu, crowds of people

attracted by the "rumours of a miraculous development" in Gopi Krishna, called at his place of residence. There was a widely held belief in his sudden Enlightenment, and probably the Pandit shared this view of his own attainment, for he now considered it was necessary to make his experience known to others. He concluded also that it was his duty to devote himself exclusively to the service of mankind, and to renounce his hapless wife and family in the process. He records of this period: "For more than a month I lived in a state of triumph and spiritual exaltation which is impossible to describe." But sadly, through lack of sleep and irregularities of diet, he soon found himself again in the grip of acute depression and debilitation. Recognizing in time what was about to happen to him, he journeyed by aeroplane back to his home and his wife, relinquishing his hope of a wandering life of renunciation "to effect the regeneration of mankind, a fantasy in my case born from the desire for power, the yearning for mental conquest, which often accompanies the activity of Kundalini in the intellectual centre . . ." (p. 218). [This last point constitutes a gross distortion. The desire for power and mental conquest has no place in an authentic *kundalini* activation. The traditional requirement is the eradication of all such egoic tendencies before this event takes place.]

Gopi Krishna's return to the bosom of his family did not resolve his problems. His transcendental experiences heightened, and he records them in detail, also the setbacks to his health and the repeated recurrences of all his devastating symptoms. On three occasions he came close to death in the midst of financial hardship amounting to grinding poverty – not aided by the "unavoidable" necessity for a special diet high in nutriments which made huge inroads into his Civil Service pension, the sole source of family income (p. 231). This further struggle lasted for nearly seven years, and only the heroism of his wife saved his life and preserved his sanity.

Despite his many tribulations, the Pandit remained convinced that he must live through all his vicissitudes in order to give to mankind the fruit of his experience. So devitalized was his physical system by these processes that he needed ten hours of sleep each night, and this need likewise continued throughout his life.

When his health in due time stabilized, Gopi Krishna occupied himself with an humanitarian enterprise supported by willing friends and, as time passed, began to record his many deductions on the value and nature of his experience, and the essential availability of this to all humankind.

It is the factor of these deductions that has caused me to dwell at such length upon Gopi Krishna, for both his *kundalini* experience and his viewpoint eventually achieved recognition in the West, where his numerous books are now in circulation and his concepts are already becoming operative. Kundalini Research Institutes have been established in the USA, Canada, and India to collate information on this subject, and to collect further case histories of individuals. Their aim is to promote scientific and medical research that will validate the statements made by Gopi Krishna, and usher in an era in the West geared to the activation of *kundalini* on a scale once found in the East.

Contrary to the views of many "experts" in this field, I would counter the wisdom of this line of action. If the premises put forward by the Pandit are valid, then the insights of my own experience are the reverse, and doubtless more educated minds than my own will pronounce upon this. My prime concern is the harm that can be done in the name of research to innocent people. I have stated my case in full in my autobiography.

Some of the convictions set out by Gopi Krishna invite strong disagreement. One such is that the arousal of *kundalini* is a "strictly biological phenomenon," and therefore open to scientific investigation. This is supported by his assertion that the commencement of the *kundalini* cycle "draws upon the procreative organs for increased production of the reproductive fluids. . . . which is converted into psychic energy." He also comments on his own greatly increased production of semen and the "intense ferment" of biological activity that preceded it. He considered the "abnormal abundance" of the "vital seed," and the subsequent sublimation, an essential prerequisite for its ultimate transmission from the base of the spine, via the spinal cord, into the brain, where it formed "an integral part" of the radiant energy he experienced (*Living with Kundalini*, p. 186). With these observations he thus perpetuated the tantric myth of *ojas*. He later states: ". . . the tremendous strain on the excessively worked reproductive organs, may continue undiminished for years" (p. 246).

James Hillman, the Jungian therapist, in his psychological

commentary on Gopi Krishna's original autobiography, *Kundalini: The Evolutionary Energy in Man*, gives further credence to this viewpoint in his observation that a seeming requirement for transitions in consciousness is a reorganization of the sexual impulse, and furthermore, that "Loss of seed means loss of that vital essence which is the source of the living liquid light" (p. 98).

This of course reinforces the concept of *urdhava-retas*, described by Gopi Krishna as the reversal of the reproductive system and the "upward" flow of seminal essence "through the spinal cord and into the brain" (*Living with Kundalini*, p. 392). He moreover states that *urdhava-retas* forms the basis of Kundalini yoga, and is the "ultimate aim" of all forms of yoga designed to achieve transcendent states of consciousness.

Without contradicting the crucial need for a sublimation of sexual energy, one may here discern a major misunderstanding on the part of yogis who seek to make a biological fact from a metaphysical issue, contracting the indications of a "subtle body" and other factors. ["According to Hindu ideas," wrote Sir John Woodroffe (Arthur Avalon) in *The Serpent Power*, "semen (Sukra) exists in a subtle form throughout the whole body. Under the influence of the sexual will it is withdrawn and elaborated into gross form in the sexual organs. To be urdhvaretas is not merely to prevent the emission of gross semen already formed but to prevent its formation as gross seed, and its absorption in the general system" (p. 199 n.1).]

We need to remember here that the sexual urge is part of human biology, and that it is the effort to control and transmute this urge which is transformative, not the factor of the urge itself, or its biological attributes.

What is necessary is a reversal of psychological and sexual orientation, not semen. Hence the traditional requirement of celibacy (for which Gopi Krishna can find no valid reason). A true celibacy can only be attained by complete "reversal" of former karmic tracks – a constant struggle with an overwhelming need for sexual expression is an unsound basis for attempting this reversal. The impressional content of one's *karma* must first be thinned, or balanced out by means of restraint, and this takes time and a gradual reorientation of personal aims, degrees of attachment, and spiritual inclination, which leads in turn to an ever-deepening awareness of an inner reality and an increasing ability to discriminate.

My personal experience of *kundalini* is that it takes place in a finer body, one that closely intermeshes with the physical but that operates under completely different laws to those of the flesh and therefore does not require semen (which my female body does not produce, nor any equivalent) to support the *kundalini* process, or indeed any conjectural transformative derivative of semen. The "forcing of the door" to the *kundalini* experience via meditation is of a different order. Gopi Krishna himself perhaps noted a relevant key to this "forcing" in his assertion that the regular practice of meditation over a period of time tended to force a *"normally silent* region in the brain to an astonishing activity" (*Living with Kundalini*, p. 361, my italics).

If this major experience does not take place in the physical body, then the cerebrospinal system will not reveal the presence of *kundalini* to modern science, though science can certainly note the diverse effects of illicit activation, which is another matter. The centuries old insistence by Tantrists and others on the value of male semen in the pursuit of enlightenment may be analogous to the devaluation of women in the eyes of ignorant priesthoods of all religions. The ancient and medieval texts relating to *kundalini* were almost invariably produced by males. These texts (Hindu and Buddhist) vary a great deal and are unsatifactory in my view. They are laden with symbolism and ritual. Gopi Krishna's modern version lacks detail to an extent that is very misleading. One may credit his aversion to the Tantric symbolism of lotuses, but his exposition is likewise contracted.

A curious factor of Gopi Krishna's experience is that he was unable to confirm the existence of *chakras*, on which issue much emphasis has been placed by medieval writers. He found "not even a vestige of one in any part of the cerebrospinal system" (p. 254), and remarked that any assumption of their existence in today's climate of physiological knowledge and research was an insult to the intelligence. It was his view that such concepts arose through the resemblance of the awakened nerve centres to certain symbols, such as a lotus in full bloom. He enlarges on this analogy, and comments that the ancient savants, lacking the physiological knowledge available today, utilized these symbols in the preparation of their students for the perception of nerve clusters and their locations. He adds that had he believed in, or had prior knowledge of, the teachings on *chakras*, he may well have mistaken these luminous formations along the spinal cord for lotuses, and might even have projected the relevant *sanskrit* letters and Hindu deities according to whatever was present in his mind.

There is much good moral sense in Gopi Krishna's autobiography, but also, in my view, much serious misconception. He makes no reference at all to the "stages of the heart" known to Sufi and Christian lore, and which are an inseparable part of inner development – which raises the question of whether he actually knew of these states, much less experienced them. He also shows no awareness of the achievement of any faculty or state save by the use of strict disciplines and dietary regimes. There is, more significantly, no functional description of a cosmic overview and evolutionary meaningfulness for humankind. Whatever he saw, however glorious, rapturous or profound, he was unable to adequately translate, or to comprehend in a wider compass. His prime concern was with knowledge of the safest methods of awakening *kundalini*. He was certain that he had received a "divine revelation," and that it was his destiny to make known his experience to mankind in general and the world of science in particular. What he advocated for the highest types of humankind, and eventually for everyone, was "a voluntarily awakened kundalini" (*Living with Kundalini*, p. 376), and he proposed a series of research experiments to prove both the truth of his statements, and find the least dangerous methods of bringing this about.

[With regard to the foregoing, it is perturbing to note that the unnamed writer of the biographical material on Gopi Krishna presented on page 209 of his posthumously published book *Kundalini – The Secret of Yoga* (1996) is guilty of distortion of facts. This was clearly done with a view to present the Pandit in a scholarly and philanthropic context for the purposes of attracting research, and makes no mention of the realities of his situation. This act of indirect dishonesty by distortion does no service to research, in fact renders it futile, as is evidenced time and again in the hazardous field of Kundalini Yoga.]

There is enormous confusion in these areas, and regrettably Gopi Krishna has not decreased this confusion with his insistence on experimentation. His greatest mistake was in thinking that all knowledge of the age-old science of *kundalini* had been lost to the human race until his advent. His inadequate version merely follows on from inadequate versions bequeathed by religious sects. This does not mean that human experience in such matters has been limited to such sects and Gopi Krishna. Informed sources *do not advocate* the random practice of advanced techniques of meditation to experimentally activate this evolutionary energy.

Gopi Krishna has done a great disservice to the next generation, for the premise on which he based all his conclusions, and on which research is already proceeding, is utterly false. In his later years, he completely ignored the earlier reality of his situation, i.e., that his own experience was *forced*, the self-induced, out-of-sequence product of a persistently used technique, and thus invalid developmentally. Moreover, he does not appear to grasp the underlying principles of such development (hence his attempt to redefine the evolutionary route for humanity), nor that his own trials and tribulations were the result of an incomplete growth that proved an unready foundation for all the stresses and strains it had to bear. Certain *absolutely specific* levels of growth must occur *before* the arousal of *kundalini*. Unless this growth is made, comprehension is distorted, higher-level faculties are inoperative, and function is non-existent. Furthermore, the *entire process* must be undone – the clock set back to pre-activation, before any authentic development can commence.

These flaws in Gopi Krishna are reflected in his work, and are heavily compounded by the uncritical academic assertions of those who have commented on his autobiography, and who are quite prepared to believe in his spiritual enlightenment. Without the necessary, indeed essential knowledge of this process, they acclaim him and promote his ideologies as if they were truths, and in the efforts of researchers to "prove" them by the experimental methods urged by Gopi Krishna, much harm will be done to young questing minds in a future decade. This type of ignorance is exemplified in James Hillman's commentary on page 69 of *Kundalini, The Evolutionary Energy in Man*. Hillman states that the route to enlightenment has been "made much shorter with modern hallucinatory drugs and other techniques." This, of course, is completely untrue. Drugs can do absolutely nothing in the area of spiritual development, save cause chaos within the organism that ingests them.

In authentic developmental situations there are *no* short cuts. It simply is not possible to moderate or alter the necessary sequence of interior growth, as I have attempted to point out. In the same book, Hillman posits Carl Gustav Jung's view of *kundalini* as "an example of the instinct of individuation" (p. 95). A close reading of Jung by anyone who has personally experienced a genuine and comprehensive *kundalini* activation will reveal that Jung himself *did not have* such an experience and was thus in no position to make such a statement. The utterances of contemporary icons are the bane of this generation. They may have rediscovered many important aspects of human psychology once known to more civilized cultures (and *always* known to all authentic teachers), but this achievement does not make them sufficiently knowledgeable to pronounce on issues like interior growth and *kundalini*. They are merely creating suppositions, or guessing, which is neither commendable nor scientific.

Gopi Krishna, having charted the way ahead for the whole of humanity, and whose dictums, in the current climate of the decline of a civilization, are on the verge of serious acceptance by qualified researchers genuinely seeking a "way out" of the human dilemma, said at the end of his autobiography: "I do not feel myself to be superior in any way to my fellow human beings. There is no idea of purity or chastity, virtue or saintliness in my mind to inflate my ego" (*Living with Kundalini*, p. 383). This comment is wholly inappropriate to one in his assumed position. Even if he did not consider himself to be a saint; he clearly thought that his ego was not inflated, which is often a deceptive assumption amongst those who have not achieved an adequate spiritual development. One can strongly query how Gopi Krishna knew himself to be in such a privileged position. He gives no indication of self-knowledge despite his psychic observations, and tells us clearly he has no teacher, and no awareness of inner guidance.

There is a missing dimension to Gopi Krishna's thought. He stresses morality, high-mindedness, benevolence and moderation, all traits of character that can be learned by example and put into practice. What he leaves out is *sensitivity*. This is well illustrated in his comments on the past general acceptance in India of heinous practices like bride burning (by families dissatisfied with a marriage settlement), *sati* (widow-burning), and infanticide, regarded at the time as "natural and normal" before these barbarities were abolished by law. The fact of such abolition does not imply any refinement in the populace as a consequence, though Krishna considers that the human mind was held in the grip of "horrible customs" and woke up to the "cruelty and stupidity" of such atrocious acts through the powerful reformative influences which "brought it to its senses with a jolt" (p. 374).

When innate sensitivity is present, it is not possible for individuals to perpetrate brutalities of this nature. It is not a matter of the mind, or custom, but of a higher range of feeling which enables humankind to become acutely aware of another's suffering, and completely unable to be the means of perpetrating such suffering, custom or no. Many war records (frequently suppressed, particularly in World War I of this century) substantiate this. In every conflict there are men (and women) who cannot do what others do, and are punished for it, often with the loss of their lives.

It is this finely developed sensitivity that distinguishes the highly evolved aspirant from the run of the mill devotee. Those who demonstrate this quality within the ranks of humanity, no matter how lowly their position in life, or how mundane their everyday existence, are the prototypes of the future, and it is *they* who will eventually qualify for higher ranges of tuition, with all that this implies.

Darrel Irving, the author of *Serpent of Fire: A Modern View of Kundalini* (1995) is another person disseminating extremely dangerous ideas about *kundalini*. He writes under the assumption that his twelve hour experience following the ingestion of LSD (no date given) – in which symptoms of *kundalini* activation became apparent – places him in a position to make valid assessments and sweeping hypotheses.

On page 45 of his book he says: ". . . the kundalini activated in my body illustrates that this cosmic force is reserved not just for the sainted few, but on the contrary, is the birthright of every person living on this planet. For at the time I experienced kundalini I was hardly saintly, nor was I religious." This comment is irrelevant under the circumstances, as his experience was artificially induced and in no sense authentic.

Many of Irving's statements are derived from information obtained during interviews between Gene Keiffer, founder-direc-

95

tor of the Kundalini Research Foundation, Ltd., New York, and Gopi Krishna, whose concepts are clearly evident throughout his text. Irving aligns this material with accounts given by Jiddu Krishnamurti (designated at an early age as a future "World Teacher" by leading Theosophists, and reared accordingly on a diet of meditation and other disciplines), and life-long Yoga practitioner Hiroshi Motoyama (referred to at length in Chapter 4 of the present book), plus his own LSD induced experience, and on these four sources formulates his thesis. [Sadly, Krishnamurti's nihilistic philosophy and covertly immoral behaviour – which included complicity in the abortions of his own offspring – should be proof enough for anyone that he is not as supposed by Darrel Irving. See R. R. Sloss, *Lives in the Shadow with J. Krishnamurti*, 1991.]

Irving states his view that *kundalini* is always active in the body – that this energy is the "veritable life force (prana) itself," but that usually this is operative at such a low frequency that the individual is unaware of it. Only when the activation becomes pronounced is the process noted.

This hypothesis is plainly linked to Gopi Krishna's assertion that *kundalini* is a biological process intrinsic to every human being (*Serpent of Fire*, p. 147) and that central to this process is the reproductive energy. According to Gopi Krishna, the sublimated sexual seed (semen) forms an integral part of the *kundalini* energy, which is thereby "transmitted through the spinal cord into the brain" (p. 150).

Irving is fully aware that this force, or energy, can be activated by the use of disciplines, and quotes *Pranayama*, Yogic postures (*Asanas*), *Mudras*, *Mantras*, *Bandhas* and sexual rites (*Tantra-Asana*) as instrumental in this (p. 13). He does not advocate them, however, and points out that certain (sexual) rites in Tantra Yoga are "reserved only for especially selected, advanced initiates" (p. 14), indicating, perhaps, his conviction of their value by the use of the word "advanced." Nor does he advocate the use of hallucinogens, being similarly aware, through personal experience, of the dangers inherent in a rashly awakened *kundalini*.

Despite these cautions, Irving boldly enters hypothetical territory with his later observations. His prime focus is on the similarity between some states of psychosis and the *kundalini* experience, and he is clearly at pains to take the matter much further. He asserts his belief that he will be able to prove his thesis, which is that "kundalini and madness, or schizophrenia, are essentially the same thing" (p. 104). According to Irving, this would inevitably have startling implications for the mentally ill, and for those who diagnose them.

Irving's theory derives from his analysis of the four case histories previously referred to, which he examines in the light of the findings of E. Fuller Torrey, a traditional clinical psychiatrist who, in his book *Surviving Schizophrenia: A Family Manual*, lists seven symptoms which are typical of those suffering schizophrenia. Irving seeks to infer that schizophrenia is part of the *kundalini* process, and attempts to link the symptoms of schizophrenia with symptoms of *kundalini* activation. Impressive though his arguments may be, they do not in my view prove his case, as any untoward disturbance in the cerebral system, malignant or psychic, could produce similar effects to those described. This is not to say that such activation is not present in a small minority of schizophrenics. Irving comments on this issue: "From this analysis, I think it is fairly obvious that we of the kundalini narratives qualify for the diagnosis of schizophrenic," further expressing the view that what he regards as the similar symptomatology of *kundalini* and schizophrenia are "two sides of the same coin" (p. 126).

Later he says, having argued his point: ". . . the fact left standing is that . . . all mental productions described in both patient and kundalini accounts, are identical. Therefore, we have traced that symptomatology to its source, and that source is not brain disease . . . This means that the symptoms attributed to schizophrenia are in actuality the symptoms . . . of the kundalini process. . . . I submit, therefore, that schizophrenia is a phase of the kundalini process – *schizophrenia is kundalini!*" (p. 137).

Such statements as the above constitute a major distortion. Schizophrenia is basically the result of a damaged psychology, not *kundalini* activation. The fact that voluntary activation (as recommended by Gopi Krishna) can actually lead to schizoid behaviour and to insanity is beyond dispute, but this is not what Irving is saying. His view is far more extreme. It is evident that the use of certain techniques will release energy associated with *kundalini*, but this does not validate such procedure as safe or correct, and does not mean that the consequences are part of the natural *kundalini* process. Delusional symptoms arise in all *forced* (artificially activated) *kundalini* experiences. These do not originate from the same syndromes as mental illness, although their overt symptoms may be very similar. Nor are they representative of *kundalini* per se.

These latter views are not shared by Gene Keiffer, the director of the Kundalini Research Foundation, who writes a glowing Introduction to Irving's book, declaring that the author has "skilfully combined thorough research with deep insight and personal experience." In Keiffer's opinion, Irving has made a convincing case with enormous implications that can "work miracles" in the wards of our mental institutions.

With such support, it is small wonder that Darrel Irving feels confident enough to state that in due time, all "yogis, schizophrenics, manic-depressives, lunatics, and delusional psychopaths" should be collectively rediagnosed as undergoing various phases of the *kundalini* process, and nurtured accordingly (p. 210).

This is a misconception of grave proportions, and demonstrates a total ignorance of the laws pertaining to spiritual growth and the specialized processes of inner development. Irving exemplifies the old adage, "a little knowledge is a dangerous thing," and in positing his viewpoint on an incomplete and meagre basis, backed by "leading authorities" who ought to know better, will lead in the wrong direction those who know even less than himself.

Similar, though less extreme, theories to those of Darrel Irving are put forward by Lee Sannella, M.D., in *The Kundalini Experience: Psychosis or Transcendence?* (1987). Dr. Sannella, a psychiatrist and ophthalmologist, co-founded the Kundalini Clinic in San Francisco, USA, in 1974, and was greatly influenced by the work of Itzhak Bentov and the writings of Gopi Krishna. (Bentov, a biomedical inventor, views the *kundalini* effect "as part of the development of the nervous system," p. 129).

Sannella presents a number of case histories of what he considers to be varying stages of the *kundalini* cycle. He notes the link between these cases and the sustained usage of meditation, yoga, or breathwork techniques which invariably preceded them, and includes in his research activations precipitated by the use of LSD. He notes, too, the records of mystics, from those of the Christian tradition to those of the !Kung people of the Kalahari

Desert who invoke n/um (a state analogous to *kundalini*) in order to achieve !kia (a condition of transcendence) by hours of dancing and by rapid shallow breathing. These latter induce power-charged states of altered consciousness conducive to healing and prophecy, also such feats as handling or walking on fire (p. 38).

Sincere and intelligent though Sannella's work is (and he appears fully aware of the dangers of ego-inflation in the more obviously unready who utilize popular systems like Transcendental Meditation [TM]), he does not appear to realize that *none of these* people should be practising meditation and/or other disciplines in the first place. Without the use of such disciplines they would not have released the energy of *kundalini*, yet the majority immediately return to these practices upon the cessation or easement of their symptoms, as did Gopi Krishna, and in his case (and that of many others) with dire consequences.

Individuals who meditate for two to three hours daily in Western environments are asking for trouble. Even in the cultures of the East there are disasters in the form of acute disorientation, though these unfortunates are far less likely to find themselves subject to psychiatric wards, antipsychotic drugs, electroshock therapy (EST) and electroconvulsive therapy (ECT). The factor of supervisory teachers or gurus of any denomination, whether Taoist, Buddhist, Hindu, Sufi, or others, does not alter this danger. Authentic teachers *do not* haphazardly dispense techniques (assuming they dispense them at all), nor do they transmit *kundalini*-evoking *shaktipat* (a subtle energy transmission from guru to disciple) to all in their contact (and it is unlikely that they ever do, as subtle energy is a troublemaker and the province of unfledged parties trying to imitate what is seldom comprehended). Most so-called disciples are vulnerable to "subtle" gurus, who can create in recipients an involuntary release of a potent force outside their control – one that furthermore may ultimately lead to their hospitalization. These are *not* "lessons" laid on for their benefit, as some like to believe, but are the result of exposure to the guru's own inchoate and similarly activated energy, over which he (or she) likewise has no control.

Gurus who are overwhelmed by sexual urges during the raising of *kundalini* are not true Gurus at all – meaning they have no legitimate function, as is later proven when they sexually succumb to the charms of submissive female (or male) devotees

99

and then seduce them. People do not realize that untoward activation of the first three *chakras* brings immense power and charisma, and is productive of the "signs and wonders" assumed by the unknowledgeable (or merely gullible) to betoken guruhood. Gurus of this type, however widely revered and venerated, do not bestow illumination (as opposed to random states) upon their followers; they cannot evoke what they have not achieved themselves – and in this field appearances are very deceptive. Such gurus are more likely to evoke havoc in the systems of unsuspecting devotees, and are rarely "found out" and exposed, at least in their lifetimes.

The presence of "miracles," and involuntary displays of *mudras*, *kriyas*, and *asanas* in pupils and their psychic or ecstatic disorientation, tends to inhibit sane observation and any attempt at assessment in those close to the guru. The state of assumed "ecstasy" is not necessarily a spiritual state, particularly where inner preparation is inadequate; it can be emotional in origin and occasionally hysterical in expression (and thus open to medical recognition), but the presiding "authority" is unlikely to analyse this. The Indian Siddha Yoga guru, Swami Muktananda, to name but one, has been guilty of all of the above, as is on record.

Currently operative ashramic practices in both East and West are all too often the left-over derivatives of past schools of inner development. These, and similar antique developmental structures from assorted origins have existed in partial form throughout many centuries. Aspirants were once diligently trained in these schools, and it was known to those in charge that certain experiential stages resultant from the use of prescribed disciplines lead to other (known) experiential stages just as surely as night follows day. Fragments of this knowledge have been preserved and are incorporated in various texts, including knowledge relating to *kundalini*. Yet it is a *partial* knowledge, not in any sense complete, and for that reason can prove dangerous when dabbled in by opportunists and the gullible. Some forms of knowledge cannot be placed into words, but can only be demonstrated by those who know, and who have the legitimate authority to do so.

In wisely conducted circles or "schools" (this word can be misleading, as no institution is here implied), pupils were carefully selected and meticulously prepared, and followed austere and highly disciplined regimes for lengthy periods as a matter of

100

course. Without an authentic teacher any such "school" will perish, and without a proper sequence of preparation, all disciplines are useless for developmental purposes, no matter how many auditory or visionary experiences are in evidence, or how many ecstatic states are attained. Prematurely administered disciplines generate false (or misaligned) growth, which must all be undone, the "growth" dismantled, and the deficiencies made good before restructuring can commence, and this cannot be emphasized often enough. There are methods by which these dysfunctional states can be rectified, but unfortunately they are not available on demand and are not obtainable from medical practitioners.

The dysfunctional states clinically presented to Dr. Sannella are of the same order, and he quite clearly used his common sense to "balance" the more extreme symptoms of his patients, in some cases with considerable mitigative success. The first and foremost requirement in such instances is to cease *all* meditations and other exercises and to "ground" the consciousness with solid (coarse) food and physical exertion. It is not sufficient, however, to merely refrain from these disciplines for a time, attempt to stabilize, and then resume them just as before. *They must cease altogether*, and permanently. [This is hard advice to persons convinced that their only route to spiritual development is via meditation or yogic practices. At the end of the day, the only way to counter this problem is through education. It is vitally necessary for the establishment of a "science" of evolutionary metaphysics, and for a careful and thorough study by qualified academics of all the material pertaining to the *kundalini* phenomenon − not just the work of Gopi Krishna, so often resorted to at the present time.]

The end product of all these "risen *kundalinis*" (where they are proven) is not the completion of the evolutionary cycle − this is not possible while the ego holds sway and sanskaric or impressional elements remain − but at best, and after much suffering, a pseudo-condition similar to Gopi Krishna's, in which a greater reality is glimpsed, yet not comprehended. If comprehension was there, the Pandit would not have introduced so many errors into his pronouncements. He would also have registered, experienced, and recorded vital evolutionary information to which he quite obviously had no access; and he would certainly not have advocated *voluntary* activation of this titanic force, for he would have known that this was contrary to evolutionary law. He would further have known that the type of research he advocated was useless, and that the clinically trained consultant, the psychotherapist, and the social worker, have no hope whatsoever of controlling the research-induced other-dimensional activity of *kundalini* on behalf of those caught up in the effects.

Researchers have stressed that some persons experience accidental activations that arise as a consequence of e.g., shock or personal injury. In reality, there is no such possibility. This force has safeguards, and is locked against "accidental" triggering, and where this seemingly occurs it is the result of past activation, whether legitimate or illegitimate, entering again into the karmic pattern of recurring events. In the first (unlikely) instance, this will be by deliberate intent on the part of a presiding teacher; in the second, a more sinister configuration altogether. This latter can be induced by breathwork, sudden shock, LSD trips, injury, anaesthetic, or whatever. The former is under far more stringent rulings, and "chance" is out of the question.

To express the matter rather differently: if one accepts the premise of reincarnation, it is conceivable that the earlier personalities of various persons could once have thronged the monastic schools and temples of past civilizations, some before, and some after their decline, and including Tantric sects and Tibetan lamaseries – and that many of these old persona will have broken into this latent syndrome in varying degrees – thus rendering the present day self prone to a similar expression of this energy. Unless the process has been set into motion legitimately, an illicitly activated *kundalini* leaves impressional imprints which are liable to replay in the same way as all other recurring events. These replays and minor activations are not going anywhere developmentally. They cannot proceed to true enlightenment or spiritual completion.

In one of his rare references to *kundalini*, Meher Baba affirmed (by means of a gesture language interpreted by Dr. C. D. Deshmukh): "*Kundalini* is a latent power in the higher body. When awakened it pierces through six *chakras* or functional centres and activates them. Without a Master, awakening of the *kundalini* cannot take anyone very far on the Path; and such indiscriminate or premature awakening is fraught with dangers of self-deception as well as misuse of powers. The *kundalini* enables man consciously to cross the lower planes and it ultimately merges into the universal cosmic power of which it is a part, and which also is at times described as *kundalini*. Ordinarily *kundalini* is the name for the power latent in the individualized soul.

"The awakened *kundalini* cannot by itself take any one to the seventh plane [where completion is effected]. When awakened and directed under the guidance of some great yogi, it can give many rare experiences which have both advantages and disadvantages. The important point is that the awakened *kundalini* is helpful only up to a certain degree, after which it cannot ensure further progress. It cannot dispense with the need for the grace of a Perfect Master" (*Beams from Meher Baba on the Spiritual Panorama*, pp. 13–14). These views, inevitably, and perhaps unfortunately, are not shared by everyone.

A Western exponent of *kundalini* who achieved a lengthy write-up on his book-jacket by Kundalini authority Lee Sannella M.D., is W. Thomas Wolfe, author of *And the Sun is Up: Kundalini Rises in the West* (1987). Wolfe, an information development course manager in computer programming, wrote an account of his personal experience, which occurred in 1975, and included the autobiographical details of the life events that preceded it and his own observations on the phenomenon as a whole. The result was evaluated by Dr. Sannella as follows: "This is a 'now' book for Westerners. It should prove of great value in further revealing this 'master process' and in informing us of its essential benign, beneficent, and deeply intelligent character."

Unfortunately, a careful reading of Wolfe's book does not confirm that he actually experienced a "classical" *kundalini* process, nor is there any indication that his experience was other than self-induced, a chaotic stirring of the *kundalini* force as a consequence of the excessive overuse of various techniques. In his November 1985 Introduction to the 1987 edition of *And the Sun is Up*, Wolfe makes unsubstantiated statements based on opinion, not fact, such as "one does not necessarily need the classical Kundalini experience in order to become enlightened" and "it is comforting to know how and why it happens, and what to expect when it does – information which you will find in this book."

Wolfe's experience occurred on February 2nd, 1975, whilst he was still in his mid-thirties. His earlier life contained numerous psychic experiences, many of an amorphous or magical nature which followed no progressive pattern and were random in operation. But life, in the main, went well for him, and for a period of years (1965–1972) "nothing seemed to be insurmountable" (p. 63). Then things began to change and Wolfe met with obstacles and frustration in a previously rewarding work situation. From 1972 onwards his days were dogged with tension and anxiety states, to which he responded with very heavy drinking and a prodigious increase in nicotine intake. This mode of existence came to a head in 1974, when in an effort to break the syndrome, in July of that year he commenced regular daily meditation, adapting for this purpose the currently popular TM (Transcendental Meditation) to suit himself, and using a *mantra* of his own choosing to repeat throughout each session. This practice produced effects with rapidity, including the introduction of what he called "attainment dreams," meaning dreams which, as Wolfe states, "reflected my desire for enlightenment" (p. 71).

Alongside this discipline, several months later, Wolfe purchased a biofeedback machine and applied himself diligently to the generation of alpha rhythms, which also swiftly induced effects. Persistent use of the machine and a series of mental exercises left him with a "residual bliss." After logging twenty hours, Wolfe noted the build-up of heat directly beneath the electrodes strapped to his head, and that the phenomenon was "usually coincident with periods of high alpha and theta generation." He further noted "an increase in euphoria during and after the sessions." In retrospect, he considered these symptoms were "reflections of similar, but more massive, Kundalini effects yet to come" (p. 71).

In mid-January 1975 he records "a low-pitched humming" in his head, and by the end of January, having now logged fifty-four hours on the machine (he had owned it for only one month), his alpha readings had quite dramatically increased. Wolfe was well aware that his practices, described even by him as "excessive," were causing changes in his cerebral mechanism. Meditation, mantric repetitions, and prolonged biofeedback sessions inevitably overstimulated his nervous system, and various effects began to spill over into his daily life. On one occasion, for instance, when driving home from his employment and "generating eyes-open alpha," he suddenly entered a "state of extreme ecstasy" that was centred in the middle of his forehead (p. 77). Not the best thing to happen on a motorway, one might conclude.

February 1st 1975 was the day prior to Wolfe's experience, and on this day he spent no less than four hours on the biofeedback machine. Upon retiring to bed he registered his own confusion of mind and the dimming of his "current reality," i.e., he found it difficult to recollect his wife and children, and everything seemed distant, even unreal, and this caused within him an extreme condition of "physical and psychological perplexity" (p. 83). This "dimming" commenced at around 11 p.m.

Wolfe announces the onset of his now imminent experience with the word "Ka-boom!," noting the time as 12:45 a.m., and recording the inception of the pulsating light he had occasionally seen during meditation. The light quickly intensified and became overpowering. Wolfe states that he no longer understood what was happening to him.

Accompanying the light were many strange sounds, loud and discordant "but somehow not unpleasant." Concurrently he experienced a powerful current oscillating between the centre of his head and his forehead, and his heart rate accelerated. He tells us he cannot explain how he knows this as he was no longer "primarily aware" of his physical body. At some point the confusion dispersed and the lights changed their configuration: "From a non-understandable pattern of random light, they snapped into an understandable, fixed holographic pattern of large, luminous balls. These balls seemed to form a corridor that I was either traveling through or part of." Wolfe regarded this state as an ego-death and a major transmutation of consciousness, in that he ceased to operate in his normal environment and body-sense and became part of the "new" environment of luminous spheres. He writes: "My consciousness had literally transferred itself from this being of flesh into an energy construction. This single event completely changed my idea of what is self" (p. 85).

The remainder of the account concerns a manifest thought that voiced a rather trite remark ("Who is thinking now, Fred?") and the fear Wolfe began to experience, plus his efforts to bring his life back into focus. For a few seconds he felt he was "trapped in the hell of being nowhere, lost and frightened," then gradually he returned to his normal body consciousness. This was seemingly the sum total of his experience.

Immediately afterwards, Wolfe got up from the bed where his wife lay sleeping beside him and wrote an account of what had transpired. The event greatly excited him – he felt he had touched "another order of existence." He later likened certain incidents in his record to classical Kundalini episodes, comparing the current experienced in his forehead to "the classical opening of the third eye," and the sound heard in the latter part of his experience to "the music of the spheres in the true interpretation of that mystical event" (p. 85). These comments, in my view, betray an ignorance of the true nature of these episodes, and what must precede them, which hold far greater substance and immensely greater implications than anything communicated in his descriptions.

Wolfe continued his meditations and mantric practices without abate (including the risky pastime of chanting and glossolalia in his car when returning from work), despite the fact that his overstressed system expressed an obvious disturbance by causing him to sleepwalk. He also continued his biofeedback sessions throughout the seven months that followed, a period he considered a continuation of his awakening. Perhaps not surprisingly, the intense heat and powerful humming vibrations in all areas of his head continued to escalate until they became a "full-blown conflagration" (p. 108), and later, a "consuming fire" (p. 112). There were also psychic and "electrical" experiences that strongly affected those in his vicinity (referred to later). Early in April 1975 he records spinal heat and a definite movement in his lower back which felt like a small animal "thrusting and thumping" in its efforts to get out. This proved to him conclusively that an active *kundalini* was the root source of his symptoms, a factor of which he had previously been uncertain.

During the weeks under record, Wolfe experimented with his heightened abilities, one of which was the discovery that he could influence his dreams by pre-sleep concentration on what he wished to dream about. On February 25th (just twenty-three days from his "awakening"), he records his decision to "try for a sex dream" and strongly fantasized "JM" (not his wife) and himself in the act of sexual intercourse. The response of his biological mechanism was swift. He awoke early in the night to severe cramps and considerable pain in his lower abdomen and genital region. Wolfe regarded this as an interpretation of his fantasies by his body-consciousness for something more tangible than sex in a dream, along with other speculative deductions. It seemingly did

106

not occur to him that the act of sexual fantasizing, and with a woman other than the wife who lay beside him on the bed, was not conducive to the spiritual and other-dimensional state he sought to cultivate, and that psychological conflict might be part of the consequence.

At the culmination of the seven month period, Wolfe felt he was facing the death of his ego, but at the same time was puzzled by the fact that he "seemed to be returning" to his former condition of being, i.e., his everyday self. In his own words, he "couldn't figure it out" (p. 123). This is hardly an observation in keeping with a recent, purportedly major, *kundalini* experience, which is known to heighten the consciousness to a pronounced degree, and for some considerable period both before and after the event.

An unusual feature of Wolfe's book is his highlighting of the uncontrolled effects of a technique-induced *kundalini* activation upon others, and likewise of effects that he personally could induce of his own volition. He tells of his experiments to successfully influence the minds of acquaintances, and (on one occasion) to create confusion in the deliberations of colleagues, around fifteen in number, at a department meeting at his place of employment. He termed the latter "a smashing success!" (p. 102). Wolfe further notes the potent, involuntary, self-generated electrical discharge which manifested in flickering light bulbs, unexplained noises (loud bangs and cracking sounds, etc., when he meditated), and his ability to manipulate events. There were other experiments, too numerous for this brief résumé, but these should suffice to indicate the overall situation.

Persons with unmonitored active *kundalini* are in fact walking pollutants, their overspills affecting all in their contact, whether wittingly or not. Such infiltration can actually activate the force in others, particularly those in close proximity who are prone to it, or in weaker individuals of passive temperament, whose psychic systems are thereby frequently thrown into states of malfunctioning or disarray. Thus all persons engaged in yogic or other practices designed to raise the force of *kundalini* are not merely posing a threat to themselves, but potentially to the whole community.

Wolfe knew that it was wrong to use his capacities in this manner and soon ceased these activities. Sadly, not all practitioners exhibit this restraint, and many misuse "siddhis" for their own ends whenever such powers become available, and some undoubtedly do so subconsciously. [Since publication of *The Destiny Challenge* in June 1992 (containing the record of my own experience), numerous letters have been sent to me from those suffering such effects as the above, or from practitioners who become frighteningly aware of the operation of these initially subconscious syndromes and find themselves unable to switch them off. This causes havoc in their lives, and creates disruptive psychological conflicts and virtually unbearable levels of stress within everyone concerned, sure recipes for disaster.]

In July 1976, Wolfe was hospitalized for three days in a coronary care unit following alarming symptoms in keeping with a heart attack or an epileptic seizure in which he became semiconscious. Soon after this came other problems, including acute long-term digestive troubles. He noted that his stomach was affected as soon as he entered meditation, whereupon his body would become "a madhouse of internal activity" (p. 126). Early in 1977, he at last cut down on his meditation periods and reduced the length and frequency of biofeedback sessions. By this time he had logged "well over 900 hours" on his machine, an excessive overuse by any reckoning. Wolfe acknowledged that these abused activities had contributed hugely to his problems.

Despite all the foregoing, W. Thomas Wolfe nevertheless promotes the invocation of *kundalini*, and the latter part of his book comprises yet another teaching/training manual, complete with limited cautions and much advice. Biofeedback is highly recommended to develop alpha and theta wave generative abilities and speed-up the *kundalini* process (p. 159), likewise meditation, mantric repetition, chanting, and a selection of dubious yogic practices. Wolfe advises investment in a high-quality biofeedback machine despite the fact that such use "is still uncharted territory to a large degree" (p. 181). There is no advice on what to do if it all goes wrong.

Wolfe escaped by a hair's breadth from serious incapacities both physical and mental, of which he was retrospectively fully cognizant, and which he incorporates in his account. Yet the dangers profiled in his book have apparently been ignored by those who sanction it so enthusiastically. It is my opinion that despite the uncritical approval of authorities like Lee Sannella M.D. and William Wolensky (Director of the Mind and Body Institute,

Poughkeepsie, New York), the recommendations contained in Wolfe's book constitute a definite hazard to prospective subjects, and reveal in the author an extensive ignorance of the science of Kundalini that he purports to teach.

As an instrument for spiritual growth, this type of tuition is about as useful as the audio cassette *Awakening Kundalini* advertised by Deep Books Ltd., London, UK, in their 1997 Catalogue. The hype commences: "In the entire realm of yoga, nothing is more misunderstood, misrepresented or sought after than kundalini, the primordial energy that is the primary life force within us." Next come all the things that yoga-awakened *kundalini* is supposed to do for you, followed by the information: "In this audiocassette, author Chris Kilham is your guide through the practical, time-honoured methods for awakening the latent kundalini force." And finally, "An experienced yoga teacher leads you through easy-to-follow breathing exercises, kundalini meditation techniques and advanced yogic practices of self-renewal." All this for £9.99 (including VAT), independent of character, motivation, constitution, level of aspiration, or whatever. And of course, no responsibility is taken no matter what crisis or sudden emergency ensues in the consumers.

Kundalini, Evolution and Enlightenment (1990) edited by John White, an author and educator in consciousness research and parascience, is described by the *Yoga Journal* as "A thought-provoking book ... a vast in-breadth presentation of a highly controversial subject," and by the *Journal of the Academy of Religion and Psychical Research* as "the most comprehensive anthology available on a subject too vital to be ignored and too essential to be misunderstood ... this book opens the window of consciousness." The jacket write-up further informs us that "Here are the most authentic and insightful writings on every aspect of this fascinating phenomenon."

White has assembled the work of "respected authorities" such as Gopi Krishna, Swami Rama, Yogi Bhajan, Christopher Hills, Ken Wilber, Swami Muktananda and others, on the subject of *kundalini*, higher states of consciousness, and personal transformation. This very popular compilation is a seemingly haphazard mix of genuine perception and assertive hypothesis, and is likely to create even greater confusion in the minds of those investi-

109

gating the matters under review. An indication of this can be found in the Research section entitled: *Kundalini as prevention and therapy for drug abuse* by John R. M. Goyeche, who states that *kundalini* in its "general manifestations . . . mimics the stimulation of the sympathetic nervous system. Thus, the kundalini experience may closely parallel the amphetamine experience and indeed may be a good substitute for it" (pp. 304–305). This comment regrettably does not generate much confidence in Goyeche's knowledge of *kundalini*.

Another statement open to question is that of Yogi Bhajan, who "has dispelled many of the misrepresentations and myths surrounding kundalini. His explicit teaching has given researchers techniques which can be tested" (p. 132). On the raising of *kundalini*, Bhajan asserts: "Is it difficult? There is no secret about it. In twenty, thirty days, if you honestly practice it about one hour, two hours each day [pranic exercises], you can be through with it. This is what I did" (p. 143).

Further on, in answer to a question about the length of hair of students of *kundalini* yoga, Bhajan (a Sikh who founded 3HO, "The Healthy, Happy, Holy Organization" whose adherents practise Kundalini Yoga) says reassuringly: "You can practice with any length hair, but the hair was the first technique to raise the kundalini energy." He then informs us that natural, full length hair, when coiled over "the anterior fontanelle for men or the posterior fontanelle for women," draws pranic energy into the spine, and the downward pull of this energy induces the energy of *kundalini* to "rise for balance." Words fail me here, though I am astonished to learn that researchers have found such material of use.

A further case in point is the updated work of Gopi Krishna (extracted by White from a paper presented by Krishna to the All-India Institute of Medical Sciences at the first research seminar on Kundalini in March 1975), which is much in evidence, and notwithstanding his well-documented *kundalini* experience upon which his reputation for knowledge is based, is as full of serious and assumptive error as his earlier books. Far from the caution expected of one who formerly stated that his experience was a warning against the ignorant use of yoga disciplines, Gopi Krishna subsequently threw all cautions to the winds, and was adamant in his theories on links between madness, psychosis,

110

trance mediumship, and the mystical experience of saints and the enlightened – hence the presumed necessity to conduct exhaustive research on volunteer participants by means of intensive yoga disciplines designed to forcibly activate the *kundalini*. He puts forward his belief that the widescale spread of this process is "the only hope for the mentally retarded or the deficient" (p. 224) – in fact that the awakening of *kundalini* is ultimately the panacea for all human ills, and the sooner we all get down to it the better. "The main targets of investigation should be the cerebrospinal fluid and the reproductive apparatus," insists Gopi Krishna, who finds that some mediums have a tendency to orgasm during trance, which information encourages him to set forth his view that the sex lives of geniuses and other talented persons would doubtless provide similar indications. "The erotic nature of mystical ecstasy is fully recognized" (p. 236), he decrees, and it seems there is no-one to gainsay him, at least amongst John White's selection of "respected authorities."

This emphasis on sexuality and Gopi Krishna's equal insistence that "reproductive juices" are "sucked up in a mysterious way and poured into the spinal canal" during the *kundalini* process, is the lead-in to another statement in which he declares that this "juicy stream" ascending through the spine is the selfsame "nectar" or "ambrosia" referred to time and again in the treatises on *kundalini* (p. 233). On this issue I must strongly beg to differ. My own experience of this phenomenon was crystal clear and repeated on several quite separate occasions. In the interests of science I must state unequivocally that this vivid other-dimensional experience was nothing at all to do with reproductive juices and had no sexual or erotic connotations whatsoever.

Apart from consolidating the tantric concepts of *urdhavareta* (semen retention), such statements as the above by the Pandit are seized on by certain individuals who also suffer various forms of excessive "genital activity" (the term used by Gopi Krishna), which they link in their minds with other auspicious symptoms and then self-diagnose their own conditions as akin to that of approaching sainthood. This is hardly surprising when one reads the personal accounts of purported enlightenment of renowned gurus like the late Swami Muktananda, who died in 1982. Under the heading of "Sensual Excitement" (p. 157) the Swami records how his body and senses "became possessed by carnal craving,"

111

and refers to the sexual torment that for a time dogged his meditations and filled his mind with fear and disgust. His own teacher explained this as the "divine grace of yoga" and reassured his pupil that under these circumstances, this "highly worthy generative organ of man" should be controlled "as much as possible" – but that if, "on touching the navel," the said organ remained in that position for a time, the "entire seminal fluid accumulated in the testicles" would commence to flow upwards to the heart. It would there become purified by the "gastric fire" and continue upwards into the brain, thus strengthening the nervous system and enhancing memory and intelligence. He later added that through undergoing this "vajroli process," Muktananda would attain to the power of *shaktipat* (the transmission of spiritual power from Guru to disciple), for his previous sexual appetite had now been uprooted by the force of *kundalini* "by means of the sexual torture which you had to endure" (p. 169).

Such exposition is seriously flawed and misleading, as this is *not* the route to spiritual enlightenment, nor is it a sound basis for the uprooting of "sexual appetite." To falsely believe that one has conquered one's own sexuality, and to have this factor later proclaimed in book form amongst one's disciples, leaves the individual devotee wide open to abuse, as Muktananda himself demonstrated if his female devotees were telling the truth. Terrorist activities and Swiss bank accounts for the purposes of tax evasion are not indicative of enlightenment either, though many devotees are seemingly still prepared to accept them as such.

[According to the Introduction to *Spiritual Choices: The Problem of Recognizing Authentic Paths to Inner Transformation* (1987), edited by Dick Anthony, Bruce Ecker, and Ken Wilber, allegations against Muktananda first became widely known in 1981 *"when one of his American swamis sent a letter to numerous professors, psychologists, schools and centers (including the Center for the Study of New Religious Movements) . . . The central charge against Muktananda is that he regularly had sex with female disciples in their teens and early twenties. Two of these young women have confirmed the allegations, in each case describing their sexual encounters with Muktananda as a molestation or even rape. Because Muktananda's spiritual teaching strongly emphasized celibacy, some people in the transpersonal community find the apparent hypocrisy more than the master's apparent promiscuity*

112

per se most objectionable. Other allegations include Muktananda's encouragement of physical violence and terror tactics, and financial chicanery involving millions of dollars in Swiss bank accounts.

"Those in Muktananda's inner circles who have remained loyal to him and to his successors claim to have no personal knowledge of his sexual habits. They do not deny the possibility of sexual relations with devotees. Even if this did occur, it is acceptable, in their view, because Muktananda as a transcendentally enlightened master was beyond considerations of good and evil; it is both futile and inappropriate for the unenlightened devotee to judge his actions. Any sexual contact with devotees could only have benefited them" (p. 22).]

My personal experience of authentic teachers is that they do not behave promiscuously with their students, or with anyone else; nor do they indulge in terror tactics and financial chicanery. To be "beyond good and evil" does not, *and has never*, pertained to such events as the above, and relates to other-dimensional levels far transcending the level of human *karma* in which "good" and "evil" are concretized polarities. These concepts and their underlying realities have been distorted and abused by pseudo-teachers and suspect gurus, who utilize these "crazy wisdom" notions for the purposes of exploitation and self-gratification.

There is much acute misunderstanding in these areas, as is demonstrated in a letter printed in the magazine *What is Enlightenment?* (Vol. 5, No. 2, Fall/Winter 1996), in response to an article by the contemporary Western guru Alan Cohen (b. 1955 in New York) which criticized the behaviour of certain other gurus, including "the great spiritual Master, Baba Muktananda." [It should be noted here that Cohen has himself recently come under valid and extremely serious criticism, and from his own mother, regarding his authoritarian and megalomanic behaviour towards his devotees – now numbered in their hundreds – a great many of whom gave up their families and careers to be with him, also surrendering their financial assets to assist his "work." See L. Tarlo, *The Mother of God* (1997).] The letter writer, seemingly taken aback by Cohen's allegations, which he felt were untrue, asserted his viewpoint as follows:

". . . It seems that the highest yogic platforms of profound love, respect and omniscience have yet to be experienced by Mr. Cohen. Had he true respect for others, the mere mention of Baba

Muktananda's name would choke up his throat, bring torrents of tears to his eyes and overwhelm him with love, gratitude and awe.

"Many who bow to a saint, offering him mind and body, consider the offering to be symbolic only, but the saint really does accept the offering and vows to shepherd the soul all the way home. This helps to explain why some promising spiritual teachers become more and more eccentric with the passage of time: the insanities, neuroses, obsessions, fixations, physical ailments and *sanskaras* [karmic traces] of the past lives of the aspirant come eventually to the self-proclaimed "guru," making him sick. How could anyone be so ungrateful to [Chogyam] Trungpa (who was endorsed by the Karmapa himself) as to say so self-assuredly that he drank himself to death? Maybe so, but it was probably his disciples' impurities that killed him!" (J. Mateson, "A crisis of trust," pp. 6–7).

While it may be considered true that *authentic* masters absorb the impressional impurities of their disciples, and the frequently excessive volume of these impurities (in the form of *sanskaras*) can make them ill, sometimes to the point of death – these are *bodily* afflictions – the outworking of karmic impulses in the flesh. They *do not* influence the teacher's mind, nor his or her behaviour. To say otherwise is a grave distortion, and a singular excuse for opportunists. *Sanskaras* release their intrinsic components, sexual or otherwise, but these are rapidly *transmuted*, not expressed, by an authentic teacher.

Of a different order are "gurus" who vampirize the energies, or vital force, of their disciples, and absorb simultaneously their impurities, which add to, and accentuate, their own unresolved propensities. Such gurus can neither selectively isolate these impurities nor transmute them. Nor can they annihilate them despite active *kundalini* (over which they have no control). At a certain pitch of intensity, they can only *express* them according to their constituents, along with their personal, unsublimated, desires; hence the extremes of immoral behaviour demonstrated by deviant "Masters" like Franklin Albert Jones (Bubba Da Free John and subsequent numerous additional appellations), Chogyam Trungpa, Swami Muktananda, and other promiscuous and/or alcoholic "crazy wisdom" gurus who have no wisdom in reality and who lead astray thousands of gullible disciples.

I would further like to clarify that it is *not* "neuroses, obsessions and fixations," and so on, that are removed by authentic teachers, but the root cause of the disciple's problems, including submerged nuclei of impressions from the past which may have crystallized and cause perpetually recurring hindrances to further development – or malformed (and usually self-initiated) structures of inner growth – again, in the great majority of cases, the result of an illicitly activated *kundalini*.

Distortions are plentiful in so-called "spiritual" writings, not least in the following documentation taken from Part IV of White's *Kundalini, Evolution and Enlightenment*, headed *Kundalini and the Occult*. It concerns a woman who mixed yoga teachings and the occult with meditation, Christian mysticism, contemplative prayer and orthodox Christianity.

Mineda McCleave is one of the persons who derived great solace from Gopi Krishna's autobiography. Under the chapter title *Christian Mysticism and Kundalini*, McCleave, who now lives in Davenport, Iona, informs us that she spent her twenty-first birthday in a state mental institution and, upon her recovery, her "aim in life became a spiritual one." Feeling herself to be a misfit in society, she "took refuge in religion," commencing a study of comparative religion, mysticism and metaphysics. Alongside these studies, McCleave delved into positive thinking, reincarnation, hypnotism, and yoga philosophy, eventually accepting Paul Brunton (d. 1981), a self-styled Western yogi and guru as her teacher, whilst retaining the Christian Bible as her handbook (p. 403). (Brunton is now considered by many former admirers to have been deluded. See J. Masson, *My Father's Guru: A Journey through Spirituality and Disillusion*, 1993).

McCleave's article is in fact her autobiography, and is very sincerely and often movingly written. She made great efforts to follow her Christian calling, to live prayerfully and place her faith in God. She tells us that she commenced her search by looking within herself, and devoting much time to prayer. She quickly discovered that through her prayer life she was moving into a deeper (or higher) aspect of her being, and began to feel an "immense love for God" which overflowed to include her family and friends, "and even my enemies." This state brought her much happiness.

Then came a problem, the beginning of which she tentatively hints at: "I noticed that the deeper I plunged into meditative prayer, with my mind focussed on God, the more I was aware of what I can only describe as sensual feeling" (p. 406).

In retrospect, she realized that she was entering into another mode of consciousness, that her normal consciousness had expanded into what she believed was "coming close to transcendental love." Retrospectively also, she recognized that she had set the *kundalini* force into motion in view of the changes that around this time commenced in her awareness – such as increasing occurrences of mental telepathy, "spiritual" dreams, and several out-of-the-body experiences. Concurrently, problems began to develop in her everyday life. There were "shifts in consciousness" during non-meditative hours, day-dreaming and absent-mindedness. McCleave was puzzled by these episodes, and observes that, not having required psychiatric care for a number of years, she was now again troubled with alternating periods of euphoria and the counterswing into anxiety, depression and despair. To her great perturbation, her "peaceful prayer life" was frequently undermined with thoughts of suicide (p. 407).

McCleave's expectation of her spiritual efforts had been that her life would be filled with constant joy; the reality was a prolonged suffering which she equates with the mystical "dark night" of the soul, and which lasted ten years. Yet what strikes one most forcefully is McCleave's naivete with regard to her own states and the states of the mystics she attempted to study and comprehend. Her mental retreat from the world involved over-long periods of prayer and meditation – but these latter, as she later acknowledged, also contained the components of yogic practices (undoubtedly derived from her copious reading and incorporated systematically into her meditations), and affected her system accordingly. With hindsight, she recognized that she had integrated certain "simple" techniques of breathwork and concentration, and that these techniques, added to long periods of prayer, had caused actual changes in her mind and body. These changes, physical, emotional and mental, were so pronounced and extreme that she was obliged to cease her employment and once more withdraw entirely from society, utterly dependent upon the care and support of her family.

McCleave declined all psychiatric help for as long as she could, but finally, in 1975 when she was thirty-seven years old, she was "hospitalized three times in the psychiatric ward of the local hospital" in the charge of her family physician. After the third incident, he insisted that she obtain psychiatric aid. For a further fortnight McCleave resisted this, finally relenting when she grasped that she could no longer cope with her mental state of agitation.

This led to eight months of therapy and acute mental stress, and it was during this period that the symptoms she attributed to *kundalini* took obvious effect. For some weeks she suffered internal heat and other symptoms, and was one day "jarred out of my prayer by what felt like a current of energy." She experienced this current as entering her body via her left foot, and likened it to an "electrical charge of nervous energy" which seemed to move with extreme rapidity upwards along the inside of her leg, through her genitals, and then dispersing in the upper region of her back. The sensation was operative for four days and nights, and generated a feeling of "great body heat" (p. 408). Her mind she described as "*hyper*hyperactive" as she tried to understand what was taking place. Her physical symptoms were distressing, and included anorexia, headaches, trembling, fever with concurrent chills, nausea and dizziness. Her emotions were in chaos, and she knowingly suffered disorientation and delusion.

At one point McCleave actually thought that she had died, and was disappointed to find that this was not so. Upon release from hospital, she was afraid to leave her home in case someone noticed her schizophrenic-like behaviour. Looking in the mirror scared her – she felt she looked "wild." In 1973 she had first read Gopi Krishna's autobiography and, not understanding it, had stowed it away. Now she retrieved it, and this time she *did* understand. She recognized similarities in parts of his experience and her own, and was assured she suffered from *kundalini* arousal, a partial and incomplete state that belonged to a greater whole.

It was when she reread of the involuntary, increased genital activity experienced by Gopi Krishna that McCleave allowed the conflict within herself (between her sexual urges and her desire for mystical states) to commence resolution. It was this sexual factor, she tells us, that had previously prevented her from seeking medical treatment. Gopi Krishna's descriptions of his sexual problems enabled her to "let go" of the secret that she had locked within herself for so many years. She believed that this decision spared her from "degenerating into schizophrenia from which there might not have been a return" (p. 410).

And it is here, in her conviction of the connection between increased genital activity and mystical experience, that McCleave moves into areas with which she is unconversant, and makes deductions (doubtless in all good faith) that are highly misleading to those seeking to comprehend the nature of mystical states. It seemingly never occurred to McCleave that her excessive "spiritual practices" were untimely, and that in these lay the prime cause of her hyper-active sexuality – in that these practices stirred into activity subliminally merged impulses that would otherwise have remained dormant. She was now reassured that this was merely a side-effect of an awakening *kundalini* and therefore perfectly in order because Gopi Krishna had described it so. Her concern from then on was to equate the phenomenon of *kundalini* with the "living waters" of Christian mysticism and the divine fire of the Holy Ghost. She sought comparisons between the experience of mystics of every religion, and the assumed erotic subsidiaries to these experiences. The many passages she quotes from her wide study of comparative religion make good sense in that their underlying meanings undoubtedly stem from a common origin, or similar mode of experience, despite the language or symbolism that cloaks them. Yet to confuse certain of that symbolism with human sexuality is incorrect, for the "heart" experience of mystical traditions, full of fiery longing and accompanying anguish, is devoid of all aspects of physical sexuality. It takes place in the innermost recesses of the human soul, and is other-dimensional in nature, as all who have genuinely undergone this process can testify. Furthermore, the entire sequence of higher range development is experienced from that level, and perception, knowledge, and certitude are accompaniments, likewise an innate stability. This latter factor is essential in order to withstand states that might well unbalance the unprepared.

To focus wholly upon a divine being – on God, or Christ, or the Master, by whatever name such an intelligence is known, in whatever religion – to be "in love with God" as this is sometimes described, is in no sense *sensual*. McCleave writes of the saints and prophets: ". . . they could have admitted that their relationship with God was a decidedly sexual one at times. They could have complemented such terms as rapture, bliss, ecstasy, and divine union with words like sensual, sexual, erotic, and orgasmic." A sentence later, she says: "The mystic who was admitted to the divine marriage was, undoubtedly, cognisant of the fact that it was in part a sexual marriage" (p. 415). This statement reveals acute misunderstanding and an over-literal interpretation of certain words. There is nothing whatever wrong with human sexuality – nor with its normal mode of expression – this has a legitimate place. But spiritual union occurs in a part of the self that has yet to be fully evolved in the greater majority of human beings, a part which comes under different laws and has its own range of experience. This range cannot be encompassed within the limits of bodily registration, and any attempt to define or describe it must of necessity use words with physical world connotations. Thus misconceptions are inevitable, as McCleave has demonstrated, and in particular amongst the self-deluded and the unprepared.

Human sexuality is the reflection of a finer reality, but only a reflection, not a route to it. It is procreative, not creative. The former is essential for the continuation of all species; the latter has a functional reality beyond the reach of the intellect, which requires to be superseded by other faculties. The lesser cannot comprehend the greater, anymore than the complex life and duties of an intelligent adult can be comprehended by a two-year-old child. Time, development, and experience are the key to this, and the eventual solution. Children grow up and become adults. The human species in due time evolves *beyond* the lesser reality of physical life into a life far greater and more real than that of the senses. The greater transcends the lesser; it also transmutes the lesser by the cultivation of finer qualities.

An extraordinary incident is described in John White's abovementioned book under the chapter heading *UFOs and Kundalini*, written by Gene Kieffer, President of the Kundalini Research Foundation Ltd., New York. Kieffer is of the view that the manifestation of UFOs (unidentified flying objects) within the field of individual consciousness is a phenomenon of the mind – in other words, the mind's attempt to translate something which it has registered that is beyond present comprehension. Kieffer links this phenomena (of UFO sighting) with the psychic confusion arising from an inadvertently activated *kundalini*, and deems that the best way to tackle the matter and obtain a more concrete and rational explanation for such events "would be for scientists to investigate kundalini." Kieffer considers that this would not prove difficult, and that furthermore, "A spontaneous arousal of kundalini under the observation of competent investigators [two or three hundred dedicated practitioners are suggested] would be a scientific 'first.' The phenomenon could be studied as never before in modern times" (p. 383). To illustrate the need for this research he records a personal experience of UFO "contact." Before this occurrence, he had learned, he says, to marginally increase his level of psychic energy, and could in fact raise it "to the fourth, or heart, chakra quite easily."

Kieffer proceeds to tell us that there is "nothing unusual" about this, and that many people achieve such an ability after only the briefest training – a statement I frankly find astounding. We are then informed that at the time of which he is speaking (1968) he "had no knowledge of kundalini" and was largely unfamiliar with psychic matters (p. 383). On this particular occasion, Kieffer decided to use his psychic energy experimentally "to carry a signal or message into space." His wish was to make communicative contact with a UFO.

Within minutes, he tells us, the contact was made, and although he saw the UFO visually (as a "luminous green, slightly pulsating, amorphous vehicle"), he later came to the conclusion that it was a self-created projection from his own mind. Soon, however, he was in telepathic contact with the UFO and was instructed to report what he had learned to a certain person in Alabama employed by NASA. This he did, by telephone, despite fear of making a fool of himself. Apparently, the report was accepted in all seriousness, and even relayed by an official to Cape Kennedy, where Apollo 8 was about to be launched on its first journey to the moon. However, this is not Kieffer's point in telling this story. His concern is with the rational understanding of such episodes. He comments that if the subjective information received via our senses and intellect is not adequately interpreted, the subsequent registrations will prove distorted, and that this is the reason "hard-nosed" scientists give little credence to psychic phenomena (p. 384). He concludes that the answers lie in a "more thorough" understanding of the human organism and the evolutionary processes at work within it; and that the envisaged research on *kundalini* would be in essence "an attempt to accelerate the evolutionary processes to an incredible degree," and thus lead to "a whole new dimension of consciousness for the race" (p. 385).

What this particular chapter illustrates most clearly is, (a) the distortion of information registered in the brain by the unprepared psychology; (b) the projection of these distortions in the form of visual and auditory (or telepathic) manifestations; (c) resultant misconception and misinformation which is passed on to others; and (d) the complete acceptance by Kieffer of Gopi Krishna's assumption of the necessity for "voluntary kundalini activation" as the core discipline of a major research programme. Other clever minds will doubtless arrive at similar conclusions on the basis of the material presented. These incorrect conclusions constitute a serious danger for the coming generation, and for university students in particular, as it is they who are likely to be the vanguard of the proposed experiment.

Kieffer's contribution also highlights the common error that *kundalini* is something that can be drummed up with a little practice and by virtually anyone. What Kieffer refers to so casually in connection with an upraising to his heart *chakra* is, by his own description, most definitely not the titanic primary energy of *kundalini*, the volcanic evolutionary force in man; and if he can make, and print, an error of such magnitude, what does this say for the research projects, scientific or otherwise, under his direction?

This brings us to the contribution of John White himself, editor of the book under review; he is described as an educator in consciousness research and parascience, and author of *Everything You Want to Know About TM* [Transcendental Meditation as taught by the Maharishi Mahesh Yogi.] White's chapter is entitled *The Divine Fire: Tumo and Kundalini*.

According to White, *tumo*, a condition recognized amongst Tibetan lamas and yogis is one of the "lesser-known but nevertheless spectacular human powers," and confers the ability to control the body temperature at will. *Tumo* is regarded as a feat for which training is given – the phenomenon of extreme and controlled heat in the human system can be induced by yogic disciplines, and has been studied, measured, and researched in this century by Westerners, usually with Tibetan monks. Much is made of the detail that those experiencing *tumo* are able to sit stark naked on ice for lengthy periods without coming to harm, or to dry out wet towels or woollen blankets by the sheer heat of the practitioner's skin.

Alexandra David-Neel popularized the notion of *tumo* in her book, *Magic and Mystery in Tibet*. (excerpted under the chapter title *Psychic Sports* in White's book). She described *tumo* as "the art of warming oneself without fire up in the snows," and further describes it as a subtle fire which "warms the generative fluid and drives the energy in it, till it runs all over the body" (p. 386). White quotes her as saying that "the secret knowledge is obtainable only from lamas with the power to confer it." The requirements are significant and include proficiency in various breathing practices, a "perfect" concentration of the mind that can move into a type of trance in which "thoughts become visualized," and the receipt of "the proper *angkur* or initiation rite which confers a secret formula" (p. 389).

These qualifications are confirmed by D. H. Rawcliffe in *Illusions and Delusions of the Supernatural and Occult*, quoted by White, in which Rawcliffe suggests that much of the process is "merely a matter of self-induced anaesthesia." There is also a lengthy quote from Perle Epstein's *Oriental Mystics and Magicians*, in which she states that the process of induction requires "long and arduous training," and gives graphic details of the intensity of the disciplines involved, e.g., "With each breath taken, the force of the flames seated in the navel grows stronger. Holding the breath for longer and longer periods, the yogi concentrates hard on the increasing fire as it moves upwards . . . The man now loses all bodily consciousness, seeing himself as nothing more than a flaming vein in a sea of fire" (*Kundalini, Evolution and Enlightenment*, pp. 309–310). Epstein likewise concludes that "the phenomenon is attributable to hypnosis" (p. 391).

After a detailed survey of various research procedures, most of which are concerned with bodily heat regulation and allied matters, White expresses the view that a knowledge of *tumo* is particularly timely, and welcomes the prospect of utilizing this ability as a means of keeping warm without the use of technology. He additionally suggests that the possibility of energy shortages in the future "may spur humanity at large to discover this little-known psychic resource" (p. 398).

Tumo is in fact rather more than a "psychic resource" or a means of keeping warm. It is a natural side-effect of *kundalini* activation and carries a distinct function, though neither this, nor other abilities that prevail during the (normally hidden) state of *tumo* are mentioned in White's text, perhaps because these capacities were either unperfected, or did not exist at all in those persons selected for research.

Individuals who deliberately induce such states as *tumo*, whether for schools of magic or other display purposes, are apt to ignore, or are unaware of, the rules for evolutionary development – of which the basic *kundalini* process is a culminating attribute. This attribute, in the form of an active, non-physical energy, both conducts and expands the limited human consciousness into the vastness of the cosmos. When this is lawfully effected in a living entity, *tumo* provides a function, one of many such. These functions, however, are not available at all times and to everyone. Nor are they described in speculative modern literature, medieval hagiographies, or antique symbolic texts – while initiation rites and secret formulae constitute further distractions invented in sectarian lore.

"Prepare to make a quantum leap in your spiritual growth" says the blurb on the jacket of *Kundalini and the Chakras: A Practical Manual—Evolution in this Lifetime* (1997), by Genevieve Lewis Paulson (b. 1927). Moreover, "The Mysteries of Kundalini Revealed" screams the heading on the back cover. For this is a special book – "A Beacon of Understanding When Sense and Sanity are Threatened." We are told this on the first page, as we are also told in subsequent paragraphs:

"It is our birthright to evolve, develop, and become super-people. Life's simplest problems may have imbalanced or blocked Kundalini flow at their root. For everyone has Kundalini, just as everyone has sexual impulses. In light of today's tenor of cosmic flux, not to know about Kundalini is tantamount to refusing teenagers sex education. The more we know, the more choices we have."

Furthermore: "... *this book is your guide to satiating the strange, new appetites which result when life-in-process 'blows open' your body's many energy centers....*

Genevieve Lewis Paulson is the Director and owner of Dimensions of Evolvement, located on 165 acres of the Ozark mountains in Arkansas, a "center of psychic, personal and spiritual learning, accrediting students in the study of Kundalini energy development." Paulson's credentials for "accrediting students" are described on the book cover as follows: She is *steeped in Western Christian tradition and once served as administrator of a United Methodist Church. With the onset of a fierce Kundalini upsurge in 1968 she began her profound energy arousal, sought accredition as a group leader in the fields of sensitivity training and conflict management – still under the purview of the Church – only later discovering the ancient literature to describe the Kundalini awakening she had been undergoing.*

Early in the 1970s, Paulson founded a "spiritual growth" center in Chicago, and rather than abandoning her Western religious ideology, "instead found a method to meld two varieties of truth, creating a synthesis of two great traditions of belief." In addition to her work of raising the *kundalini* force in students and accrediting them to do the same for others, Paulson *"lives like an itinerant preacher in her second home, a red pickup truck, counseling and giving workshops ... on a circuit of cities from Florida to Arizona."*

This author has written several books, among them *Introduction to Out of Body Travel*, which perhaps is an indicator of the "New Age" ethereal nature of her expertise, for throughout the two-hundred or so pages of *Kundalini and the Chakras* there is no evidence at all of the higher-level range of knowledge invariably bequeathed by an authentic full-scale experience of *kundalini*.

Paulson states that the condition was totally unknown to her at the time she first "became aware" of its power, but that she *did* have the help of direct guidance from "Beings" through the media of clairaudience. Also, much of the information in her book "came to me originally from these Beings" (p. xv). She cites Gopi Krishna as a "modern exponent of this evolutionary energy" and affirms that his experiences and writings "have been very beneficial" and will also "give you a deeper understanding of this process as it functions in the Aquarian Age. Ancient texts will give you background and foundation" (pp. 4, 188). Other "verification" came to Paulson through her work with students – which seems a somewhat dangerous way to learn, particularly for the students. No other information is given on her actual experience.

Doubtless with Gopi Krishna's work in mind, Paulson gives a list of symptoms which are, in her view, indicative of early release of *kundalini* before the physical system is ready for it. This list in general reads like problems symptomatic of severe forms of psychosis, and includes "Evidence of multiple personalities," excessive mood swings, difficulty in coping with everyday life, loss or distortion of memory, disorientation, and erratic behaviour. What is needed, therefore, is "Kundalini cleansing," and that is primarily what Paulson's book is about.

In the view of the present author, such "cleansing" is not possible; and many of the practices described, and their effects, are clearly of the same order as the purported removal of "energy blocks" by hypnotherapists and others. When satisfied of sufficient cleansing, Paulson instigates minor "releases" of the *kundalini* force, which the student gauges for himself/herself and increases by stages (theoretically, at least). As the energy accumulates, Paulson states that "homosexuality and lesbianism may appear as Kundalini energy brings about an androgynous state." The reason given is that "Kundalini forces people to deal with both masculine and feminine polarities" (p. 19). The assumption here is that homosexuality and lesbianism are stepping stones to an androgynous state, which is simply not true, and betrays a distressing ignorance (in view of the numerous students in her charge) of what constitutes these evolutionary anomalies. Normal masculinity and normal femininity *do not change* their intrinsic characteristics through any kind of "balancing" or fusion, whether of the left-brain/right-brain variety, or anything else.

Advice is given on "Facing Demons," a situation which arises, according to Paulson, in stages of preparation. She tells us: "A person in the midst of cleansing is very aware of this demonic side, which may involve deep feelings of bitter hatred, sexual perversion, sadism, or other unacceptable tendencies" (p. 45). This seems a very strange basis for *kundalini* activation, and grappling with the ensuing situation is left entirely to the student – though it is conceded that "some people" may prefer professional counselling "when dealing with this aspect of life."

Paulson's casualness in matters of such seriousness is shocking. Individuals suffering these tendencies should never be exposed to the powerful break-in techniques that she so ignorantly

125

promotes. The dangers are titanic, and no form of counselling, however professional, can hope to control the consequences.

Similarly, when cleansing is advanced, and kundalini "releases" are actually in operation, *those who have been on hard drugs may experience too much release in the beginning and should be extra cautious*" (p. 172, Paulson's italics). What Paulson is doing teaching *kundalini* release to students damaged by drugs is anyone's guess, but it is very irresponsible and further demonstrates her ignorance of the very fundamentals of what she purports to *know* by her own experience.

The attributes and abilities which the average human being is deemed able to command, verges on the ridiculous. "When you are aware of what the energies feel like, and when you are able to move energy around, you stand a much better chance of controlling additional release. *Once released, there is no putting the energy back.*" The pupil is informed of the possible consequences of over-release, one of which is that the *kundalini* energy can "turn back on itself; this is very unsafe and creates risk." Immediately following is the assertion: "You may use the power of Kundalini to hold back the Kundalini itself for a period of time, but such a concentration of energy increases the risk of bodily harm" (p. 172). [I would here like to state categorically that the live, other-dimensional energy of *kundalini* **cannot** be manipulated or held in check by *any* student, of whatever calibre, by the methods described, nor indeed by any methods at all, and to initiate this process in students, and in the general public which constitutes the readership of Paulson's books, is in my view a criminal activity and a breaking of evolutionary law. The assertions about the "Soul Body," the "Divine Body," the "Monadic Body," and what can be done with them by the practitioner, are nothing short of nonsensical, as indeed is "Blissing out the Chakras" and similar idiocies. Tragically, the fact that these are idiocies will not negate the effects of the exercises given.]

Paulson includes among her recommendations the dubious practice of tantric *Maithuna*. She is also plainly heavily influenced by Gopi Krishna in her methodology. The required attributes and abilities are all encompassed by breathing exercises, "thinking" a requirement into being, and visualization, all of which require skill, determination, and dedicated focus. Kundalini is literally "forced" into activity in some instances, e.g., "Alternately tighten

126

and release the Kundalini reservoir [via the anus], forcing the Kundalini into the end of your spine, into Sushumna [the central column] and up the spine and out the top of the head" (p. 181). In this distasteful schema, enlightenment, when it comes, will allegedly include such acquirements as the following:

". . . walking in the air or on water, levitation, ability to be invisible in a crowd, ability to generate enough body heat to melt a snow-field, command over the environment; healing, speaking in tongues, casting out devils; imperviousness to poisons," and so forth (p. 188).

Of the other promised "gifts," of which there are a number, several have clearly not yet been bestowed upon Paulson, or she would not zealously promote the activation of *kundalini* amongst the general populace, nor seek to bring awareness of these energies into every sphere of life, even the world of childhood, and the darker world of criminals – *kundalini* check-up's, for instance, would be "a valuable part of a child's education" in the future. She also recommends the training of Kundalini Specialists and Kundalini therapists (trained by whom, one might ask?), and considers that virtually all ills can be cured by Kundalini therapy in the charge of a qualified Kundalini practitioner. All of which would probably have been roundly cheered by Gopi Krishna, and gladly supported by Gene Keiffer of the Kundalini Research Foundation.

Nevertheless, regardless of how the individual chooses to use the exercises and recommended practices in Paulson's book, or however inept their attempts to regulate the flow of their "releases," their teacher asserts ". . . you must always remember that the responsibility for it remains yours. You cannot delegate the responsibility to a guru or leader" (p. 197). They must, in other words, face the consequences themselves, which could be grim to say the least.

I was appalled by Paulson's book. Although in the ninth printing (first published in 1991) and therefore very popular and widely read, the content is so utterly distorted, both theory-wise and in the advocated practices (many of which are extremely potent), one despairs for the students who trustingly place their wellbeing in Paulson's hands.

The following book in this brief survey of contemporary knowledge provided by presumed "authorities" on *kundalini*, pinpoints certain dysfunctional syndromes whilst at the same time promoting *kundalini* activation. *The Yoga of Power: Tantra, Shakti, and the Secret Way* (1992) by the Italian thinker, Julius Evola, (d. 1974), in its English translation is an unusually comprehensible treatise on the subjects referred to in the title. The jacket describes Evola as a "controversial renegade scholar, philosopher, and social thinker" [whom some contemporaries considered a racist and a Fascist] and states that he has "long been regarded as a master of European esotericism and occultism as well as a leading authority on Tantra and magic." The author "introduces two Hindu movements – Tantrism and Shaktism – both of which emphasize a path of action as well as mastery over secret energies latent in the body . . . Evola focuses on the perilous practices of the Tantric school known as Vamachara – the 'Way of the Left Hand' – which uses human passions and the power of Nature to conquer the world of the senses."

Drawn from original texts allegedly dating from the fourth century onwards, Evola's book contains the usual sexual emphases on the subject of Tantra, and it is possible to see in certain sections of his text where misconceptions arose in what was once a pure system, devoid of any sexual connotation. Having made this statement, it is disturbing to find yet another influential work giving specific information on raising the *kundalini* energy under such chapter headings as *Techniques employed to awaken the Serpent Power*, particularly as these deal almost exclusively with *sadhanas* associated with *pranayama*, including breath suspension and precise breathing rhythms designed to "break down the blocked doors of the subconscious" (p. 160). These are the very techniques which create the most problems.

Scholarship is not absolved from the need to discriminate. Evola does at least refer to the dangers of these operations if certain "obstacles" are not surmounted before the commencement of such programmes – these "correspond respectively to the bonds of sexual desire, of self-love, and of the intellect (especially in the form of pride)" (p. 173). Should these obstacles remain untransmuted, "one would incur one of the greatest dangers inherent to these yogic exercises." For instead of liberation, says Evola, the end result "would be obsession – obsession with sex, with selfishness (the opposite of this bond is a false universal and sentimental love, encompassing everything and everybody), and with a cold and detached intellectual pride (hubris)." One's entire being, in fact, will become dominated by one of these hugely amplified determinants, which "having escaped control are now absolutized . . ."

Evola stresses the dangers of the partial awakening of a *chakra*, and the lack of control of whatever propensities are released. He also warns of the effective result of neglect of the preliminary discipline of purification, and asserts that "every leftover residue will 'vampirize' the awakened energy and feed demons. This belief is also found in other initiatory traditions." He then emphasizes the strength of the onslaught, and the "extent to which these phenomena can go." He asks us to remember his earlier comments concerning the "samskaras and the *vasanas*, the subconscious roots whose origin often antedates the present life. These underground roots are responsible for causing the relapse into tendencies or states that were believed to be left behind once and for all." They are also responsible for attitudes and attributes never before manifest in this lifetime, avers Evola, such predispositions having been "galvanized by the new energy now circulating one's body . . ."

Yet the emergence of such residues is not confined to physical life alone, and subtler processes are frequently involved of an intensely frightening or deviant nature, some of which take the form of "visions and apparitions during the yogic process, thus causing more deviations" (pp. 174–175). This is an understatement of the horrors to which he alludes.

Relevant to the above, and certainly potentially disastrous in effect, is the "modern" instruction given in *Tantric Yoga: The Royal Path to Raising Kundalini Power* (1989) by Gavin and Yvonne Frost. I include this book solely because of the uncensored explicitness of the presentation, and the fact that publication by Weiser has ensured its widespread circulation despite the nature of the contents.

The Frosts exhibit wholly permissive viewpoints and overwhelming contempt for all taboos, and their left hand appetites have provided a detailed course of indulgence in all aspects of the debacle known as *Reconstructed or Neo-Tantric Yoga*, "considered by many to be the highest and most rapid path to enlightenment." Much is made of the opportunity for single persons

129

or couples to join with the Frosts in a scheme of community living for the purpose of practising Tantra Yoga as a fulltime, daily life system of development.

In preparation for this venture, in the late 1950s Gavin and Yvonne Frost "independently researched Eastern religions," and over a period of sixteen years Gavin Frost made numerous visits to India and Pakistan in search of the "remnant teachings" on Tantra. By-passing "tourist traps," he eventually found what he sought in Thailand in the teachings of the Western tantric exponent John Blofeld, and later still met practitioners of what he considered a "true path" in Bengal. Everything he learned and deduced was promptly adapted and put into practise with his partner, and after several years of "work and experiment" the system now known and used as *Reconstructed Neo-Tantric Yoga* came into being. This led to the inception of a series of "Tantric Houses" in which groups of Westerners live communally and follow set time tables and lunar workcycles, including copulating according to prescribed rituals with each and every member of the commune.

Special to the book, as stated on the cover blurb, "are rituals and meditations for ascending and descending the chakras," and the authors "particularly devote themselves to discussing how to work with activating the kundalini energy *safely*." [Safety, however, is a word that has no meaning amongst those who believe that morality is unsafe.] Comprehensive exercises are given for separate activation of each *chakra*, and the end results are confidently delineated.

In the preliminary foreword "About the Authors," the information is proffered that in 1985 a course on Tantra was made available by the School of Wicca (presumably tutored by the Frosts). We are told that: "To date over 100 students have completed the course and made their recommendations for changes in the system as taught. The School also invited gays and single practitioners to try the course. Both groups have been successful in achieving spiritual enlightenment."

[According to the *New Age Almanac* (1991) by J. Gordon Melton, Jerome Clark and Aidan A. Kelly, the Church and School of Wicca "was founded by Gavin Frost and Yvonne Frost in the early 1970s. It is a form of Neo-Pagan Witchcraft that operates with a theology derived from the Druidic school of Iolo Morganwg, and

130

utilizes rituals derived from British ceremonial magic rather than the Gardnerian Witchcraft system based on the work of Margaret Murray and Robert Graves. These differences in operation led to some initial misunderstandings with other Neo-Pagans in the early 1970s." The scholarly *Almanac* further informs us that: "The Church and School of Wicca is one of the largest and most accessible of the current Witchcraft groups, and sponsors some of the largest festivals." It also states that Gavin Frost "is regarded by many as one of the most intelligent of the current leaders of the Craft movement" (p. 340).]

The Preface to *Tantric Yoga* furthers the information on the qualifications of the authors. Apart from research in all matters Tantric, some of the material used in the text was derived "through our own enlightenment," and some was culled "from the enlightenment of our students." Thus the claims (and aims) are allegedly of the highest nature by reason of this supposed enlightenment.

The rules are unequivocally explained. *Nirvana*, it is stated, "is gained by the Tantrist through a regular cycle of indulgence and abstinence" (p. xv). This routine is designed to achieve control over all the passions, "and through that ability to gain control of all other body functions, including temperature and pulse rate . . ."

The book in question is rather more than the usual DIY manual; it is intended to take the place of a personal Guru, and is claimed to provide all necessary instruction in this particular branch of Neo-Tantra. This is because the centuries old concept of the need for a teacher (as the text makes clear) is now outmoded. Since the advent of the printed word such entities are regarded as obsolete. Despite this dictum, it is quite evident that the authors have arrogated to themselves the function dismissed, for in 300 or so pages an entire course is presented; one that is rigorously adhered to in all the Tantric houses indoctrinated by it. *Maithuna* (sexual) rituals of every description cram the pages, likewise *chakra* meditations, cleansing rituals, breathing techniques, directions for raising *kundalini*, and "authoritative" advice.

Tantric Yoga is a very objectionable book. The content breaks all taboos yet is convincing to persons steeped in modern ideologies, also to those drawn to ritualism and certain types of ultra-erotic experience. Under the pretence of learning self-control, everything sexual is permitted and nothing sexual is denied. The license is group based and circle oriented, and a glib slogan used is that "the thing that drives the circle is sexual desire." The objective is hormonal increase, for which the requirement is orgasms that constitute "the most exquisite, deep, mind-blowing, earth shattering experience that stirs every part of each one's very being" (pp. 125–126).

Group sexual contact is therefore endemic, and partners are exchanged with very great frequency in order to weld the group and keep sexual interest at peak level. There is really little else in evidence, whatever the Tantric rhetoric. In some Tantric houses the ritual copulations of the four-weekly (lunar) all-day Kundalini Circle are required to be conducted in public, and if six couples participate, the aim is that all produce orgasms as near the same minute as possible, after which the participants rest briefly then meditate for sixteen minutes. The entire process is now repeated in full with a different partner until every male has coupled with every female. The whole involves "a concentrated effort to gain total satiation and to be totally drained sexually so that Nirvana can be entered" (p. 128).

At the conclusion of a number of such libertine cycles comes the "great meditational release," when everyone present commences to meditate and to "open" themselves to whatever "comes through." In this condition (strangely akin to states found in Spiritualism), guides are encountered and guidance obtained. It is claimed that many practitioners at this stage achieve *Nirvana* or "ultimate bliss" (p. 128), a statement which defies belief.

The intention behind these ritualistic processes is the raising of *kundalini*, without which the experience of *Nirvana* is not possible, and for which event, in the Tantric system of forced activation, much higher levels of sexual hormones are believed to be required than is the norm. In a circle using strictly-followed *Maithuna* rituals, hormonal levels will rise and act as a propulsive fuel – one which, combined with the effects of other disciplines, will precipitate the arousal of *kundalini* and literally force open the lower *chakras* – to the detriment of all concerned.

In order to raise such levels in the individual, consistently repeating orgasms are resorted to, and likewise the counter-practice of withholding orgasm when the body is on the verge of expressing it. These rituals, occurring with frequency and sustained at peak levels for quite lengthy periods, soon flood the systems of those participating with sexual hormones, creating levels of excess within the entire group, and making of it a dangerous instrument of obsessive energy not otherwise obtainable.

The Frosts inform us that as training in the activities of sexual Tantra increases, so does the level of desire and the need for yet more sexual activity – the hormonal release increasing accordingly. The reality of this is such that warnings are given if members consider leaving the group without first "winding down." The effects of cyclic *Maithuna* are similar to a regular high intake of steroids: to cut them off suddenly is to risk the health of the body, and the greater the intake, the more likelihood of serious illness or collapse.

To deepen and further these experiences, at the appropriate moon phase, the "Ascending Kundalini" is dynamically forced upwards (we are told) from base to crown (*muladhara* to *sahasrara*) as each *chakra* in turn is activated, and a series of actions, emotions, and meditations set into motion or experienced. In the *Ritual for Activating the Base Chakra*, for instance, the house members remain unwashed following a period of manual labour, and rub grime and heavy fish oils onto their stomachs and buttocks in preparation for the ritual. The more odiferous they are from extensive sweating, and the more grossly they behave, the more potent the ritual is believed to be. Members, both male and female, hit, pummel and buffet each other and "bruising is encouraged"; the meaningful objective is "real, significant pain." Eventually the whole group falls upon one another in a "writhing frenzy," and any part of the lower body can be "slapped or grabbed and twisted." Even the testicles of the males can be squeezed until the owner is obliged to give ground. The intention here is to "open" the posterior *yoni* (or anus), considered the external route to the internal base *chakra*. It is also considered that this ritual provides the means of transcending the primordial passions by first experiencing them. The folly of all this is indescribable

To enable participants to obtain the desired hormonal upsurge in the next phase of activation, after ritual cleansing, all inhibitions are released, and complete loss of control encouraged in "the frenzy of sexual activity" that hallmarks this stage. For

133

example, when it becomes obvious that "all members are ready and eager for sexual contact" in the *Ritual for Activating the Pelvic Chakra*, the circle is broken by the leading yogini who "grabs at the lingam [male sex organ] of the yogi to her right and pumps it quite violently. The other yoginis immediately follow her example. The yogis fall to the floor with the yoginis on top of them" (p. 168). Loincloths are torn off, and each *yoni* [female sex organ] forced "down over the lingam in a violent motion," so violent that lubricant is applied beforehand in some houses to the genitalia of all concerned. In this ritual uncontrolled urges and primal emotions reign supreme, yet initially the male is required to remain passive, the female "ravening and violent," as after "eight strokes" each yogin moves clockwise to the next yogi and treats him in similar fashion. Soon the yogi is "rutting in need" – the rest of the paragraph more suited to a hard-core porn magazine than a sacred ritual. Nothing is barred, however profane or perverted. No act is prohibited. At this point in the proceedings, "many houses allow the use of the whip to encourage and rouse the yogi." Even in this environment the sturdiest male will occasionally falter beneath the all-too-insistent demands of the flesh. The publisher of *Tantric Yoga*, Samuel Weiser Inc., should be prosecuted for promoting such activities.

Outside the monthly cycle of sexual rituals, the occupants of a Tantric house can make love as they please – a "group can make love as a group" (meaning collectively) or two males can experiment together, likewise two females. Most commune members are partially bi-sexual, or at least willing to try bi-sexual activities (pp. 129–131).

A portion of the Frost manual is given solely to homosexuals, and there are special instructions on the use of the anus for homosexual yogis. For yoginis of a lesbian persuasion, the double-sided artificial phallus is recommended. It is further mentioned that sexual contact between brother and sister is considered quite in order, providing no pregnancy ensues. AIDS tests for both male and female are deemed essential before community inclusion in any House.

In the midst of all this sexual activity, an occasional unsought pregnancy can arise. Though babies are usually welcomed in a Tantric commune, it is conveniently believed by Tantrists that the foetus is unconnected to a spirit until it is born and has taken its first few breaths. Before this, it "amounts to a growth on the uterus" and can therefore be aborted if wished by the mother, without conscience or regret (p. 23).

Maithuna training and sexual meditations (which latter include the preparatory option of masturbation) are an unlikely basis for spiritual enlightenment. The Frosts lead gullible readers to believe that *Nirvana* is virtually guaranteed within a four to six month period. This may be regarded as a deception of the worst type. Nowhere is the actual Nirvanic experience described in terms other than ecstasy or bliss, designates equally applicable to states far lower in the scale than *Nirvana*. Yet the promised *kundalini* activation, however partial, is an almost certain consequence for the confused adherents of the disciplines advocated, which in their Tantra-based, hormonal, and meditational requirements must ultimately invoke this energy, and at the same time *hone the will* to an obsessive degree quite useless to anything spiritual, and indeed inimical to anything refined. The obsessiveness is extremely unhealthy in itself, but when aggravated by occult factors like *kundalini*, is sufficient to trigger problems far worse than the AIDS virus, being equally infectious and possibly lasting for much longer – should reincarnation prove a fact.

The deviant one-pointing of the will is exacerbated by exercises derived from European Wicca. The art of Witchcraft admixed with Tantra Yoga is a formidable factor, as is evidenced by the description of "skills of single pointed concentration and visualization" (p. 43), the power they bequeath, and the uses to which such skills are applied, i.e., to fulfil lust; reduce tumours; undergo abortion, or eliminate one's enemy (p. 45). Exercises are outlined in the use of pranic force, which include the "telepathic control of another person" (p. 32). Group usage of the force is also dealt with, and participants are taught how to increase the volume and velocity of this potency for use of the entire commune. In this type of ritual, members form a circle and a repetitive chant sets the force into circulation and recharges the exponents. As the chanting rises in volume to a crescendo, a selected person moves out of the circle, thus breaking its circuit, and "sends the force out explosively" to do whatever has been willed by the participants (p. 40). As there is no belief in *karma* (according to the Frosts) in such unsavory circles, there is no fear of breaking planetary law, and the possible consequences of this mode of

135

activity when indulged in by an unregenerate group – whether or not they have activated the power of *kundalini* – should make anybody sane keep their distance.

Information is given of a far more detailed nature than the above, and covering a wide range of possibilities. These disparate aims make nonsense of the rules of all authentic spiritual development, though such development is firmly claimed. There is no "surrender to God," of course. No "heart" experience either, but enlightenment nevertheless (we are assured). The following advice encapsulates the barren outlook under discussion: "Even when you display emotions like anger, they must not make you angry and they must be completely under your command. From anger [or any other emotion] you must be able immediately to change into cold, hard objectivity" (p. 202).

Cold, hard objectivity is a gross distortion of the dispassionate objectivity arrived at by means quite other than those described by the Frosts. At the back of their book a Questionnaire is included for "those who are interested in founding or joining a house." Supposed advantages of this type of group-living are enumerated on page xix of the Introduction, among them, "never again to be alone," and the achievement "of complete equality with the opposite gender." Please note: it is made clear that males who have the genetic impediment of undersized genitalia (and their female counterparts) have little or no hope of attaining enlightenment in the Frost system, as all Tantric houses are likely to refuse them. Similar rulings are made for the reverse end of the spectrum, and a pathetic gauge, taken from the classifications of the *Kama Sutra*, is provided to enable applicants (both male and female) to self-assess these supposedly vital statistics and declare them on the application form, no doubt with a view to forming a separate establishment if enough potential rejects are found.

The book in question is the end-of-the-line in Tantric tuition. The information disseminated in *Tantra Yoga: The Royal Path to Raising Kundalini Power* exemplifies the root and substance of this system, and clearly reveals the pivotal point towards which all, or most, Western Tantric practitioners (and too many Eastern ones) gravitate. Amidst all the exercises and disciplines, is the corrupt core of the matter: free sexual licence – the unrestrained, unrestricted, and uninhibited release of all lusts and perversions, without criticism or indictment, utterly without guilt; all wrapped up in the gilt paper guise of learning self-control and a means of self-enlightenment. ***This is the biggest lie in the whole book of lies that comprises sexual Tantra.*** People who still harbour desires for frenzied orgies, and who are willing and prepared to indulge in them on these pretexts, are nowhere near the point where authentic spiritual training can commence, no matter how many miniature fasts and austerities are interspersed in the monthly cycle to give the impression of spiritual "work."

That the Frosts are aware that these practices are exciting goads and whet the appetite for the next bout of licence is indicated on page 171 – where it is stated that the "uninhibited enjoyment" found when opening the lower *chakras* is for some the be-all and end-all of the practice of Tantra; that many participants simply go through the motions of all other "work" in order to again take part in these recurring rituals. The danger is acknowledged, as also are other dangers, some of which are extreme. Yet all responsibility is said to rest squarely on the ignorant members, not the gurus proffering Tantric Houses, Tantric experience, and Do-It-Yourself manuals promoting (in fullest detail) *kundalini* activation, *chakra* opening, ceremonial Wicca, and group sex.

The irresponsible Frosts are patently wrong in their assumptions of what constitutes *Nirvana* and spiritual development. This being so, does it really matter what happens to those who so willingly "open" themselves up to the unknown through such false recommendations? Or to those who establish Tantric Houses as the Frosts suggest, and find themselves (and their members) in dire difficulties? One could say that they have been foolish, but the damage is done once *kundalini* has been prematurely activated, a far-reaching consequence out of all proportion to the human weakness of sexual permissiveness. The former is not the natural outcome of the latter, and would not have occurred outside the continuous practise of Tantra Yoga.

Unfortunately, the type of presentation at issue here is very attractive to a small but significant section of the populace, and is unlikely for long to confine itself to unsubstantial groupings, or even to the USA. The end product of this training can only too readily make its mark upon a declining Western culture, and leave widespread and unconsidered havoc in its wake.

Tantric Yoga was imported from the East into the West, but

137

the articulate, magic-oriented, and explicitly pornographic variant found in the Frosts' newly adapted *Reconstructed or Neo-Tantric Yoga*, has recently been exported from the West back to the East again via the undiscerning auspices of the Delhi based academic Indological publisher, Motilal Banarsidass. [If publishers believe in karma, they would surely undo some of their commercial strategies.]

The form of tuition under review is certainly something both East and West could do without.

Erratum

(*page 113, line 26*)

"Alan Cohen" should read:
Andrew Cohen

Chapter Four

Incomplete Forms of Enlightenment

Dysfunctional states (i.e., disoriented, delusive, and chaotic states of altered consciousness) are regrettably the end product of most forms of *kundalini* activation, and the more responsible exponents have stressed the need for a teacher, or guru, in the interests of safety. Too little is known of this phenomenon, aside from antique texts, to enable investigators to chart such development comprehensively. Diverse lore exists in Tibetan Buddhism, Hindu Tantra, and also Sufism (via the conceptual framework of the *lataif*) that allegedly prepares the human vehicle for the stimulation of the evolutionary force. What is seldom, if ever, attested are the results of these processes, the degrees of illumination attained, and the proportion of practitioners who run into major difficulties. One reason for this is that much of what occurs of this nature takes place in closed environments such as ashrams, and, increasingly in the West, in monastic centres of Buddhist orientation, now currently operative at several major venues, and under teachers whose unquestioned credentials are confusing to most Westerners. I refer here to the geshes, lamas, and gurus, by whatever title they are found, who are the product of traditional methodologies concerned with spiritual advancement. These teachers frequently emerge from long years of practice of time-honoured techniques, either in monastic communities or isolated retreats where much of the discipline is done in solitude – techniques such as those found in Kundalini yoga, i.e., visualization, meditation, breathing exercises, the use of *mantras*. Some are life-long celibates and highly dedicated to their calling. Many commence their training in childhood and know no other form of life than the monastic mode found in Tibetan monasteries. They often gain organizational roles of authority. These persons are usually honest and abstemious, though there have been disconcerting exceptions to this, notably the hedonistic "crazy wisdom" exponent Chogyam Trungpa (d. 1989).

What happens to the unsuspecting Western pupils of these teachers? Are they miraculously salvaged from the perils of a premature activation of the evolutionary force? Sadly, the indications are otherwise; genuine aspirants are likely to be far more sensitive to the effects of powerful disciplines than the traditionalist tutor himself.

Many teachers in various religious orders have acquired their status through learning by rote in much the same manner as secular teachers. They can teach by the letter, and nothing more. This is well demonstrated in some Buddhist orders, where traditional training in *mantra* and meditation, the memorizing of complex texts and a literal understanding of their meaning, is considered a basis for tutorship, and subsequently for spiritual direction, a situation I have personally encountered and observed. Many of these tutors have not themselves experienced the nonordinary states induced in the more sensitive by their curriculum, and have absolutely no idea how to regulate these states when they occur. Such states can leave the pupil in an almost permanent condition of disorientation, or even worse. These are states that, in the West, achieve hospitalization or the attention of psychiatrists, and should never have arisen in the first place.

The fact that a tutor can experience and describe a seemingly advanced non-ordinary state of consciousness does not of itself signify a great deal. Such states by the score are arrived at through the use of potent "break-in" procedures. Only those with awakened inner sight and a high-level degree of knowledge and comprehension can ascertain the value of that state, whether an actual achievement on the path, or otherwise; and to experience even an "advanced" state does not qualify the individual concerned to regulate the states of others (even assuming that this is possible). There are many grades and qualifications on the spiritual path, a fact seldom registered by most Western aspirants (and certainly not taught by most Western teachers), who consequently place their own development at risk by taking too many things on trust. "All that glitters is not gold," is a sound maxim in these instances.

Problems are particularly likely in the case of a scholarly but unillumined monastic director whose indiscriminately applied programmes will unerringly produce lopsided growth, thus leaving his unfortunate pupils in similar situations to those who live in the world and illicitly induce, either wilfully or unwittingly, the evolutionary energy of *kundalini*. Even when the novice is sound (that is to say, correctly oriented), traditional, potent, long term directives given by an unperceptive tutor can prove a disaster.

Some psychological states evoked by various disciplines create distortions that abound in undiscerning "spiritual" organizations, and also in monastic retreats of both Eastern and Western orientation. Delusions are manifold on the spiritual path, and especially when that path is rendered even more problematic by the introduction of assorted techniques of great potency. This is particularly evident in some contemporary Indian ashrams, as many records written by disillusioned one-time resident Western aspirants testify. There is a serious lack of knowledge in our present culture of the necessity for preparation, or even what constitutes such preparation. In the past, in all the major religions, the religious life was essentially a serious vocation. As Mary Scott observes in her book, *Kundalini in the Physical World* (1989), the first task of the Hindu aspirant was "working at oneself until one has the necessary qualities to satisfy a guru that one is ready for the systematic development of higher powers. . . . It includes enough to keep most of us busy working on ourselves for a lifetime and still be modest about our attainments at the end of it." The prescribed self-discipline "involves the acquisition of certain moral attributes. It comprises an oriental equivalent of the Ten Commandments and the Sermon on the Mount. The qualities aimed at require both the practice of avoidances and the positive exercise of virtues. For instance, one must avoid inflicting injury on any creature; one must not covet what others have and one has not; one must avoid excesses of all sorts; one must be prepared to forego sexual satisfactions. . . . On the positive side one must be truthful, brave, kind and pure. Some of this is reminiscent of St. Paul in Corinthians" (p. 208).

This is just the beginning of work on oneself, the basic preliminaries. A far cry indeed from a few weekend courses on "Opening the Chakras" under a New Age facilitator, and without any prior preparation at all.

Nevertheless, traditional developmental systems of the East *do* precipitate the awakening of *kundalini* and these systems are fraught with danger for the Westerner. It is alarming that organizations claiming affiliation with Sufism, and specifically the London Sufi Centre, the vehicle of Pir Vilayat Inayat Khan (the purported Head of the Sufi Order in the West), submit raw beginners from the general public who attend their weekend courses to intensive *chakra* meditations designed to swiftly activate the *kundalini*. Those seriously interested naturally continue to use these meditations when at home and, indeed, are encouraged to do so. Newcomers are also welcomed to the "Sufi" summer camps and immediately introduced to *zikrs, wazifers, mantras,* and other "spiritual" exercises. There is no screening or selection of those participating; anyone can take part. Vilayat Khan, in fact, openly promotes *chakra* and *kundalini* exercises at his fee-charging lecture sessions in London, the USA, and elsewhere. All this is folly in the extreme, and results in effects not described in the advertising leaflets or the course prospectus, and which are unlikely to be remedied by those persons currently in charge (most of whom are Westerners), no matter what the traditional grades of spiritual ability claimed by the adopted prefixes to their (also adopted) Middle Eastern names. Persons who have legitimately acquired such status would not initiate this type of activity, nor use it as the means of a lucrative livelihood.

Buddhist Orders are no less guilty in certain respects, but here some claims are more extensive. The disciples of Geshe Kelsang Gyatso of the Manjushri Mahayana Buddhist Centre in Cumbria, England, equate their teacher with the Buddha and turn to him as their highest authority. They have furthermore listed him in the lineage of a stream of allegedly enlightened tantric teachers comprising the Kadampa Tradition (a lineage said to have originated with the 10th century Indian Buddhist reformer Atisha, and to have also later included the yogi-scholar Lama Tsong Khapa, the 14th century Buddhist reformer who founded the Gelugpa sect, one of the four major schools within Tibetan Buddhism). The Geshe's status is emphasized in the introductory pages of one of his books, *Tantric Grounds and Paths* (1995), where we are informed by Roy Tyson, the Administrative Director of the Manjushri Centre, that "The author describes directly from his own experience all the stages of the path to enlightenment. Never before in the history of Buddhist literature has such a clear, profound, and comprehensive guide been published" (p. vii).

Geshe Kelsang Gyatso was born in Tibet where he was ordained at a very early age. He completed his studies at Sera-Je monastery, and then practiced meditation in the Himalayas for eighteen years. According to the write-ups on the jackets of his books, the Geshe is a fully accomplished Tantric Master and foremost teacher of Kadampa Buddhism. He is also a scholar of the Mahayana Buddhist tradition and has given extensive teachings on the major scriptures of the Mahayana. Since 1977, he has been resident at the Manjushri Centre in England, and now has thousands of disciples in many countries, and has founded numerous Buddhist Centres throughout the world.

The books written by the Geshe are considered unique by his disciples, and on the Acknowledgements page of *Clear Light of Bliss* (1995), described as an invaluable guide to those travelling the Tantric swift path to full enlightenment, we find: "For this incomparable book, the like of which has never before been seen in this world, we offer heartfelt thanks to the author." This well-written and meticulously detailed treatise, and the many others penned by the Geshe, are "primarily for the benefit of Western Dharma practice" and contain specific instructions which, if followed, are said to prepare the Western student for Highest Yoga Tantra empowerment from a Vajra Master (Geshe Kelsang Gyatso). After further practices, the attainment of direct realization of the Union of Mahamudra (spiritual enlightenment) is virtually guaranteed. The entire process, step by step from beginning to end, is set forth in these two books (*Clear Light of Bliss* and *Tantric Grounds and Paths*), and we are assured that diligent practice will achieve fruition within the current life span if the practices are adhered to. This form of Union is synonymous with Buddhahood, and a very real incentive to the pupils involved – for the Geshe makes clear that "If we keep our Tantric vows and commitments purely, and on this basis practise the generation and completion stages, we can attain Buddhahood in this life" (*Tantric Grounds and Paths*, p. 55).

Kadampa Buddhists are greatly concerned with accumulating merit by means of various rituals and dedications, making offerings and prostrations to Deities, and performing the disciplines of visualization and meditation. These practices are said to strengthen the powers of concentration and to engender a focused pitch of intensity whereby altered states are created in the mind, and visualized images are brought into concretized perception.

The objective of these disciplines is to extend the consciousness into increasingly subtle realms, and thereby actualize an equivalent vehicle, or "drop," as a levering point for the creation of a yet finer "body," and thence to the most rarified and lustrous body of all, in which enlightenment is attained.

These "drops" equate with the etheric, subtle, and mental bodies of other systems, but in Tibetan Buddhism each minute segment of each intermediary "whole" is scrupulously pinpointed, and appropriate disciplines are provided that ensure the objectification and establishment of each part, like creating rungs on a ladder. The principal difference between this system and certain others is that the entire procedure is engineered in the mind, and the karmic process (the outworking of which occurs in the physical world), and any possibilities inherent in the final balancing or concluding of that process, are assumed superfluous and are altogether sidestepped.

Training in "Divine Pride" is another Kadampa activity, and one that can easily be misunderstood, particularly by the Western intellect inadequately versed in humility which might conceivably utilize this exercise for purposes other than intended, including self-aggrandizement. "Divine Pride is a special way of regarding oneself in which we imagine that we are a Tantric Deity and that our environment is his or her Pure Land," says the Geshe (*Tantric Grounds and Paths*, p. 94), who provides the interested public with a series of complex meditations designed to make this an actuality. He further states: "The only way to reach liberation is to follow correct internal paths, which are explained only in Dharma [the Buddha's teachings]" (p. 7). It is made quite clear in the ensuing text that no other route is considered viable.

The similarities between tantric Buddhist practice and certain forms of magical ritual cannot be ignored, as the process is one of evocation (via visualization), and willed activation, rather than all-round balanced growth. The route to be followed is sectioned in detail, and is identical for each and every practitioner, no matter what their type, state or stage upon arrival at the Geshe's door.

There appears to be no process of selection nor concern with the candidate's suitability for tuition. The pressures of the practices themselves are the means of ascertaining who proceeds, and who drops out. All are given the same disciplines in sequence, the same meditations, the same empowerments, the same acts of dedication – and the same advice and directions. The complete process moves from preliminary practice (which includes the study of root [lineage] Buddhist texts or their nearest equivalent), through mandala offerings and recitations, to yogic concentration on the "winds" (the subtle energies that move along psychic nerve channels carrying cellular "drops" of awareness, and said to be the basis of the subtle mind); there are also exotic features such as igniting the inner fire of *tummo* (the latter by means of intensive meditation), penetrating the precise points of one's body, and penetrating the precise points of a partner's body (via the wisdom mudra and action mudra of sexual tantra), and the ultimate Mahamudra which leads to "the place where Buddhahood is attained" (*Clear Light of Bliss*, p. 251). All this is followed by every novice monk and nun, regardless of the nature of past *karma*, any present lack of development, and other considerations not occurring to the insistent formulators of such an over-intensive and inappropriate lifestyle.

This means that these powerful concentrative disciplines will inevitably affect all practitioners and further their indoctrination, complete with the expectation of what each stage of meditation should produce. Nowhere is there any mention of going beyond the mind (though doubtless this is implicit by the alleged nature of the results) – the focus is upon differing degrees of emptiness and differing degrees of bliss. Even the end product, the Complete Enjoyment Body in which a practitioner attains enlightenment, is adorned by identical attributes: "Such characteristics include the crown protuberance (ushnisha), wisdom hair curl, elongated ears, and other signs that signify the unsurpassable qualities of a fully enlightened Buddha" (*Clear Light of Bliss*, p. 237). In my view, such texts are a ludicrous guide to enlightenment. They attest indoctrination, not wisdom. Reliance upon inadequate texts, antique or otherwise, will lead nowhere save to confusion, and will create grave problems for the Western student trained to think for himself or herself and make independent analytical assessments. For example, what is he or she

145

to make of the constituents of certain "root downfalls," or falls from grace, all of which are considered extremely serious for the disciple. These include:

*"**Scorning the Dharma of Sutra or Tantra.** If we criticize any teaching of Buddha, claiming that it is not the word of Buddha, and if someone else hears our criticism, we incur a root Tantric downfall . . ."*

*"**Destroying others' faith.** If we cause someone's faith in Secret Mantra to degenerate by telling them that the practice of Secret Mantra is very dangerous and advising them to remain with Sutra practices we incur a root downfall."* (*Tantric Grounds and Paths*, pp. 64–66).

Equally uncompromising are more mundane injunctions:

*"**Not maintaining commitment objects.** One way to incur this downfall is to refuse to accept the various commitment substances passed round during an empowerment or the substances offered in a tsog offering puja, thinking that these substances are unclean. Another way is not to keep a vajra and bell, thinking that these objects are meaningless. Yogis or Yoginis . . . also incur this downfall if they refuse to accept an action mudra* [relating to sexual intercourse] *without good reason,"* and so on. There are many others. One can imagine the Western disciple questioning the hygiene of the *tsog* substances, and displaying unwillingness to imbue inanimate objects with the required degree of reverence; likewise an adamance, perhaps, in those more morally and aspirationally inclined, against accepting a sexual partner for ritual purposes towards whom one felt neither love nor attraction. If the above was the case, despite the fact that during such mandatory acts of intercourse the nominal practitioner must utilize "Divine Pride" and imagine himself and the consort as Tantric Deities (and also regardless of the tantric insistence upon transcending moral and social conventions), more appropriately such disciples would view the stipulated bodily responses as lustful, and find it impossible to comply.

On page 137 of *Clear Light of Bliss*, there is reference to the *Heruka Root Tantra* which contains a definitive explanation of the different classes of action mudra, as well as "complete instructions on where, when and how we should enter into that practice." According to this text, "each part of the consort's body should have a specific shape, including even the eyes," and furthermore, "in addition to having attained a certain level of inner realization, the consort should be skilled in the sixty-four arts of love." (This latter seems a curious requirement, more in keeping with the medieval practice of temple prostitution than with contemporary aspiration). These days, it is very difficult to find such a consort, says the Geshe, and acceptable alternatives are detailed. These rulings and suggestions are delicately and traditionally expressed, yet the confusion in priorities is rather painfully apparant. One may conclude that the "downfalls" are part of an extremely questionable exegesis inherited from degenerate Indian environments not described by the Geshe, as the historical reality is not part of Tantric fantasy and visualization.

"Gross downfalls," which the Geshe refers to next, are slightly less serious than their root counterparts, and include "Fighting or arguing during a tsog offering ceremony," and "Staying seven days in the home of someone who rejects the Vajrayana" (*Tantric Grounds and Paths*, p. 71).

[Buddhism may broadly be divided into three Yanas (*yana* = vehicle: a means to Buddhahood) – Hinayana, Mahayana and Vajrayana. The lastmentioned is the Adamantine or Diamond path associated with the Buddhist Tantras. Most of the Buddhist Tantras claim to have been spoken by Sakyamuni Buddha himself, but as John Powers remarks in his book, *Introduction to Tibetan Buddhism* (1995): "This claim is accepted by most Tibetan scholars, but is generally rejected by contemporary historically oriented scholars, because no solid historical evidence supports the appearance of tantras for at least a millennium after the death of Sakyamuni" (p. 220). The Buddhist Tantras represent a quite evident corruption of the original teachings of Buddha, who did not permit the use of mantras, mantraic rituals, or of fish, meat, wine, and sexual intercourse with the opposite sex, on the part of monks.]

This latter downfall (rejecting the Vajrayana) is clearly concerned with novice converts falling under the influence of those closest to them who are critical of their Buddhist beliefs. Some of these beliefs are of course anathema to other religions – one such belief being that of transmigration after death into lower forms of life. The Geshe observes: "Though we grasp very tightly to our human body today, tomorrow we may already have lost it and moved into the body of an animal!" (*Tantric Grounds*,

147

p. 180).

(Compare the explanation of Meher Baba, who stated categorically that the evolution of man is progressive, i.e., that the incarnating soul having attained to human existence continues, and completes, evolution in human form – and does not regress into animal forms as a consequence of *karma*).

A Buddhist practice equally strange and distasteful is that of acquiring the ability to transfer the body consciousness elsewhere at the point of death (thus escaping the "ordinary death process") by means of a discipline involving "transferring our mind into a recently dead corpse and reanimating it." This practice "is not very difficult," we are told, and "used to be quite widespread" (p. 182). [This seems a similar practice to necromancy.]

Other potential attainments are listed elsewhere in the book, and one can only assume that these encourage many recruits of a certain type when presented as factual attributes. The power to "bless pills," for instance, and "cure disease and increase the lifespan and good fortune of whoever tastes them," and to bless "medicinal substances" such as eye-lotion so that whoever applies such substances to their eyes "can see for a great distance, and even through mountains"; plus the attainment of "seeing beneath the ground" that "enables us to see hidden treasures" (p. 42). There are also the attainments of flying, of invisibility, and longevity, of subduing our enemies and averting wars "simply by holding aloft a ritual sword." This reliance on magic is retrogressive, and also implies that the generated thoughtforms are not merely comprised of mental structures that influence minds (for concentrated minds focusing upon the same concepts will plug into such structures with the greatest of ease), but contain potent subtle energies which conceivably could have far more sinister effect.

Considerable information on the core of Vajrayana Buddhist practice, namely Secret Mantra and Highest Yoga Tantra, is given in the Geshe's books, which also describe the four stages said to transform sexual bliss into the pure bliss of Buddhahood. In stage one (Action Tantra), the meditator, if male, "generates bliss" by visualizing a Goddess in a beautiful feminine form, and then transforms that bliss by meditating upon emptiness. Having achieved this, stage two is embarked upon and bliss is generated by exchanging smiles with the Goddess (Performance Tantra), which again is transformed by meditating upon emptiness. Stage three generates a yet greater bliss by holding hands with her, then proceeding as before (Yoga Tantra). But in Highest Yoga Tantra "the meditator generates bliss by imagining sexual embrace with a consort and, at advanced stages, by engaging in actual embrace; and then transforms that bliss into the spiritual path" (*Clear Light of Bliss*, p. 4). This is further qualified in *Tantric Grounds and Paths*: "When we can transform the bliss of embracing a visualized consort, we can try to transform the bliss of actual sexual intercourse into the quick path to Buddhahood" (p. 22).

Permission to put this latter into practice requires the bestowal of the necessary empowerment from the Spiritual Guide in the form of an action mudra, and the consort is preferably one who is undergoing the same completion stage practices of the pupil concerned. It is said that "great results" can be obtained from union with a consort, for the necessary preliminary of the "generation of bliss" is in most cases more powerful with a living partner, and both requires and can produce, stronger efforts from the practitioner to transform the lesser (sexual) bliss into the greater (spiritual) bliss via the meditational focus upon emptiness. To rely upon an "unqualified consort" for whom one may feel attachment is not regarded as useful, and can, conversely, introduce "great obstacles to our daily practice." (*Tantric Grounds and Paths*, p. 73). The anomaly of such attitudes within monastic Buddhism invite a more cautious approach than is demonstrated by Western converts.

In this disconcerting system, each stage is completed to the tutor's satisfaction before a further stage is attempted. Yet there remains the puzzling factor that at each stage, sexual "bliss" is the commencing point. Does this mean that desire has actually to be activated, or stimulated, by means of visualizations? Or is it that the mere sight of a beautiful woman (or, in the case of a female practitioner, an equivalent man) whether visualized, or in the flesh, is sufficient to evoke a sexual response? If the former is the situation, it seems a retrogressive step, as sexual desire is surely not concomitant with spiritual disciplines, and if the latter, then control of one's sexual impulses is still a long way off. This being the case, one might ask why novices are undertaking the demanding cerebral disciplines of sustained visualization, concentration, and meditation that invariably precede Secret Mantra and Highest Yoga Tantra, only to invoke sexual desire (or "bliss") at the culminating point of their work. Why utilize sexual desire at all? The regulation of such desire is a matter of self-discipline and re-focused orientation, but is nothing at all to do with higher range states, which occur spontaneously when the pupil has made the appropriate degree of growth. It would appear that the dubious intention is to bring the sexual energies under complete control by means of "Divine Pride" and "wisdom mudra" visualizations, and to thus create an increasing ability to retain seminal fluid, no matter how strong the excitation. When an action mudra is operative, the seminal fluid should not be released. With semen retention, according to the Geshe, the deified "bliss" can be sustained indefinitely with practice.

[However, there are known problems with this, as noted by Charles Breaux in *Journey into Consciousness: The Chakras, Tantra and Jungian Psychology* (1989): "techniques for blocking the natural expulsion of semen after the contraction of the sex glands, tensing rectal muscles or thrusting one's finger into the perineum below the root of the penis, may cause sexual fluids to back up into the bladder and prevent the prostrate gland from emptying itself. As a frequent practice, this can cause congestion, and hence, disease in these organs" (p. 74).]

The reliance upon a consort at an equivalent stage of training to the practitioner implies that intercourse occurs between monks and nuns who are normally celibate. If this is so, the possibility of pregnancy must surely arise on (at least) the first occasion the action mudra is put into practice, and one wonders how this eventuality would be dealt with. Whatever the case here, the literary format is clearly one of a monastic borrowing from "left hand" sources, and thus indicative of a serious confusion.

Some "left hand" male yogis considered it their prerogative to "vampirize" their consorts and absorb their vital energies during sexual activity, thereby to enable a more potent activation of *kundalini*. These practices, and others, are referred to by Kevin Shepherd in *Minds and Sociocultures Vol. 1* (1995), pp. 18–19, 421ff., who refers also to Taoist yoga, which has similarities to Tantra. Moreover, according to Charles Breaux, a practising Tantrist, male practitioners are required to refrain from orgasm, whereas female orgasm is encouraged in both Tantric and Taoist sexual rituals. Breaux comments that the feminine essence "is considered to have a vitalizing effect on the lovemaking, nurturing the circulation of psychic energies through the conjoined subtle bodies of both practitioners." Theoretically, the feminine essence is "inexhaustible," unlike male energy which requires replenishment. This replenishment is accomplished by means of certain techniques used in sexual yoga. See C. Breaux, *Journey into Consciousness*, pp. 73–74.

Tantric practitioners are manifestly in error with their reliance upon sexual bliss as a means to gain enlightenment. They have little hope of comprehending a different condition altogether, known to genuine contemplative mystics as the "heart" experience – the most intense and all-encompassing longing for God. The two perspectives are poles apart.

With regard to the Vajrayana of Kadampa Buddhism, one may ask pertinent questions. What happens to unfledged individuals who have partially awakened the subtle "winds" of *kundalini* (*tummo*), and leave their monasteries in states of doubt and disturbance through what is happening (or not happening) in their systems? Who takes responsibility for this, and what are the likely effects? Once set into motion, these activations do not obligingly subside when we find them distressing.

Some persons I have known, both male and female, are perhaps indicative of what can occur as a result of such dabbling (especially for believers in reincarnation). These people frequently exhibit certain aptitudes from early childhood; for instance, they have very strong minds and pronounced capacities to concentrate. They early recognize the effects of their minds upon others, and some use this recognition to get what they want by various means. Many also have marked abilities to visualize, and to sustain that visualization. Young males in particular use this ability to create sexual fantasies, often of an extremely erotic and pornographic nature, and to such an extent that their lives are consumed by it. [Two men in their early twenties told me, quite independently, that the female created in their fantasies was almost tangible, and could be perceived between sleeping and waking "like a living entity."]

Here we have minds imprinted with the excesses of contemporary magazines and television, which bring to this imprintation a very similar faculty to that trained to dwell upon tantric sexual bliss. A trans-sexual orientation is another problem in Tantric

151

practices. Young males were [and are] encouraged to project themselves imaginatively as feminine deities, in which roles their sexual consorts are males. These syndromes can spontaneously replay associatively in the minds of heterosexual males in the current era, and cause much puzzlement and distress. In my view, there are also possibilities of a reincarnational regression in which former monks who have had their developmental potential hopelessly wrecked by traditional disciplines accepted in trust (and which did not achieve their promised conclusion) – subliminally register their present-day predicament, and what this entails – and abandon all faith as a consequence. The fault here lies with the tutors, rather than the taught, and constitutes a tragedy of immense proportions.

Some of these persons actually recognize that in some forgotten past existence they must have had specific training. Those I refer to were in each case aspirational, yet despite this factor, were largely unable to control their worst characteristics and fell victims to extremes of sexual permissiveness, including bi-sexual activity. Some also fell victim to drugs like LSD, and other consciousness-altering lures. Several produced isolated and entirely spontaneous major metaphysical experiences in puberty, which tended to unbalance them and to ruin future career prospects. Several had what they now know to be *kundalini* experiences, acknowledged to have been terrifying at the time, and which left grievous mental pressures as an aftermath. One intellectually brilliant middle-aged woman (whose problems commenced with the practise of yogic *asanas* in a British "Keep Fit" class) suffered many years of absolute torture as she struggled to rear a family and stave off what she feared was insanity.

Other young persons consciously experiencing these activations incurred extremely alarming occult visions and related phenomena in the midst of ordinary everyday life. Some had highly developed psychic faculties that produced appalling dichotomies in their 20th Century modes of thought. These, and similar syndromes that people normally keep secret (if their health permits) were proffered to me in the form of written autobiographies from persons interested in developmental metaphysics, who recognized that I might have some understanding of their situations. For the above-illustrated and many other confidential reasons, I cannot stress strongly enough that Westerners should not submit themselves to Eastern disciplines, or indeed to any disciplines designed to activate *kundalini* before the time is "ripe" for them. When this time comes they will need an authentic teacher to guide and protect them. Such teachers do not place their pupils at risk by out-of-sequence development, nor do they raise *kundalini* by the methods above-described.

I would like now to draw upon the experience of Charles Breaux, who in his book, *Journey into Consciousness: The Chakras, Tantra and Jungian Psychology*, provides experiential insight into widely practised contemporary Tantric processes, and their effects on his own psychology.

Breaux's interest in spiritual matters commenced in his youth. As a teenager he discovered a book on yoga and was fascinated by an illustration of a meditating yogi complete with seven lotuses along his spine. This struck a latent chord in him, evoking memories that he did not understand, and precipitating a search for further literature on a subject he found increasingly engrossing, confusing, and profound. At college he studied philosophy, psychology and world religions, subjects which, after graduating, caused him in his "youthful idealism" to seek enlightenment, an aim he considered "the only worthwhile goal" (*Journey into Consciousness*, Introduction, p. x). He thus became a "modern-day recluse" and for a period of three years committed himself to seclusion and intensive meditation, which latter resulted in the awakening of *kundalini*. Breaux writes: "For several days and nights a flaming pain burned in my pelvis and lower abdomen." This pain eventually moved upwards along his spine and seemingly out of the top of his head, leaving him in a "state of rapture" which endured for some weeks. Significantly, he adds: "I had expected to be transformed into some magical 'enlightened' being, instead I found myself only at the beginning of an incredible journey" (p. x).

This encounter with *kundalini* brought with it "clairvoyant and healing abilities," and not long afterwards, severe digestive problems that Breaux associated with opening certain *chakras*. Medical assistance proved ineffective, and he therefore utilized his new abilities to heal himself. Within a very short time he began "working with others" and then commenced to tutor classes in psychic awareness and healing. During this period he experimented with various methods of working with the *chakras*, interpreting the results in sympathy with Jungian psychology, which he believed to be "especially pertinent."

Breaux was shortly introduced to Tibetan Tantra by a friend, and became as a consequence the pupil of Gyalwa Karmapa, whom he describes as the 16th incarnation of the head of the Kagyu lineage of Tibetan Buddhism, and from whom he received "instructions and initiations." He later studied under several other lamas and attended various meditation retreats, the result being that over a span of several months in 1981, he underwent further *kundalini* activations, and "a series of Tantric initiations while in meditation" (p. xi). He states that he also "relived" several lifetimes as a yogi and a lama, which lent greater insight into his pursuit of Tantra in his present life.

It was soon realized by Breaux that an awakened *kundalini* could cause problematic side-effects quite other than digestive troubles, as old karmic patterns raised their heads and his subconscious threw into focus certain of its content. He observes somewhat ruefully that "if we are not diligent in integrating the increased emergence of unconscious contents . . . we may very well be cast mercilessly into a real live nightmare" (p. xi). He additionally comments that the mere awakening of the power of *kundalini* "does not automatically insure spiritual perfection. This primordial power may indeed be venomous, activating unconscious contents which may cause severe psychological imbalances . . ." (p. 34).

Breaux nevertheless persevered in his Tantric endeavours, and eventually his practices brought forth powerful experiences which he deemed to be positive. *En route* to describing these experiences, he points out that Tantric meditation produces alpha and theta rhythms in the brain which "give access to areas of the psyche" not normally reachable. And it is *here*, says Breaux, in the subliminal depths of the psyche, "that the images and ritual activities of Tantra work their magic." Then comes a most intriguing statement on the use of Tantric deities as continual objects of visualization. Breaux found that these numinous images could be utilized as sources of psychic energy, charged as they are with "the potent meditations of Tantric yogis for well over a thousand years." Such potency could be drawn upon for the purpose of transformation of the body-mind into a "clear" vehicle for the forces operative in Tantric practices (p. 35).

Clear vehicle or no, these "batteries" undoubtedly played some part in Breaux's personal experiences (many of them of a sexual nature) which are discussed at some length, along with detailed information on Tantric sexual rituals (meditative or otherwise), breathing techniques, and other practices. In the meditative discipline, which "may include the whole spectrum of possible expression of the contra-sexual side of yourself," it is suggested that the reader "can choose one of the forms in which the god or goddess appears to you and imagine in detail a Tantric sexual experience" (p. 78). It is further suggested that the "feeling of completeness and love" experienced in the meditation can be extended into everyday life "by imagining (and acting as if) your consort accompanies you throughout the day." On retiring at night, the consort is imagined as being there beside you, and in the morning, the day is begun by greeting the consort. A journal is recommended for recording the experiences that will arise at this time in meditation.

As the practitioner's creative abilities became more advanced, the imaginative projection of oneself as one's chosen deity (alternately male or female) is increasingly intensified and extended throughout all areas of the everyday life. Thus, as Breaux explains, when eating, one is actually making offerings to oneself as a deity. When defecating, one is "expelling obscurations from the world of sentient beings through your divine power." Even when opening a door, one is "clearing the way to liberation" for everyone else (p. 193). In this way, says Breaux, you will think, and act, at all times as if one were in truth the deity itself – a practice not without serious dangers to a random readership (or for Breaux), one would think, particularly for those of an insecure temperament or who are egoistically inclined.

In view of the emphasis on fantasized sexual intercourse with abstract deities, it is not surprising to learn that Breaux's consort externalized in the form of a *dakini* (a female spirit who imparts secret knowledge) in a series of experiences he recorded in diary form. In sharing these details he is hoping to "impress upon the reader that these deities, i.e., their qualities of consciousness, do indeed exist in the more sublime dimensions of the psyche" (p. 223).

Breaux's experiences occurred while he was meditating. They

are clearly not imaginary in the usual sense of the word, as they have a reality consistent with the type of experience generated by a partially and artifically awakened *kundalini*. Entities encountered through an intentional process that strongly stimulates the lower *chakras* are frequently energized images which attain a concretized actuality for the experiencer when in a particular state of mind. (Such images can also be ensouled – that is, utilized as a cloak by a spirit, or spirits, in the astral realms of existence who seek grosser types of experience, perhaps those with occult powers awaiting rebirth, or more tenuous types cast adrift by magical practices). Breaux's *dakini* is recorded as appearing on twenty or so consecutive days, whenever he sat in deep meditation. Her activities included sitting astride Breaux in the *yabyum* position (of tantric sexual embrace) on most of the occasions when she manifested. She is also reported as generating between Breaux and herself an intense exchange of psychic energy; also of drawing a circle around him on the floor and interlacing it with a six-pointed star; of activating his *chakras* and moving energy into a central channel; releasing "blockages" and enabling the rising of a golden light that burst forth from the top of his head; mutually embracing in a shower of golden energy till he "felt like a Buddha radiating light out in all directions." On one occasion she danced erotically before him in her "beautiful etheric form" and deliberately aroused his sexuality; on another she was "healing and balancing" his subtle bodies and *chakras*, and prompting him to visualize himself as the deity Vajradhara – the "holder of the vajra," the power of the indestructible Void (pp. 225–238).

Interspersed with the above were more abstract episodes. Breaux describes an expansion of consciousness that continued until his body "was the entire cosmos," with planets spiralling around the sun. Whorls of energy moved up and down the length of his spine, and were so powerful his "whole body was gyrating" (p. 227). He tells us of his profound sense that everything was contained within him, at which point his *dakini* told him that the "Vajrasattva yabyum was all encompassing, that it is the state prior to entering the Void. She then brought me into the Void." He speaks of the powerful feelings of love that rose from deep within him – feelings that he had sought for in relationships, and his overwhelming gratitude at finding that what he had lacked was within himself.

Among the numerous spiritual events that Breaux recorded is a curious reference to the misuse of power, in which he posits that following a spiritual breakthrough (or even enlightenment) in any particular life, there may be later lives in which these developed levels of realization are not fully expressed – with the "probability" that inherent power and knowledge may subsequently be misused for self-aggrandizement, thus "creating more potent *karma*" (p. 229).

Such dangers, in reality, can only exist if *kundalini* is awakened prematurely, that is, before the completion of essential stages and the ensuing annihilation of the ego. This latter process, conducted in rightful sequence, and by an appropriate authority, leaves the conscience and integrity intact, and the will surrendered to a higher intelligence – all essential attributes for higher range experience. When these are present, the possibility of egoic inflation, or any form of "self-aggrandizement," is non-existent.

This is not to say that people cannot have powerful experiences and later behave in ways at variance with the profundities of that experience. Until an advanced stage of growth is reached, all development is uneven; states cannot be maintained, and aspirants inevitably move into other areas of their psychologies, and of their lives, where former certitudes are unreachable and, indeed, no longer real to them. But this is *normal* development, not a backstepping following supposed enlightenment. What is *not* normal (speaking metaphysically) is the deliberate use of a mentally and sexually oriented system such as Tantric Yoga to obtain the presumed benefits of that system (e.g., power, *siddhis*, superconsciousness), or simply to escape from the world and confrontation with all responsibilities by means of the system, and without any interior (or spiritual) motivation at all. It is the "X" factor of a subsequently activated *kundalini* that creates all the problems, and reveals in the long-term (and quite inevitably) the defect of the pseudo-aspirant. This is an unpopular view but one nevertheless worthy of consideration.

The diary excerpts of Breaux conclude with a vision that arose during meditation. At the time of occurrence he experienced a concurrent awareness of the transformative fire of a powerful deity burning within him. He felt he was undergoing an initiation, and "kept getting the impression it had something to do with teaching" (p. 238) – that, in fact, he was being empowered to teach

Tantra. Breaux makes the comment that he "mistrusted these thoughts" and suspected his ego was "again" being tempted. Yet it is evident by the scope of the teaching manual which his book comprises that Breaux was actually convinced of his mission in this respect. When completing the manuscript some seven years later, he informs his readers on the closing page that following his interlude with the *dakini*, came six months of "the most incredible" peak experiences; but after this, "the dross began spewing out into my external life." It seems that the seven years were packed with "one intense drama after another," and that the "deepest and darkest" karmic patterns within him were relentlessly brought forward through the act of arousing the force of *kundalini*.

Many levels of *chakra* experience are claimed by Breaux, yet despite his seeming attainments, much of his ability really boils down to powerful imagery rather than other-dimensional comprehension. The terminology used, in particular with relation to the higher centres (e.g., "the nectar from it [the sixth *chakra*] drips down to produce pleasurable sexual feelings" (p. 191), does not indicate an experience of the level the author wishes to imply. Some of his statements on the *chakras* are highly questionable, as is his view that "a healthy sense of self-esteem and personal power" are indicative of "a successfully awakened third chakra" (p. 81). This smacks more of Jungian therapy than anything else, and one is left with the impression that this extremely informative book is not a true picture of an unimpeded path to liberation, but rather one that will require much of its structural content to be undone before the writer can hope to achieve both the state, and the function, he so patently desires.

Delusion is a side-effect of incorrect development. As such, it cannot be compared to the defective knowledge, and the errors that arise from it, that are usual at an early stage of normal developmental growth. These errors and misconceptions will inevitably achieve rectification when a further stage is reached. Delusion, however, is not amenable to re-structuring. It blocks all possibility of further progression, and its origins, or foundations, can only be countered by removing them completely.

A classic example of yogic training is exemplified by Hiroshi Motoyama. He is described by his biographer and pupil, Rande

Brown Ouchi (founder and director of East-West Communications in New York City), as "a man of science and of religion: a [Shinto] priest, a philosopher, a yogi, a physiological psychologist, a computer specialist, a researcher of oriental medicine, a parapsychologist who trained with Rhine in the 1960s, an electrical engineer, a spiritual healer and a seer." (Editor's Introduction, Hiroshi Motoyama, *Karma and Reincarnation*, 1992, p. vii).

Motoyama holds doctorates in psychology and philosophy, and established a research Institute in Tokyo in 1960 to "investigate the evolution of human consciousness." His work there, including authorship of over thirty books, has won him international awards and acclaim, and a worldwide following. He is said to have "awoken to states of consciousness that enable him to see beyond the limits of space and time," abilities which he regularly uses during spiritual consultations, of which there have now been many thousands.

Motoyama was born in 1925 on the island of Shodoshima in the Seto Inland sea in Japan, and began his spiritual education when he was five years old. His mother and her friend (a female mystic and healer who founded a Shrine for the Tamamitsu Sect of Shintoism on the island) instructed the child in forms of spiritual practice and asceticism, such as "the traditional rite of chanting sutras while standing almost naked under a freezing waterfall." The young Motoyama "responded ardently," and soon began to have experiences of the non-physical dimension of existence. He also commenced to experience clairvoyance and telepathy, and "was able to communicate with disembodied spirits in the higher dimension." These attributes were of course remarkable in so young a child. By 1935, the trio had settled permanently in Tokyo, where another Tamamitsu Shrine was established, which continues in strength to the present day.

In his teens, the diligent Hiroshi initiated "a daily regime of early morning yogic exercises, prayer and meditation," attaining to "major spiritual breakthroughs" in his twenties. He eventually became Head Priest of the Shrine, and successor to the founder. His mother, following the demise of her friend, was now Head Priestess. It is stated that both mother and son continued to "broaden and deepen their experiences of the nature of reality through daily practice."

In the course of his work, Motoyama has drawn two major

conclusions; firstly, "that human beings are born onto the earth many times"; and secondly, "that the continuum of birth, life, death, and rebirth is governed by the universal principle of karma, the moral law of cause and effect that assumes that every action an individual takes will bear an equivalent result at some point in time" (pp. x–xi). Upon these two conclusions (with which I have no quarrel at all) he has based much of his research investigation, and the content of his book *Karma and Reincarnation*, which is largely comprised of spiritually delineated case histories and the perceived operation of *karma*.

These case histories are of interest to researchers, particularly when compared to other achieved insights following the raising of *kundalini*, a process described by Motoyama in his *Theories of the Chakras: Bridge to Higher Consciousness* (1995), which also incorporates his own personal *kundalini* experience (referred to shortly). Some of the psychic perceptions he records seem somewhat bizarre to Western minds, including those which involve outraged water spirits that require appeasement by the chanting of *sutras* (*Karma & Reincarnation*, p. 67), and that of the soul of a samurai warrior who took revenge upon an entire family when the tomb in which his "soul was resting" was disturbed (pp. 74–75). Motoyama declares that there are many people suffering present-day problems "as a result of angering the spirits of their ancestors." He illustrates this with the story of a man who consulted him with regard to the emotional and psychological symptoms currently suffered by the man and his family. These symptoms commenced shortly after having accepted a "high-ranking position in one of Japan's new religions." Upon psychic investigation, Motoyama discovered that land and other property belonging to the family for generations had been donated to the church of this religious organization, and that his client, in effect, had "sold his birthright" in order to obtain a position of prominence. This act had "outraged" the spirit of the former head of the family (the originator of the fortune), who vented his anger at this loss of wealth upon all concerned, whether innocent or guilty, causing them to suffer prodigiously as described (pp. 56–57).

As this type of ancestral activity is outside my experience, I cannot comment other than to say that the scenario proffered *could* be attributable to other causes, or could merely reflect Shintoist beliefs. Either way, the majority of insights recorded relate to the "astral" realms inhabited by the earthbound and the newly dead, and do not require (in my view at least) the highly developed faculties of the higher *chakras* to register them.

Motoyama nevertheless has done much more than spread knowledge of reincarnation and the action of *karma*. He is also a scientist, trained in empirical methodology, and his scientific endeavours resulted in the establishment of the International Association for Religion and Parapsychology, an organization whose members perform research in these and related fields. In recognition of this work, UNESCO selected him in 1974 as one of the world's ten foremost parapsychologists, and he has since been honoured by several renowned scientific and religious organizations and serves as an advisor to various international associations and institutes. Motoyama is therefore taken very seriously indeed. Moreover, he is actively concerned with the promotion of yogic techniques, and his much-quoted work, *Theories of the Chakras: Bridge to Higher Consciousness* contains precise and illustrated details of the entire practice of Tantra Yoga.

The Foreword to *Theories of the Chakras* is enthusiastically written by Swami Satyananda Saraswati, founder of the Bihar School of Yoga in India, under whose guidance many yoga centres and ashrams have been established throughout the world. Saraswati commences with the words: "It gives me great pleasure to introduce the work of Dr. Hiroshi Motoyama to the scholars, scientists, and spiritual seekers of the English-speaking world . . ." and expresses his view that Motoyama's "pioneering discoveries" over the past decade have "carried orthodox science to the threshold of the spiritual dimension, and will serve as a basis for future investigations." He further states: "This present book . . . is an outstanding document from both the scientific and spiritual points of view. In the first place, it presents a unique and authentic record of the spiritual experiences of an adept in whom the kundalini has been awakened by yogic practices. And second, it is the unique record of the pioneering experiments conducted at the Institute for Religious Psychology, Tokyo."

The Swami then proceeds to make several thought-provoking statements, among them his conviction that in the near future many scientists will validate "the theory of kundalini and the chakras," and that yoga will achieve great prominence, and the

161

widespread practice of this discipline "will change the course of world events" (p. 15).

What follows is a comprehensive treatise on the practice of Tantra Yoga. It is very well written, with an Introduction primarily aimed at clarification for those new to the subject, and with the information that in later chapters details will be given on awakening the *chakras*, and their related effects on body and mind.

In Chapter One is an excellent exposition on the discipline of *Yama* ("restraint"), the moral observances of non-violence, truthfulness, non-stealing, chastity, and non-covetousness, first codified by Patanjali, along with other disciplines, in the fifth or sixth century B.C. These disciplines were based upon the teachings of various Yoga sects (according to Motoyama) and included in his *Yoga Sutra*. A detailed section is given to each of them. Curiously enough, Motoyama reveals that in actual practice, certain disciplines are amalgamated in "powerful configurations" called *mudras* (ritual gestures). These practices are very important, says the writer, and traditionally "taught only to outstanding disciples." In view of their effectiveness, which is greater by far than *pranayama* (breath control) or *asanas* (postures) practised in isolation, they were thus considered "potentially dangerous for those not adequately prepared." He then tells us that these practices are now openly taught worldwide to "earnest disciples by various gurus," and that the *mudras* referred to are "types of gestures that generate great psychic power and deeply 'spiritual' emotions." They are also utilized as "the core of the techniques for awakening the chakras" (p. 33). [In my view this whole subject is fraught with error and superstition.]

Motoyama makes no personal claims in the greater part of this treatise; he utilizes the Upanishads and other works, and writes largely from the third person. An entire chapter is accorded to Swami Satyananda Saraswati on the *chakras* and the *nadis*, and another chapter is given to the views of the Reverend C.W. Leadbeater, an early member of the Theosophical Society (which he joined in 1882) and who later produced a book called *The Chakras* (first published 1927) based upon allegedly clairvoyant observations. It is chapter nine that falls to Motoyama, and under the title *Experience and Experiments of the Chakras*, he relates his personal experience of *kundalini* activation. But first he tells

162

us of his early life, and how he was taught conjointly by his mother and foster-mother to chant Buddhist *sutras* and Shinto prayers with them for hours on end. He was also "taught about and experienced the existence of non-human entities, of entities who reside in higher dimensions." At little more than five years old, this must have been quite overwhelming. Of his later years he informs us that at twenty-five years of age he regularly arose at 3 a.m. to practise *asanas* for thirty minutes, and meditation for three to four hours. The first half of the meditation was devoted to breathwork, and "the latter to concentration on a specific *chakra*" (p. 240). He then gives very precise details of the *pranayama* practised, and the way this enabled the period of breath retention (*kumbhaka*) to increase. During this period he began to notice new sensations, such as itchings and tinglings in various parts of the body, and a feverish sensation in the lower abdomen. He also heard sounds like the buzzing of bees at the base of his spine, and his sense of smell became hyper-sensitive to the point of causing discomfort.

After several months of concentrated practice, one day while Motoyama sat in meditation, he experienced the first major upward movement of *kundalini*. He describes this in terms of an incredible power that rushed through his spine to the top of his head. This lasted only a second or so, but his body levitated a few centimetres from the floor, causing him great terror. By now he was burningly hot and suffered severe headache, to such an extent that he felt his skull would "explode with energy" (p. 241). Hitting himself around the top of the head was the only measure that brought relief.

Motoyama briefly describes the awakening of each *chakra* in turn, each one at a different period of time. After awakening the second *chakra* (*svadhishthana*), which apparently occurred *before* the activation of *kundalini* described above, he became "overly sensitive, both physically and mentally." His emotions were unstable and he was easily excited. He began to have prophetic dreams and involuntary ESP experiences (such as telepathy), and "to realize the spontaneous fulfillment of wishes."

Six months into yoga practice, a new series of sensations commenced. Motoyama began to see a reddish light centred within his navel that would become so brilliantly white that he would grow dizzy with its intensity. He likewise experienced a purple light radiating between his eyebrows. As the *manipura chakra* opened, he was troubled with what he describes as "ghosts" (lower astral beings) similar to those that had appeared to him in childhood. These he saw with increasing frequency during meditation, and often tried to ease their suffering by chanting purificatory prayers and *sutras* for them. Sometimes, however, these spirits were forceful, and adversely affected Motoyama instead; so much so that he would feel great anger for no reason, his body would become ill, and his mind unstable. Conversely, "positive" spirits who sought to help others, affected him with feelings of peace.

As a result of awakening the *manipura chakra*, Motoyama reports that "clairvoyance, telepathy, and spiritual insight," were enhanced, and he now records an extraordinary experience which much affected his later life. Whilst playing a Japanese game which resembles the use of a Ouija board with an elderly assistant at the Shrine, he fell into a semi-trance in which his right hand started to move violently and his body felt on fire (p. 243).

What happened next foreshadowed his later work of consultation with the spirits of those long dead – suddenly he experienced an extrasensory vision of a man wearing antiquated white clothing, whom he saw as clearly as if in the flesh. The ensuing dialogue, registered telepathically, continued for some minutes. The man appeared to be standing in a pine grove, and conveyed that he wished Motoyama to re-find this place, a former shrine, where both had lived many centuries ago – the entity (Hakuo) was a tribal leader, and Motoyama had been ruler of all the tribes in the neighbourhood, including Hakuo's. Motoyama here interjects that as an academic researcher he found all of this strange, but in a higher part of his mind he registered that what the spirit was communicating to him was true (p. 244).

The following day, Motoyama went by bicycle to Jindaiji temple, a place he had never visited before, and found himself entering the shrine he had seen in his vision. This experience he heralded as an affirmation of the existence of the spiritual world, which he believed was made open to him through the awakening of the *manipura chakra* (p. 245).

About two years after commencing yoga practice, Motoyama became aware that his heart was functioning abnormally and that he had pain in his chest despite feeling otherwise fit and well.

It was the coldest period of winter at the time, and he was practising the traditional water asceticism for "about an hour" at dawn each morning, by "pouring icy water" over his semi-naked form. One morning, whilst thus engaged, Motoyama saw "a kind of heat energy" which rose from the base of his spine to his heart, causing his heart to shine a brilliant gold. As the *kundalini* current upsurged through his body, his consciousness rose with it and entered a higher dimension, "worshipping the Divine," and leaving his physical form standing immobile and forgotten in the cold wind. This is the point at which Motoyama felt his heart *chakra* (*anahata*) was awakened (p. 247).

Following this awakening, he learned to control his abilities, and to heal others psychically. He comments on the reversal of the effect which proved so troublesome after awakening the *manipura chakra* (that of spirits entering his psychic system). In contrast, his own energies, via the medium of his "astral" body, could now enter the system of another "to effect curative changes" within that individual (p. 248).

During the fourth and fifth years of yoga practice, Motoyama began to concentrate on the *vishuddhi* (throat) *chakra* after the daily discipline of *pranayama*. He subsequently developed an irritation in his throat and breathing became difficult. After some months he noted various effects. Psychically, he saw purple light spreading about his head, and all consciousness of his body ceased – his mind became stilled, and he experienced "the state of nothingness." After several repetitions of this state, he found himself confronting an abyss "of absolute void." This Voidness generated such fear in him that he wished to discontinue his yoga activities, and the paralysing effect only diminished when he learned by degrees to surrender himself completely to God.

A strange feature of Motoyama's account is that during the *vishuddhi* process he encountered a terrifying devil-like being, and it required all his faith to pass through this "frightening and dangerous period" unscathed (p. 250). The ultimate outcome was the achievement of non-attachment, and the ability, when giving spiritual consultations to members of the shrine, to see their past, present, and future lives as one continuous stream (p. 251).

To specifically accelerate the awakening of the *ajna* (brow) *chakra*, Motoyama embarked on further disciplines of concentration, one of which combined visualization with *pranayama*, focusing on the *chakra* itself. This latter exercise was performed for one hour daily for several months, and produced a fresh upsurge of the *kundalini* energy, this time reaching the relevant *chakra* and forcing it into activity. Motoyama tells us that he was immersed in a dark purple light, and heard a voice call him as if echoing from a valley. This filled him with ecstasy, a condition that endured for well over an hour, and indicated, he thought, an initial awakening of the *chakra*. While in this state, his consciousness widened and deepened, encompassing the essence of all things, and the simultaneous awareness of the *karma* of nations and of the world. By means of concentration upon the *ajna*, Motoyama registered that one of his tasks in life was to help make this knowledge available to humankind through the media of science. He also noted that his already perceived power to affect and alter the *karma* of others was "greatly enhanced" through the activation of this *chakra* (pp. 252–253).

Bearing in mind that the functional ability to realign *karma* is the sole prerogative of authentic instructors, we come next to the description of the arousal of the seventh *chakra*, the *sahasrara*, and the claim is made that Motoyama actually opened this *chakra* less than a year after his initial commencement of the practice of yoga and well in advance of the lower *chakras*. Once again precise details are given of the practices used and how this was achieved. Motoyama's description of the effects is very similar to that of the previous *chakra*, in that he lost all sensation of his body and attained to a state of superconsciousness. In this state, he perceived his spiritual self rise out of his body through the top of his head "to be restored in Heaven."

Now comes the culmination of this state; the apex of the *kundalini* experience as recorded by Motoyama. Unfortunately, he does not enlarge upon the details, save to say that he heard a powerful and tender Voice "resounding through the universe," and that whilst listening to that Voice: "I realized spontaneously my mission, my previous lives, my own spiritual state, and many other things" (p. 254). After a time, he felt the necessity to return to physical life. He descended, by means of the same route, and had to consciously reactivate his body with spiritual energy because it had stiffened to the point of paralysis.

Motoyama states that as a consequence of opening the *sahasrara chakra*, his "astral body" was able to leave the physical self via the "Brahman Gate" at the top of his head. This enabled him to perceive the outer world as well as the inner. In relation to this, he describes a stranger in the Shrine whom he "saw" from this state, and relates the original extrasensory experience that appeared in *Reincarnation and Karma* about the farmer who removed an old tumulus from one of his fields in order to enlarge his property (this was the father of the stranger observed). "The scene shifted," says Motoyama, "and I saw that later one of his descendants and a few of the villagers had gone insane." At this point he realized that he was looking at an old battlefield where a Takeda warrior had been slain about 400 years ago, and subsequently buried beneath the tumulus. When the farmer removed it, the soul of the warrior became angry, and commenced to "haunt the farmer and his descendants." As a consequence, the grandson of the farmer became schizophrenic, which fact had induced the stranger to pray at the shrine for assistance. The upshot was that Motoyama "negotiated intensively with the warrior's soul" and eventually persuaded him to depart. Soon after this, the youth began to recover (p. 255).

The reason I have included this episode is my astonishment that it should be recorded in this context – that of the *sahasrara chakra*. However, on the following page Motoyama informs us that as the *sahasrara* became more fully activated the following abilities were made operative:

    (a) he was enabled to "enter and affect" the bodies of others;
    (b) to extend his existence and to "include others within it";
    (c) to work unbound by the trammels of *karma* and "the restrictions of the body";
    (d) "to be granted union with Divine power" (p. 256).

The remainder of the book (*Theories of the Chakras*) is concerned with scientific experiment with the use of newly developed apparatus. Not being a scientist, I am unable to deduce what the professional world of science will make of the resultant data. Motoyama expresses the hope that his research centre will clearly demonstrate that the act of persistent concentration upon a *chakra* "awakens" that *chakra*, and induces "the psi abilities associated with it" to begin to manifest (p. 274).

From the foregoing it is apparent that yoga disciplines strongly activate the interior energies of both *kundalini* and the *chakras*, and that Hiroshi Motoyama is a dedicated exponent of these questionable practices.

But what of the "heart" experience of genuine Sufis, and the equivalent "burning heart" of the Hindu mystics and contemplative Christian saints? What place has this vital episode of the soul's existence in the mental and physical disciplines of Buddhism and Tantra? It does not appear to have been included.

And what did Motoyama see of our planetary future in the state where past, present and future co-exist? Or in the dimension beyond this, did he observe the planetary necessity to rapidly produce an overall higher level of human development? Did he register an hierarchical intervention to sweep clean the results of past illicit *kundalini* activations and the massive misuse of wrongfully acquired *siddhis*? Did he see the racial distortions and evolutionary blocks that arose as a consequence of such misuse? Or the engenderment of false growth that now tips the balance and threatens to destroy our very existence as a species? These matters were not mentioned, nor have I seen them referred to in other Tantric or Buddhist books and studies. Or, for that matter, in any studies at all, of whatever persuasion.

Yet Motoyama's book is a valuable book in that it clearly records aspects of a process which can be forced through the use of willpower and yogic exercises. It is also an extremely dangerous book, as these methods have been misused and abused through the centuries and are now in process of widescale reprojection in the West. Despite relevant cautions scattered throughout the work, detailed instructions on all aspects of yoga are given *in toto*, and in such lucid and straightforward form that certain readers (particularly young intellectuals) will inevitably put them to use – with consequences, as Motoyama himself has indicated, that can prove calamitous. Yet on page 29 he conveys that in the event of no qualified person being available to the reader, "he should feel free to enquire without hesitation at this institute ... where instruction and guidance in the awakening of chakras is given on a regular basis."

So here we have it. Motoyama himself is teaching this system, as is Swami Satyananda Saraswati (who lavished praise on Motoyama in his Foreword), and doubtless others who have been, or are being, trained to replace them or to share the tuitional load in the present. As we are told by Jonn Mumford (of tongue-piercing fame) in *A Chakra and Kundalini Workbook* (Mumford was initiated by Swami Saraswati in Monghyr, Bihar State, India, in 1973) in reference to certain of Saraswati's teachings: these should "only be practiced under the direct guidance of an initiated Swami of our order" (p. 250). This refers to the teachings on Kriya Yoga in *Kundalini Tantra* written by Saraswati, and unarguably indicates that "initiated Swamis" are considered competent to deal with any effects, adverse or otherwise.

Mumford himself stemmed from the Bihar School and is a Swami of the Saraswati Order, and in this capacity has roundly praised such sinister influences as Aleister Crowley. Of Crowley's *Eight Lectures on Yoga* he wrote: "Priceless and witty commentary by one of the most controversial geniuses of this century . . ." He also asserts that his reading of this book thirty-five years ago enabled him "to dismiss literal interpretations of the Yama and Niyamas" (*A Chakra and Kundalini Workbook*, p. 251). This is a most surprising statement from a Swami of a Hindu traditional order, as these are respectively the moral rules of social and personal conduct, the bedrock of all religious persuasions, which the infamous occultist-cum-magician and sexual sadist Aleister Crowley flouted at every opportunity.

Motoyama has himself stressed the necessity of the above rules. He further placed on record his view that Swami Saraswati has "distilled the essence" of traditional yoga practice, and that the system Saraswati teaches – *"his own system of tantra"* (my italics) is adapted from the original to suit the requirements of contemporary society. Motoyama went to the extent of linking his self-founded Institute for Religious Psychology in Tokyo with Satyananda Saraswati's organization, thus cementing a relationship "whereby we utilize his yoga teachings, and he has free access to our scientific research" (*Theories of the Chakras*, p. 209). Thus yet another adaptation of this ancient (and suspect) developmental system has been introduced into the West, and firmly consolidated in the East.

Before leaving this subject I should point out a pertinent observation on the *anahata chakra* made by Swami Saraswati. He tells us that before attempting to awaken this *chakra* it is "imperative" to have first developed certain mental capacities, i.e., "correct thinking and judiciousness." Disharmonious and vicious thoughts create conflict and ill-will, and this syndrome is disas-

169

trously amplified when an individual prone to such thinking has awakened the *anahata chakra* and "wills his mistaken thoughts and desires into full actualization" (*Theories of the Chakras*, p. 230).

As the Swami has earlier said that a practitioner with an awakened *anahata* is capable of directly perceiving the operation of earthly *karma*, and can at the same time "free himself of it," and moreover that at this level "the jiva [embodied soul] can control worldly karma and exert its own will in this realm to fulfill its wishes," it is apparent that some very serious situations can arise. A few lines further on, Saraswati continues: "When this power is acquired, it is said that the subject's wish will be granted, whether good or evil" (*Theories*, pp. 229–230).

If the foregoing is placed in the context of the warnings given in chapter seven of Motoyama's book (written by the Theosophist C. W. Leadbeater, a controversial figure alleged to have practised yoga for many years under a guru in India), a formidable configuration emerges for those who are inadequately prepared. "Once awakened," says Leadbeater, "the serpent power is uncontrollable," and proceeds to tell us some of the likely consequences of such lack of preparation, including excruciating pain, and even death. He also warns of dangers less frequently emphasized, such as the "permanent damage" sometimes sustained in "dimensions higher than the physical," and of the extreme intensification of undesirable traits to the extent of "deteriorating the very nucleus of the life process" (pp. 206–207).

It is clear, then, that practising yogis (and even theorists such as Leadbeater) well know the extremities of the dangers attendant upon premature awakening of *kundalini* – yet still they publicise the methods of so doing, and for anyone and everyone, stable or unstable, aspirational or vicious, to experiment with. This is hardly a responsible act, and the scattered provisos and offers of supervision do not, in my view, justify the release of such information.

An even more disturbing factor is that in the other-dimensional states of consciousness that are operative when the higher *chakras* are functioning – states that are claimed as personal experience by a great many yogis – knowledge becomes available on the matter of human development which negates entirely the validity of currently taught yoga systems. If this statement is true (and

170

it stems from my own, fully recorded, *kundalini* experience and is supported by the experience of others known to me), how does one account for the fact that the teachers of Kundalini yoga (including Hiroshi Motoyama) appear unaware of such factors? For if the direct knowledge of this dimension, which is available to all who attain to this stratum, is actually registered by the brain, it would not be possible for those in experiential possession of such knowledge to act against what they know. And if they do *not* know, and my statement is correct – there must surely be a missing dimension in their experience, and thus a missing ingredient in their development.

Yoga is a composite system. The methods have been altered, adjusted, added to, and subtracted from, throughout the centuries of its existence, as the many differing schools of yoga bear witness. It is my contention that a significant number of the dire consequences of past yogic practices in those same schools now lie karmically concealed beneath the surface of our Western culture – in certain forms of mental illness, psychosis, schizophrenia, and other problems. But there are other ways also in which these backfiring syndromes manifest, ways that are culturally adverse in the extreme, and these I have covered elsewhere.

An attempt to correlate various types of *kundalini* experience has recently been made by Arjan Dass Malik in his monograph *Kundalini and Meditation* (1994). Malik (b. 1938) studied at Delhi University and obtained an MA degree in Political Science, and was later British Council Scholar at the University of Edinburgh where he took his post-graduate diploma in Community Development. Joining the Punjab Civil Service in 1961, Malik is now Commissioner and Secretary to the Government of Haryana.

The author met his Guru (whom he considers to be an enlightened Master) early in 1984, and was swiftly initiated into the practice of "mystic meditation" and subsequently awakened the energy of *kundalini*. In order to achieve this, Malik took leave of his official duties for the period of one year, and undertook an intensive *sadhana* within the confines of his home and amid the setting of family life with his wife and two children. Throughout his *sadhana*, he was in the personal charge of his Guru, who visited him when necessary. The unnamed Guru also supervised "every step" of the writing of the resultant book.

171

Malik commences: "It was entirely by the grace of my Guru that I experienced the awakening of my Kundalini after about a month of my initiation into the discipline of mystic meditation" (p. 9). This initiation took place in the room in Malik's home that was exclusively set apart for meditation. His Guru told him to keep a window open "so as to allow unhindered flow of the divine cosmic energy." He was also asked to sweep and clean the room himself and to keep it for his own private use. This precaution was "aimed at preventing the vibrations of outsiders [including his wife and children] from disturbing the cosmic energy circle" created by the Guru.

On the day designated for the initiation, Malik was instructed to place sanctified ash on various specified parts of his body, and to sprinkle it in all four corners of the room, while prayers were chanted by the Guru. He then touched Malik's forehead and the lower part of his spine and "thereby infused his spiritual energy" into his disciple's body. The intention of this transmission was to "send signals to the dormant Kundalini" and thus cause it to awaken. The ritual was followed by five minutes of meditation, and both then left the room for a festive meal prepared by Malik's wife.

The sprinkling of ash "amidst chanting of sacred words," as Malik tells us, was to give the meditation room "a protective cover against evil souls and negative vibrations," as these could create disturbances in the mind during meditation. Malik states that the significance of what occurred is profound – "an outward ceremony which transforms the initiate inwardly." Immediately afterwards, he found that his body emitted a subtle fragrance, undetectable to his wife but clearly evident to his Guru, who told him that this was the fragrance of his soul, and that the presence of this emission was "a sure sign of a successful initiation" (p. 11).

Malik was now ready for his *sadhana*, which consisted mainly of meditation. No special technique was given him, nor was he asked to adhere to any specific discipline. The requirement was to use only the prepared meditation room, to sit in a certain posture, and to commence each session with his *Guru-mantra*. He was at liberty to meditate as often as he wished, and for as long as he wished – providing he could comfortably maintain his posture. This ruling was to be adhered to until the awakening

172

of *kundalini*. Once this occurred, he could lie down to meditate in what is known as the "corpse-posture."

With one year's leave at his disposal, Malik was somewhat at a loss to fill his time. Having no instruction save "wait for the Grace of God," he read books on meditation and practised the techniques described, in order to engage his mind. These included watching the breath, concentration, invocation, and just sitting still and doing nothing. The new disciple was now "troubled by unwanted thoughts," often to the point of agitation. Frequently, he became bored. He was also prone to bouts of irritation, and any small noise in the house would provoke him to shout at those responsible. Despite this behaviour towards his family, "with a rare sense of sacrifice they all cooperated with me and helped me through my meditation," says Malik. After about a month from the time of his initiation a "subtle transformation" occurred in him, and enabled a state of "effortless concentration" (p. 17).

It is to this juncture that Malik attributes his *kundalini* awakening, of which, at the time it commenced, he was completely unaware (he was informed of the activation by his Guru). Yet despite his "blissful ignorance" of the actual situation, he none-theless accepted that he "must have been spiritually progressing" even though unconscious of any movement within his body.

The awakening was first detected by the Guru, who on one of his regular weekly visits, announced that since their last meeting Malik's *kundalini* had "taken the prescribed route of ascent and descent." This news caused Malik to feel "happy and exalted" and he expressed his gratitude by touching the Guru's feet. Moreover, he was told that not only had the *kundalini* awakened but that the *ajna chakra* had also become active and thus opened "the aperture between the eyebrows." This latter, said the Guru, was of great significance with regard to spiritual progress, and indicated the completion of an energy circuit that made possible the final, upward route to the *sahasrara*, the highest *chakra* in the head. (The details in all their intricacies are fully described on page 19 of Malik's book. I am unable to comment upon them as they are entirely outside my own experience).

Malik remembered the striking experiences described by Gopi Krishna in his autobiography, and now hesitantly enquired of his Guru how it was that his *kundalini* had been awakened without his knowledge. The Guru explained that he had so regulated

173

matters that the "initial upward flow" was minimal and thus caused no harm to his disciple. Malik then thanked his stars that he "was under the benevolent protection of a perfect Master," one who "could not only awaken the Kundalini but could also keep its movements under check to prevent mishap."

Even so, Malik "earnestly desired" to have these experiences, and at their next meeting fervently requested that he be given "perceptible experience of the movements of the Kundalini," to which the Guru readily agreed. Malik was asked to enter the state of meditation there and then, and within a few seconds he felt a movement within his spinal cord and energy moving upwards into his head. This experience he describes as "soothing, gentle and mild." From there the energy moved downwards until it "vanished into the space between the root of the sex organs and the anus."

"It was as simple as that," says Malik. As he breathed in, "the energy waves arising from their source would move up and instantly reach the top of the brain." And as he breathed out, the energy travelled back by the same route in reverse. "That was all the time it took," he asserts, and the rising and falling continued throughout the five minutes or so of his meditation. Malik found the process most enjoyable and wished to continue, but terminated the procedure in order to inform his Guru that the "desired experience" had been obtained. He wept tears of joy, and the Guru was also happy in Malik's bliss-filled pleasure and conviction. Since then, declares Malik, the experience of *kundalini* activation has come to him whenever he enters meditation.

Following this first episode, Malik wished to correlate his experience with that of others, and commenced to study books on the subject, including the classic text by Sir John Woodroffe, *The Serpent Power.* And here he met with a problem, for the experiences did not synchronize. By this time, roughly a month from the initial awakening, and two months from the original initiation, Malik had become aware of increasingly powerful interior movements that generated side-effects. Half-an-hour into his meditation period (there were now three sessions daily, each of 100 minutes duration) he would experience several "ejaculations" of *kundalini* energy shooting into his brain, "as if the spine was a syringe." This would engender a pronounced feeling of heaviness in his head, which persisted for some while. What follows

174

is a complex description of what he believes was taking place, and pages of discursive comments derived from his extensive studies, and the questionable viewpoint of his Guru on the varying types of yoga practice – these latter ranging from Taoist *Tantra* to Chinese *Shen*. Malik argues fervently in favour of the grace of the Guru, who provides a "natural" way of experiencing the awakening of *kundalini*, and stresses his own good fortune in finding such a being – ignoring, however, the additional factor of his one year *sadhana* and prolonged and intensive meditation sessions. The happy result of all the foregoing, as he assures us, is that he can now "increase and decrease" the *kundalini* flow at will, and plug in directly to the cosmos.

Nevertheless, on page 40 Malik admits that prior to meeting with his Guru, he commenced the practice of *Kundalini yoga* under the tutelage of a *Hatha-yogi* friend, and during these practices felt "some sort of burning hot liquid" slowly move upwards in his spine. Over weeks of practice the heat in the lower part of the spinal cord intensified, and to such a degree that it caused actual pain, and he thus discontinued the discipline, at the same time giving up hope of awakening *kundalini* and acquiring cosmic consciousness. This episode must of course have affected his system and added an impetus to later events, such as the receipt of *shaktipat* from his Guru, though he makes no mention of this probability.

On the matter of *chakras* Malik is equally reticent, but reveals the unusual order in which his own *chakras* were awakened (*ajna*, *vishuddha*, *muladhara*, *manipura*, and lastly, *anahata*), giving no details save that there were lengthy intervals of many weeks duration between the opening of each *chakra*. He also tells us that no "siddhis" were involved; that none of the supersensory dynamics associated with *chakra* awakening came his way. In order to achieve such powers (according to Malik's Guru) it is first necessary to have recourse to *Mantra-Yoga* or the technique of *Tantra*, which he did not recommend (p. 25). Even opening the "third eye" itself, an occurrence that rendered this organ "ablaze, like a candle," yielded no visionary experience in Malik's case.

The details of the "push" preceding the opening of the *sahasrara* are rather more complex. Suffice it to say that the "flowering" of this *chakra* combined an almost complete loss of bodily consciousness with immersion in a sea of light and ineffable bliss.

175

From the heights of this state, Malik records that he wished to test the possibility of moving his limbs, and therefore cautiously moved his smallest finger. As he did so, even more powerful energy rose within him, and a cloud of cosmic energy simultaneously engulfed him from above. He became one with the cosmos and duality was dissolved. Yet despite this profound and long sought-after experience, to his great disappointment the awareness of "I-ness" remained. Malik thus considered that he had experienced *Savikalpa-Samadhi*, and the highest state of all was yet to be attained.

Having made these statements, the author mentions that the language used is symbolic, and that when he says that light currents or waves of energy ascended his spine, he means only that there is a "feeling of something like that acting within me" (p. 27). This comment unfortunately confuses rather than clarifies the situation.

In Chapter 8, under the title "Post-Samadhi Situation," a further singular statement is made, in which it is claimed that the "upward and downward" flow of *kundalini* can be regulated via the *ajna chakra* by the use of a certain technique – one in which the point between the eyebrows is gently pressed by the fingers in a particular manner. The caution is added that this area should not be touched at all during the period between the first experience of opening the *sahasrara* and the "final *Nirvikalpa Samadhi*" as the self-regulatory system is easily disrupted at this time. This curious advice implies a physiological process, an assumption given emphasis by a further statement that spiritual energy needs continual replenishment, and that severe loss of energy occurs when a practitioner moves around in a crowded place. To compensate this, a yogi must needs learn the techniques of specialized breathing exercises in order to absorb more cosmic energy. The ultimate objective is to enter *samadhi* instantaneously upon closing one's eyes (p. 75).

The remainder of Malik's book contains many more statements and explanations, most of which I find problematical. In the world of yogis it seems that nothing can be done, or achieved, without concentration on a *chakra*. There is apparently no such thing as natural insight and intuition, and nothing spiritual is attainable save with *mantra*, posture, breathwork, and meditation. Whether with, or without, the advantage of a Guru, these practices appear to be the norm.

Although Arjan Dass Malik undoubtedly had some form of *kundalini* experience and provides us with the elevatory observations of his Guru, it is abundantly clear that whatever happened to him was first initiated, then aided, by the use of various techniques. His descriptions of his own experience, and the pedantic dissertations of his Guru, leave me unconvinced that Malik attained an overall consciousness of the cosmos, much less *Nirvikalpa Samadhi*, or enlightenment.

* * * * *

Lilian Silburn, Honorary Research Director of the Centre National de la Recherche Scientifique in Paris, and author of *Kundalini: The Energy of the Depths* (1988), has this to say on the subject of *kundalini*: ". . . this mysterious energy aroused by Kundalini yoga manifests with a violence beyond belief and cannot be manipulated without incurring certain risks. (Some deviations of Kundalini are even termed 'demoniac', as they lead to depression and insanity). Therefore, to probe into her secrets, one must seek the help of a master belonging to a special lineage and endowed with unfailing knowledge."

Silburn's book appears very knowledgeable and contains a great deal of interesting information, but the basic premise exhibited is the relation of *kundalini* to sexual expression. Her theme is the Tantric use of sexuality in combination with various techniques as a means of awakening and controlling this energy. Silburn, according to the jacket of her book, is an academic authority on *kundalini*, and has for many years achieved worldwide respect "as a leader in studies of the Shaivism of Kashmir." She has additionally published many academic books and articles on the subject. In the book under review, she "draws together passages from the Trika, Krama, and Kaula systems ranging through Abhinavagupta and Lalla and provides both translation and commentary for them." These systems appear to be seriously defective. Under the section headed *Incomplete and Defective Ways* (in reference to the upward movement of *kundalini* and the problems that can arise in the ascent of this energy) we read that: "There exist a number of incomplete courses frequently followed by the Kundalini of a yogin who lacks vigilance *or even*

177

by that of a master when he is busy with worldly tasks" (p. 68, my italics).

This is surely bad news for all potential pupils of such masters, and does not say a great deal for their abilities. Silburn goes on to describe the "incomplete process," which is apparently the result of a fault in breathing (*pranayama*) that "effectuates" only a partial ascent of *kundalini* "from the navel to the heart or from the heart to the throat" (p. 69).

"*Truly defective*" (my italics), asserts Silburn, "is the way known as *pisacavesa*, demoniac penetration." This condition is the result of a complex type of "misfiring" arising from "accumulated breath," and is described in detail. The passage concludes: "Even if the yogin is in *samadhi*, the breath goes out through the nose and the yogin comes back to the ordinary state without deriving any benefit from this practice – neither power nor bliss – for all movement which passes downward through the centers generates either depression, fatigue, or disgust" (p. 69).

Samadhi is explained in the index of Silburn's text as "Deep, undifferentiated absorption," and as such is considered to be a state of Union or ecstatic bliss, which again signals a strange combination of knowledge and ignorance, i.e., knowledge of the existence of higher states, and ignorance of what constitutes them. One can argue that the ignorance is extensive in promoting vulgar activity of the lower *chakras* and confusing this with something more advanced.

Silburn enlarges upon the work of Abhinavagupta and gives excerpts from the *Tantraloka* (Ch. 29 v. 237–38) on the methods used to evoke *kundalini*. ("Evoke" is a key word here, for it is evident that all the systems referred to used specific procedures for the activation of this force). On page 81 she writes: "The awakening of the coiled-up energy, achieved through the use of formulas, gives a glimpse into the main phases of its unfolding." Following this is a series of visualizations and meditations, and on page 87, an illuminating insight into the master/disciple relationship: "The indescribable transmission from master to disciple takes place from heart to heart, from body to body. Since in reality there exists only one Consciousness – the infinite realm of illumination – one can understand how the master's illumined consciousness is able to penetrate the disciple's obscured consciousness in order to enlighten it." Yet a few pages later we learn:

178

"This initiation by penetration, described here and there in the treatises, and in many ways, should be performed by a master well-versed [in this field]. When duly performed, it consists of penetrating higher and higher into the disciple, who clearly and unmistakably feels it through his centers. This is how he acquires supernatural power. . . . However, according to the *Ratnamala-tantra*, if he fails to bring about the rising from wheel to wheel [i.e., *chakra* to *chakra*], the penetration then goes downward and will be termed as demoniac" (p. 92).

This extraordinary statement is reinforced with a quotation from a verse by Jayaratha, which refers to the "two antagonistic movements," and states that: "the ascending course bestows liberation and awareness, while the untoward descending course is related to penetration by a demon" (inferring a form of demonic possession). Silburn continues: "Indeed, if instead of moving upward the flow of energy goes down from wheel to wheel, no fruit is born; worse still, this flow becomes an obstacle to spiritual life, leading to depression and a dissipation of energy. Such a process endangers both master and disciple, for the benefits as well as the risks involved in these initiations are shared by both. A failure is due either to the master being *not sufficiently experienced* [my italics] or to the disciple not sufficiently prepared" (p. 92).

Once again, the proficiency of Tantric "masters" is brought into question, and the danger of inexperienced teachers in superstitious Tantric initiations is a combination best avoided. The "masters" referred to in many ancient and medieval texts were not necessarily proficient at all, in much the same sort of situation as the "masters," "adepts," and "teachers" today, who claim or accept the designations conferring this distinction without the relevant qualifications or the inherent attributes. Authentic masters do not, for instance, conduct initiations, which are the means of perpetuation for many sects and cults, and which are often of a very extroverted nature.

The latter part of Silburn's book is concerned with sexual Tantra, to which she gives credence, misleading many readers. She proffers the uninspiring information that anal contractions in conjunction with specific breathing disciplines are used in some systems as a sure-fire means of *kundalini* activation (which practice is perhaps a precursor of "anal sex" in certain rites). The

179

abnormal psychologies at work in such activities must have left their mark in so many unedifying Tantric texts, and have rendered their study a pointless exercise.

The phenomenon of Tantric Yoga, in all the many variations, provides a fraught short-cut to *kundalini* activation and awakening of the *chakras*. Yogic systems claim an intensive programme designed to produce results, e.g., to nullify the karmic seeds and impressions stored within the lower *chakras* in the shortest time possible by means that (arbitrarily) extinguish them.

Some systems deviate from the natural order of *chakra* awakening, and through the induced (or forced) prior activation of the *anahata*, assume that they can neutralize the stored impressions normally requiring confrontation long before the *anahata* is reached, supposedly nullifying the karmic content of the lower *chakras* with the more powerful stimulus of one much higher. Thus the end goal is attained (it is claimed) and all *karma* annihilated. The seemingly unending cycles of incarnation are at an end, or so we are told.

The "evidence" put forward as proof of the above, and kindred assertions, is invariably flawed, though there are few persons who are seemingly prepared to take this seriously. More and more books are written on Yoga and related subjects, and both these, and the recent research undertaken by professionals are construed as consolidating the premise that enlightenment (or what is assumed to be enlightenment) can be reached by these processes.

An eminent German Professor has produced a two volume work that is currently attracting much attention and achieving considerable acclaim. Klaus Engel's *Meditation: Vol. 1 History and Present Time*, and *Meditation: Vol. 2 Empirical Research and Theory* have recently appeared in an English translation (1997) complete with detailed research documentation and an invitation to his readers to participate in an ongoing research programme. Regrettably, however, Engel has approached the entire subject from the "ground floor" of intellectual assessment and without any intrinsic knowledge of what he attempts to research. Thus, his descriptions of the *chakras*, for instance, are derived from the writings of Gopi Krishna, and his material on *kundalini* (titled "The Path of Psychosexual Energy") is clearly influenced by the same source. This erudite work is wholly based on the evaluation

180

of artifically induced activations of interior forces, generated principally by means of meditation. Despite the use of measuring instruments (and other laboratory procedures) for the resultant assumed "Definitions of Altered States of Consciousness," realistically this type of investigation can lead nowhere in terms of genuine knowledge. Unfortunately, it nevertheless consolidates the credence given to twentieth century gurus whose reputations are built upon the phenomenon of *kundalini*.

It is widely believed that such gurus are fully "enlightened" and therefore competent to direct all areas of the inner and outer lives of their pupils. This, regrettably, is rarely, if ever, the case. Acclaimed gurus who have opened the three lower *chakras* may have attained to great charisma and certain paranormal abilities associated with guruship, i.e., healing, thought transference, the spontaneous production of *kriyas* and *mudras* in devotees, plus haphazard stirrings of the *kundalini* energy in those close to them; but although such attributes are impressive in demonstration, they are quite meaningless in the field of evolutionary metaphysics. They will not of themselves engender in others an enduring basis for spiritual growth.

The live, organic stimulus essential for spiritual progression can only be provided by an authentic teacher. Such stimulus essentially derives from an evolved, or higher level of evolution. The *shaktipat* of gurus who have artifically awakened the power of *kundalini* is not of the same order, and can only produce in others (owing to its inchoate nature) a hybrid form of lopsided growth incapable of maturation.

Scholarly research has notwithstanding provided much valuable information regarding New Religious Movements and their figureheads. One of the more useful investigations is Judith Coney's *Sahaja Yoga*, an excellent and impartially presented account of the movement surrounding the female Indian guru, Sri Mataji Nirmala Devi (b. 1923 in Chindwara, India). [Mataji, the eldest daughter of a leading Indian barrister, also happens to be the wife of Mr. Chandika Prasad Srivastava, the Secretary General of the United Nations International Maritime Organisation.]

Dr. Coney teaches in the Department of the Study of Religions, SOAS, University of London, and her book, which is largely based on participant observation with devotees, clearly defines all sociological aspects of this movement which claims up to one hundred thousand members throughout the world, a membership that wholly accepts the self-professed avataric divinity of Sri Mataji and permits her total control of their lives. This extends even to arranged inter-racial marriages for Westerners as well as for her Hindu following, and her total dictatorship on the rearing of all children of her devotees (this to the extent of sending two-year-olds to the sect-run boarding school in Rome, and five-year-olds to similar indoctrinal institutions in India). Parents are told by their guru, Sri Mataji, ". . . don't get too involved with your children, that's a dangerous thing. . . . The children are mine, not yours, so you just don't get involved with them, that's a temptation for you, too much involvement with the children, that's a sign of degradation" (*Sahaja Yoga*, quoted by Coney, p. 149). [Such injunctions also ensure that devotee focus is maintained exclusively upon Mataji.] Children in the Sahaja Yoga movement are considered to be "realised" souls, and thus "require an upbringing which Sri Mataji, due to her authority and divine wisdom, is most qualified to dictate" (p. 149). Daily practices for all, both young and old, are a seemingly endless round of rituals, feet washing ceremonies, meditations, and attempts at *kundalini* arousal.

Mataji's claims are all based on her alleged personal experience of the raising of *kundalini*, and her assumed ability to awaken the *kundalini* of her devotees "almost instantly" and to grant them "realization" *en masse*. The descriptions of these events as given by Mataji and her devotees, however, are not convincing. The prime concern is with the "vibratory awareness" of cool breezes on the hands and the head, which are accepted as proof of successful activation. Apart from the described physiological effects (subjective or otherwise), there is no indication of any consequent altered or intensified state of consciousness in the experiencer.

Of Mataji's own self-proclaimed "realization," she records: "I saw the *kundalini*, which is the primordial force within us, which is the Holy Ghost within us, rising like a telescope opening out. And then I saw the whole thing open and a big torrential rain of beams started flowing through my head all over. I felt, I am lost, I am no more. There is only the grace. I saw it completely happening to me" (quoted by Coney, p. 27).

Despite being "fully realized," when Dr. Coney requested permission by letter to conduct a scholarly study of the movement, she was required to forward her photograph so that Mataji could "feel" the state of Dr. Coney's vibrations (p. 209), a psychometric factor scarcely in keeping with the attributes of enlightenment, or with this guru's messianic declaration of Divinity in December 1979 in London, when she claimed that she was the "One" who had come to save the whole of humanity (p. 27).

A more disturbing factor is the fear amongst devotees of Mataji's presumed retributive psychic powers; that if they wish to leave the organization "the long arm of the Goddess will reach out and terrifyingly punish them for their disobedience" (p. 180). Mataji herself has said (amongst other, similar threats and warnings): "Those who come to Sahaja Yoga and do not meditate and do not rise are destroyed or they are thrown out of Sahaja Yoga" (quoted by Coney, p. 171) and, "Those who have not recognized me will not be blessed," meaning they will not participate in the prom-ised new life of the future (p. 225, note 46). These fears are likely to have been amplified by certain mantric requirements for devotees. On page 231, note 25 of *Sahaja Yoga*, we read:

"In a book of mantras published for devotees there is a list of satanic leaders and groups and the mantras to be used to 'destroy' them. As well as the Maharishi Mahesh Yogi and Rajneesh the list includes Muktananda, Sri Chinmoy, Krishna-murti, Sathya Sai Baba, the Dalai Lama, Findhorn [Foundation], the Pope, the Catholic Church and Adolf Hitler."

This requirement to participate in what is in reality a form of left-hand magical practice, speaks volumes for the mind-set of Mataji, and negates entirely (at least in the view of the present writer) her claims of enlightenment.

According to Osho Rajneesh, Nirmala Mataji was his pupil for ten years, a detail which is similarly no recommendation for her declaration of "Divinity." Rajneesh stated: "I know her perfectly well – for ten years she was my student. There is nothing in it, no spirituality, no meditativeness . . . but she got the idea [of becoming a guru] from Muktananda" (quoted by Coney, p. 26, who also relates that Mataji has confirmed her contact with Mukt-ananda, p. 220, note 7).

An exercise given by Mataji to her followers, and special to her organization, epitomizes the level of knowledge of the guru. This is the purportedly protective technique known as "tying up the *kundalini*" (which precedes meditation and all attempts at *kundalini* activation) in which the devotee is instructed, with the use of both hands, to "tie the *kundalini* in a knot above the head" (p. 72) – a symbolic rite which illustrates the type of fantasy to which Mataji and her devotees subscribe.

One can therefore conclude, quite justifiably, that paranormal effects, where they exist, are merely the product of the ego-powered, technique-induced *shaktipat* of yet another yogi – along with the delusion, self-aggrandizement, and vast monetary gain that invariably accompanies such illicit manifestations.

Chapter Five

The Heart Experience

The "heart" experience comprises the essential core of all interior growth, and is a stage which cannot be by-passed on the route to spiritual enlightenment. Attempts to describe this experience have been made by centuries of mystics, and there are many records, frequently partial or incomplete, which delineate the sufferings of the soul approaching the ground of its existence, the abode of the Beloved, its very source.

Viewed from one angle, this is wholly an illusion, for the essential spirit is at all times a pervasive Unity, permeating every particle of our human form and every atom of our very existence. Yet the fact remains that as members of the human species we are almost 100% unaware of the truth of this, and only when traversing the latter stages of the tenuous interior path that links the lesser self to an innermost core does the soul recognize the intrinsic divinity of its origin, and the essential wholeness and benevolent nature of the entire Universe, and beyond.

The created Universe is itself part of the Great Illusion, as is the Universal mindstream in which all human mentation is contained. In order to attain to the totality of being that is our birthright, the fruit of evolutionary completion, the soul in human form must experientially penetrate to the boundaries of that Universe and transcend *all* form, and *all* substance, physical, subtle, and mental; must forge its way to the ultimate essence of the Divine.

To do this it seemingly journeys through all these levels, drawn on by an increasingly urgent and irresistible awareness of the All-Pervading Reality to which it aspires, till it reaches the mystical Void, the boundary line, that lies between the ultimate strivings of the uncompleted entity, and the completeness of Union with the eternal Beloved.

Here, on the edge of the Abyss, the soul can see God "face to face"; can perceive the Beloved everywhere and in everything – pervading every particle of Creation . . . while yet still experiencing itself as alone, and utterly separate from that Everything . . .

It is here that the heart experience begins in earnest.

*   *   *   *   *

This profound experience constitutes the "bridge" that spans the Void. The few that undergo it at any one time, in all its intensity, literally burn themselves to nothingness, are annihilated in the agonized longing and all-consuming love which climaxes the evolutionary journey and brings the entire process to completion.

This is the true annihilation of the lesser self, or ego. It is always carefully monitored. The route, both externally and internally, constitutes the apex of spiritual endurance, and extends to the limit of the capacity of the almost completed human entity.

This state, as with all major states that signify vital stations of the path, reflects into the lower planes of being, where are enacted lesser degrees and variations of the same order. The stages are reworked again and again on an ascending spiral. Thus, the experience of anguished isolation and separation, of deep yearning and an overwhelming love, will arise in a less pronounced form (matched to the capacity of the aspirant) in earlier phases of development, and help prepare the soul for its final move towards consummation.

To attempt to express this matter more intelligibly: we should remember that *all* experience other than the purely physical is internal, or interior, and the states and planes of being (as described by various authentic teachers) are all reachable (and traversed) within oneself, and are externalized via the human emotions and other psychological processes. It is in the so-called mental body, the non-physical higher vehicle of the individual soul, that the heart experience is undergone. It is within the subtle body that the non-physical energy of *kundalini* is initially raised. Both conditions (the heart experience and the raising of *kundalini*)

186

affect the physical body vicariously, and reveal their reality in mirrored events and situations in everyday life.

There are few contemporary records of this process, and even these, in the main, are complicated by the problems of yogic practices. The forced activation of the heart *chakra* (*anahata*) by a yogic master and the concurrent arousal of *kundalini*, can mimic this process in a disciple and precipitate that disciple into states for which he/she is spiritually unready, with long-term consequences. Many people commence to teach others after emerging from these counterfeit experiences, under the belief that this is their rightful destiny. But it is not the *anahata chakra* that produces the lattermost stages of the "heart" experience and ultimate completion; it is the *ajna chakra*, unreachable in a meaningful sense through any artificial process, that enables the soul to enter the Void, and see God "face to face."

This field of knowledge has been barely touched upon in our present culture, and as more and more aspirants take note of the existence of the heart experience, further information is vital in the interests of all concerned. Without basic understanding of spiritual evolution, even genuine students can become side-tracked. People are frequently dazzled by the spurious – by the purported experiences of well-known instructors and their apparent knowledge and expertise. They cannot discriminate between the lesser and the greater, the counterfeit and the genuine, the half-baked and the fully-fledged, and therefore ingest indiscriminately the distorted concepts proffered them by fakes and ignoramuses. The New Age view that inner development is easy and teachers are dispensable – that growth is painless and outmoded ideas on suffering should be jettisoned – is entirely erroneous. Growth is *not* easy, and one cannot develop to any degree without knowledgeable assistance (*self*-development is a figment of New Age imagination). Likewise, self-esteem and self-assertion (to name but two of the current delusions) are ego-oriented constructs leading entirely in the wrong direction [the above constructs are therapeutic supports for over-passive and unintegrated egos, not for aspirants who should have already attained to integration.]

People indoctrinated with false ideas will not recognize the states and stages of a path that is anathema to them. Such a path holds no interest and will be repudiated by all but the most sincere. In today's climate of easy options, who wants the struggle and effort required to forge a genuine integrity? Who is prepared to heed a conscience that if acted upon will inevitably cause loss of prestige or position? And if the spiritual path is given no credence, and its states, stages, and stations remain unrecognized, how can these phases be prepared for? Until some move is made to counter this dilemma, casualties will continue to be heavy, and the yield in terms of spiritual growth and development very small indeed. What, for instance, is the average New Age-fed aspirant likely to make of the following, set in southern England in the latter part of the twentieth century?

"The inner fire increased, creating such overwhelming longing, I was distraught, and could barely conceal my state from even the unperceptive eyes of colleagues. It was rooted in my heart, and had no linkage with human desire, though it raged like a conflagration towards an ultimate zenith of consummation, projecting itself as a total grief, a pining away, an **annihilation** *... the moth consumed by the flame, a searing agony inextricably bound with bliss, a delectable wound that made one weak with its pain ..."* (A. J. Peterson, *Approach to Reality*, 1983, p. 152).

The above book contains accurate descriptions of a wide variety of authentic yet little-known mystical states, including a vivid encapsulation of the heart experience. Unfortunately, though factually based, it is only semi-autobiographical (as the publisher makes clear in an appended note) and is therefore unsuitable for the type of analysis required, which depends upon 100% direct personal experience, and absolute authenticity. This does not, however, negate the book's value as a form of documentation.

In paving the way for greater awareness of the "burning heart" interlude, a close study of clearly expressed records is imperative. And here the serious student confronts once again the recurring problem of what constitutes spiritual authenticity. For not all records are what they may seem, or purport to be, as has been demonstrated in the foregoing chapters.

Two very contemporary autobiographical accounts of this major experience are provided by Irina Tweedie (d. 1999), latterly designated a Nasqhbandi Sufi, and her personally appointed successor, Llewellyn Vaughan-Lee (b. 1953), founder of the Golden Sufi

Center, California. These books are, respectively, *Daughter of Fire: A Diary of a Spiritual Training with a Sufi Master* (1986), and *The Face Before I Was Born: A Spiritual Autobiography* (1998).

Tweedie did not declare herself a Sufi teacher, insisting always she was but a disciple of her own (deceased) teacher, known as Bhai Sahib, in whom she was "merged," and from whom she took directions when in meditation. Even so, according to her students she behaved authoritatively and in every respect as if she held this function, projecting her work in much the same manner as she had witnessed it in Bhai Sahib's ashram in India. For well over two decades her home in north London was in use for four days each week as an "open" centre, and here she daily gave teachings that eventually attracted literally hundreds of disciples who were trained by her for varying periods. [Bhai Sahib was acknowledged within his community as a Naqshbandi Sufi of the "Golden," or "silent," Sufi lineage (silent, because they practised a silent *zikr* known as prayer of the heart: *zikr-bil-qalb*).]

Irina Tweedie was born in Russia in 1907 and educated in Vienna and Paris. She moved to England in the early 1930s as the lively young wife of a British banker and lived "a life of frivolity and pleasure." Following his death in World War II, she fell deeply in love with an English naval officer, and married for the second time, again very happily, until his premature death in 1954. There were no children of either marriage to comfort her, and utterly grief-stricken and distraught, she sought spiritual consolation and a meaning to life. This she found in the teachings of H. P. Blavatsky and the Theosophical Society at their venue in London, England, and later, within the Theosophical community at Adyar in India. Tweedie learned from the Theosophists of the "hidden Masters," a supposed hierarchy of immortal beings who allegedly dwelt in the uninterrupted seclusion of the Himalayas for the sole purpose of service to mankind, and who had made themselves known to various of the original Theosophists by a series of "miraculously" received communications known as the "Mahatma letters."

In 1961, a friend suggested she should visit Bhai Sahib in the small city in northern India where he lived, and whom she duly approached in the hope that he would instruct her in Yoga. Instead, as she tells us, he made her "descend into hell" and obliged her to "face the darkness" within herself. Bhai Sahib (which means Elder Brother, the name bestowed on him by Irina Tweedie in her book to conceal his identity from the curious) nevertheless gave the desired instruction, for she practised yogic *asanas* every day before visiting the ashram, and recounts how she told Bhai Sahib that, elderly as she was, her body could accomplish all the exercises relatively easily without having learned them – an ability she felt implied her proficiency in yoga in a former lifespan. As one of the exercises was the *shirsha-asana* (standing on the head), this was no mean achievement at the age of fifty-four (p. 47).

Tweedie soon noted the slowing down of her thinking process when in the presence of Bhai Sahib (p. 12) and also the strange states of seeming unconsciousness entered into by others who visited him and sat in his vicinity. These meditative states were called *Dhyana*, but Tweedie was never subject to them. Bhai Sahib said that he had chosen for her a different route, one of complete renunciation.

In the first few weeks of Tweedie's experience of the guru she suffered much doubt and disappointment. Continually within herself she queried if she could trust him – if she dared to take the training he offered and submit herself to his care. She felt he had "some kind of terrible power" which did not seem human, and which made her restless and afraid. What if he misused it? Tweedie feared he might in some way cause the loss of all she had; that he could "put me in a state where I would give all my money away, or do something mad . . ." (p. 25).

Conversely, her swift introduction to the powerful atmosphere generated by Bhai Sahib when in meditation or *samadhi* (which invariably she found quite overwhelming) soon resolved into states of peace. Her heart, as she noted in the days following, seemed to have been affected by the atmosphere, and began to beat with great rapidity – to flutter, to miss beats, to stop altogether for some moments. There was a strange sensation in her throat, stirrings of heat deep in her body, and the commencement of a curious yearning.

Yet still the doubt persisted, combined with a terrible fear – that he could do anything he chose with her, "anything at all, that I am completely helpless in his hand . . ." (p. 28).

In a surprisingly short time, however, events and conversations created a change of viewpoint, and before long Tweedie had satisfied herself that her new teacher was the equivalent of the Theosophical Himalayan Masters, and a member of the current reigning spiritual hierarchy, and made the decision to transfer to him her allegiance. She even showed him her treasured copy of the *Mahatma Letters* (see A. T. Barker, ed., *Mahatma Letters to Mr. Sinnett from the Mahatmas M. and K. H.*, 1924), complete with facsimiles of their signatures. Bhai Sahib appeared to accept the legitimacy of the content, and moreover commented on the superior status of the "Master K. H." (Koot Hoomi) as opposed to the "Master M" (Morya), having intently scrutinized their handwriting (pp. 40–42). Tweedie seemed unaware of the long-standing controversy surrounding the letters – or perhaps like many Theosophists declined to consider they might be fraudulent. [These letters, now lodged in the British Museum, were eventually exposed as fakes by Richard Hodgson of The Society for Psychical Research (SPR), being written by Blavatsky herself, or in some cases, by others under her instructions. Details regarding both the letters and the Mahatmas can be found in Bruce F. Campbell's *Ancient Wisdom Revived: The History of the Theosophical Movement* (1980) pp. 53–61. The same conclusions are voiced by Janet Oppenheim in *The Other World: Spiritualism and Psychical Research in England, 1850–1914* (1985) pp. 176–182.]

In the midst of the ebb and flow of doubt and experience, and of her earliest taste of her Guru's intermittent display of indifference towards her, Tweedie somewhat angrily challenged Bhai Sahib to produce in her the mystical love he spoke of – the intense love and longing of the heart. She pressed the point, laughing but defiant, and after a few moments of consideration, the challenge was accepted. Tweedie immediately felt uneasy, knowing full well that something outside her control had been set into motion (pp. 93–94). [At this point, she appears not to have realized the significance of her earlier symptoms, or of the processes already triggered in her system, which would soon accelerate and become manifest.]

Very early in their relationship, Bhai Sahib instructed Tweedie to keep a diary (p. 127) which he later assured her would one day be read by others. This she dutifully did, in great detail, and *Daughter of Fire: A Diary of a Spiritual Training with a Sufi Master* (first published in a much abridged edition as *The Chasm of Fire*, Element, 1979) is the result. On a day to day basis she recorded the events of her life at the ashram over the next nineteen months, complete with accompanying states, thoughts, feelings, and the words of Bhai Sahib both to herself and to others. This provides impressive documentation and runs to well over eight hundred pages. The primary interest of that work lies in the ongoing account of a powerful *kundalini* activation, and the heart experience to which it was linked.

The significance of this documentation is stressed in several places much further into the book. On page 266 Bhai Sahib tells Tweedie: "Some knowledge has to be given out to the world. I want you to do it. You will have to take my message to the world." She was also told that she was "the first woman" to receive the ancient, traditional training: that such experiences are not recorded anywhere save in Persian writings, most of which are untranslated. To enable this "System" to reach the West, Bhai Sahib said he had done "the easiest thing." He had given her direct experience of the System so that she could write a full account of it, and need not depend upon books (p. 269).

Although known as a Sufi, Bhai Sahib referred to the training system he used as a Path of Yoga, and on one occasion demonstrated the exercise he was given when young by his own guru, in which he learned to remain for well over an hour without breathing. He remarked that this exercise was suitable only for those under eighteen who had never been married, and "is a quick way to take up all the sex power to *Brahmarandhra*"(the Crown *chakra*), a process facilitated by "singing certain sentences in a certain way" (pp. 120–121).

He also describes some very strange yogic powers such as that demonstrated by a yogi to him in his youth, and which he put into practice soon afterwards. This was purportedly an act of instantaneous teleportation from one venue to another by means of a specially prepared leather pouch concealed in the mouth, the latter gifted to him by the yogi, and for which display of yogic showmanship he was rebuked by his father, an eminent guru.

[It must be remembered that the cultural background of India encouraged the commitment of entire families to the care of a guru – in Bhai Sahib's case, his father and uncle became revered teachers, his brother was trained alongside himself, and his cousin (less reverable) considered himself a *mahatma* by right of lineage following his father's death, rather than by right of qualification

(p. 703) – a situation sadly evident in many Sufi circles.]

Much of the teaching given by Bhai Sahib is confusing. Intermixed with clear and logical expositions of Sufism are more magical matters, such as the preparation of *Yantras* for those with smallpox (pieces of paper carefully cut and folded, blown upon and blessed, which must be tied around the neck for children under twelve, and under the right armpit for boys, and the left armpit for girls who are over this age). "Nobody can die of smallpox if given this Yantra," declared Bhai Sahib, "It is more than magic. It is magic helped by the Divine Power" (p. 655). Likewise the matter of ensuring by certain means that an unborn child (already in the womb) would be male (pp. 32, 646). There are numerous questionable comments scattered throughout the book, a large number of which are on the subject of *chakras* and *kundalini*. According to Bhai Sahib, in his System only one *chakra* is activated by the Master, the heart *chakra*, which gradually awakens all the others. "It is done with Yogic Power," he tells Tweedie (p. 55).

Inevitably, this process is applied to Tweedie, who details very vividly her experiences as each *chakra* is stimulated. Bhai Sahib acknowledged some yogic force had been used on her – that something in her had to be forced, for her ultimate benefit: "This force which has been used on you," he tells her, "will make you doubt, will cause disturbances of many kinds, but it was necessary" (p. 35).

What it did was precipitate Tweedie into a nightmare situation that endured for some months, with only the briefest respites. This involved confrontation with the sexual energies formerly locked in the *muladhara*, now violently awakened. The onset was sudden, without warning. She was lying in bed feeling comfortably sleepy when she noticed a vibration, a soft movement, then a *sound*, like a muted hiss, within her lower abdomen. Something seemed to be spinning, and it crossed Tweedie's mind that it boded real trouble... "There was a deep, dark fear..." (p. 108).

What came next flooded her with terror. With no prior indication she was seized with a powerful sexual desire, "to no object in particular... uncontrollable, a kind of wild, cosmic force... This was not just desire – it was madness in its lowest, animal form, a paroxysm of sex-craving... a wild howling of everything

193

female in me, for a male." Yet inexplicably, the idea of any kind of intercourse was repellent, though her body shook, and she bit her pillow to prevent herself from howling like a wild animal, quite beside herself with sensual craving. It went on for hours, leaving her helpless and trembling, a fiery force burning in her bowels, and sensations of heat that "increased and decreased in waves" (pp. 108–109). The end result was psychological turmoil.

Worse was to come, the following night beyond endurance. She was "beyond" herself with unexpressed desire, at times only partially conscious. Then suddenly, in the dark room arose "whirling, dark, grey mist," and within the mist moved hideous shapes, leering and obscene, performing wild sexual orgies. Tweedie thought she was going mad. She had not known such practises were possible – "with dogs, humans, men and women, horses . . . Things I never knew could be done, could exist – the most lecherous filth, I had to witness . . ." (p. 111).

The awareness that knowledge of these experiences must have been somewhere within herself, undid her completely. She was swamped with a sense of helplessness and black depression. Weak and shaky, she sought out Bhai Sahib next morning, her heart thudding furiously, her head spinning, a feeling of bitterness against him for plunging her into this torment. Bhai Sahib was unperturbed, and not disposed to be friendly.

In the daytime the horror ceased, yet Tweedie knew that in the darkness it would return, as indeed it did. Once more the night was "a perfect hell" – the creatures closer now, all around her bed – so close that at times she was compelled to hide under the sheet in terror. With trembling body and inoperative mind, perilously close to vomiting, she again sought Bhai Sahib, who told her to be patient; it would pass.

But not immediately, of course. Nightly, Tweedie dreaded to go home, and nightly, almost without break, the same situation ensued. The body grew weaker, heat raged relentlessly within her, she was beset with giddiness and felt unsteady on her feet. On February 26th (1962) she tells us: "Once more the fear of going insane was haunting me" (p. 144).

Other symptoms amplified her misery. There was the consciousness of her heart *chakra* spinning round at terrific speed, her physical heart beating madly in response. The power exuded by Bhai Sahib was tangibly experienced, progressively intense. In his

194

presence Tweedie's breathing was affected and she could only inhale with difficulty. She could no longer think coherently; sometimes she could not speak.

As the process heightened, Tweedie found to her amazement that at night, when alone in her room, her entire nervous system became visible to her, pulsating with light, until it "looked like a luminous web encircling the body, inside and out" (p. 127). She became aware that this liquid light was burning her, "as if currents of hot lava were flowing through every nerve, every fibre, hotter and hotter, more and more unbearable ..." (p. 128).

The account covers very many pages, and is quite impossible to condense without losing detail. Yet apart from the above, and the fact that Tweedie frequently saw light exuding from Bhai Sahib, at times almost blinding in its brilliance, she experienced none of the more traditional states pertaining to *kundalini*, and very few mystical insights and visions. Her descriptions of the awakening of each *chakra* are invariably physiological, full of pain and distress, and the ever-present burning. Alongside these vicissitudes was a depth of longing that continued unabated, and which ultimately proved the greatest agony of all.

There was shortly to be considerable encouragement. Before long, Bhai Sahib told Tweedie that he had "something in mind" for her future, and that if she knew what it was she would never cry or feel upset. He spoke of a former European disciple – a man who had died of a brain tumour seven years previously, and who was "the best" of all his European disciples "until now," the implication being that Tweedie was of real consequence to his work (p. 155).

Early in her account, Tweedie comments on her fear of clairvoyance, and her suspicion that she had been led astray by "powers" in a previous existence (p. 42). [Even in her old age, after decades of functioning as a teacher, when interviewed by Surya Green, she states: "I have no clairvoyance, no clairaudience, I know nothing. If I am *told*, I know. Told by whom? By my teacher. Because the relationship with the teacher remains forever. He is not in the world any more; that does not matter. One can always reach the teacher, always." (Surya Green, *The Call of the Sun: A Woman's Journey to the Heart of Wisdom*, 1997, p. 306). This is long, long after the demise of Bhai Sahib, whom, according to

195

Tweedie, she could contact in meditation when the need arose. On the same page she confides to Green: "The spirit evolution – angels and jinns and ghosts and all those – is a parallel evolution to human beings. They do exist. And they can be seen. But when I began to see and to know such things, my teacher took this away from me. 'Are you after child's play or are you after Truth?' he said." As this interview was taped, these are Tweedie's own words.]

Intimations of future events soon made themselves apparent. Tweedie records how Bhai Sahib repeatedly emphasized the necessity of trust in the Teacher, and that one should not think of tomorrow and its needs, but learn to live in faith. In due time her earlier fears that she would lose all her money became realized. She voluntarily sold her stocks and shares, disbursed her financial securities, and transferred all funds to Bhai Sahib, who promptly distributed them to the needy. We are not given precise details, only the fact that she released her resources by stages, and underwent acute anxiety and resentment concerning how she would live, and what would happen to her if her Guru died. This escalated enormously when her (substantial) funds had all been given, whereupon Bhai Sahib then informed her that she was to leave India in a few months time and "go home" to England, there to prepare for her future work. He also made a surprising statement that Tweedie simply records, without comment: "You are sent back to atone for the life you have led previously, and which was not justified" (p. 448).

[Tweedie was not left entirely penniless. Bhai Sahib gave her small amounts when necessary (though he made her wait for them) and funded her return to England. She also retained her war-widow's pension.]

Parallel to these events were the punishing states above-mentioned, when her mind ceased to function normally, and she was internally consumed with ever more heat. Even more disturbingly, for a (mercifully brief) period the alarming copulating "creatures" were with her day and night, without respite. At the height of this phase the terrified Tweedie, whose physical condition was fast deteriorating, broke down disastrously, announcing to Bhai Sahib in no uncertain terms that she could continue no longer, that she was going mad, and that he, "with his powers" was the cause. The upshot was a flaming row, a scene in fact (the first of several) in which, desperate with anger, fear, and frustration, she attacked him verbally with loud and violent accusations. He was in the garden holding his grandchild at the time, and Tweedie's hysteria provoked an uproar. The alarmed child screamed relentlessly. Bhai Sahib walked away with the child and entered his house, closing the door behind him, and Tweedie "slumped down in helpless sobbing" (pp. 152–153).

But this was not the end of it. After a while the Guru returned in order to talk with another disciple, and mentioned in Tweedie's hearing the lack of perseverance in women that made them unsuitable for spiritual life. Indignation and rage revived Tweedie. "Boiling" with anger, and aware that she alone of all his disciples would be left without money, she informed him sharply that she, as he well knew, was made of the stuff of "Saints and Martyrs," and had demonstrated the very reverse of what she was accused. She then went home earlier than her usual time, and slept "in perfect peace" – a vitally necessary breathing space before the next onslaught on her mind and emotions.

Bhai Sahib told Tweedie that many of the problems she experienced, such as the powerful sex-urge and the nocturnal visitations, were the result of latencies within herself, and that the uprisings of hatred and resentment that escalated with the upward movement of the inner fire, were all part and parcel of the same process. "This is a purifying fire, this suffering," he said to her one morning, "and you will need a lot more" (p. 173). Despite this explanation there were to be further major altercations between them, some of which seem quite unbelievable in the light of the reported ongoing inflooding of love, and the developing heart experience.

What emerges most clearly in *Daughter of Fire* is Tweedie's enormous struggle against certain attributes within her own nature, which arose to confront her at every turn. It is apparent that she underwent a traditional yogic process which included the forced arousal of *kundalini* and a deliberately contrived opening of her heart *chakra*. The stress and suffering involved, however, were of a kind not normally associated with these procedures, and point unerringly to an unwisely premature activation. This raises the question of the legitimacy of her guru. The fact that he could initiate such a process does not mean that he had the

197

right to do so.

Bhai Sahib was a powerful yogi (according to Tweedie, a Sufi Master) who blew "hot and cold" with her in traditional fashion, and subjected his elderly disciple to every kind of bodily discomfort and to numerous incidents she found deeply humiliating. These things he did openly, if sometimes obscurely, and always made sure that Tweedie recognized that this was intended, and thus understood to some small degree what was going on. Understood, that is, in the sense that she knew that it was *he* who placed her in these situations, and that he knew quite well what she suffered as a consequence. The extent of her doubt in him is thus quite horrifying under the circumstances, likewise the violence of her anger, the depth of her hatred, and the accusations of error that she made against him, also her excessive arrogance and pride – all of which manifested concurrently with the *kundalini* activations, and intermingled most puzzlingly with the heart experience.

Tweedie also records the bitterness she felt as others were given consideration and she was left out (p. 134), and the acute resentment she experienced at Bhai Sahib's harsh treatment of her in front of her fellow disciples, most of whom were of Indian nationality, and male. On one occasion he called her "ignorant and impertinent" when she publicly criticized his wife for asking silly and unintelligent questions, and she in return made sharp criticisms of her Guru in an attitude of frank defiance (pp. 234–235).

Tweedie chronicles the magnitude of the fear she felt because she could not understand the states she experienced – states of non-being, of emptiness, of mental fragmentation – "for they are a nothing, a complete insecurity, from the point of view of the mind" (p. 287). On the following page she accuses Bhai Sahib to his face of human fallibility and susceptibility to error. Upon his rebuke for her lack of respect and reverence (he called her a "stupid, dense and ignorant woman"), she retaliated with hostility and informed him that he was "an arrogant autocrat." The interchange between them enraged Tweedie to the point of being "beyond" herself with fury – and she insisted again to Bhai Sahib that he was responsible for her plight and gave her no chance to recuperate. The Guru's response was that her own sins were coming back to her – the "evils" were in her blood, and so on. Tweedie could not take this, and assured Bhai Sahib that what

198

he saw was his own reflection – that all the hatred and evil perceived in others, was in him, too (pp. 288–289).

Throughout her tirade there were continuous interruptions from his family which fuelled her irritation to the point of paroxysm, and forced at length a crescendo of uncontrollable weeping. She brought out to Bhai Sahib her loneliness, the hopelessness of her situation, "the lack of money and the most elementary physical comforts" . . . the dust and the flies – the hours each day on her own in the dusty garden, and the treatment he meted out to her that was worse by far than to anyone else.

At home she could not eat, her body trembled without cease, and the savage heat of the surging inner fire seemed about to consume her. The pain, she tells us, was excruciating. She felt once more that she could not continue. The whole thing was utterly unbearable. Later that same evening she returned to the ashram and tried again to speak with Bhai Sahib. This time his anger was titanic; he did not wish to hear any more. But Tweedie brought out more accusations, and one that was shocking in the extreme – that he took advantage of the fact that she was on her own and helpless. She threatened to ask one of his "more intelligent" disciples to act as her relative, and to intervene on her behalf to protect her against him. At this juncture Bhai Sahib shouted furiously at Tweedie, declaring her no better than a street woman, a person "known to be expert" at defamation.

Tweedie was astounded by this allegation, and stopped in her tracks. It was *she* who was wronged, not he. The Guru insisted that she was "lying shamelessly," and Tweedie at once demanded the presence of the "intelligent pupil," a Professor, to bear witness to his words.

Bhai Sahib, not surprisingly, had had enough. He informed her coldly never to enter his premises again. Tweedie believes she fainted, or at any rate lost consciousness when she heard these words, and when she came to herself, all was as usual in the courtyard, with people sitting in *dhyana* and Bhai Sahib explaining things to pupils in his normal manner.

At length he turned to her and suggested she went home now. She refused, and said she would stay all night in protest at what she had suffered at his hands. Bhai Sahib left and went indoors, returning after a while with his wife and his sons, telling her quietly that it would be best for her not to stay. There was authority in his voice, and it seemed to Tweedie a note of warning, which she chose to ignore. She refused again to leave, exploding verbally in despair, telling him the whole town should know what he was doing and how badly he had treated her. The Guru turned abruptly and walked away. Later still came the wife and sons on their own and attempted to persuade her to see sense and go. Tweedie was adamant, and remained overnight in the ashram garden until 5:30 a.m., when she gave up of her own accord and departed (p. 292). During the morning she returned. No-one would speak to her, however, including Bhai Sahib, and the following day she learned he was confined to bed with severe heart pain and fever, quite possibly brought on by these stressful events. For nearly a month he was very ill indeed, his condition complicated by acute amoebic hepatitis; he escaped death by a hair's breadth.

Even in retrospect Tweedie does not seem to grasp the anomaly of her behaviour, believing, as she states, that the situation arose as some form of needful emotional release – part of her "crucifixion" and the final yielding up of the self. The next few pages are full of her anxiety for Bhai Sahib, her implorations that he should continue to live and complete her training, her desire for surrender and her feeling of merging into his identity . . . then came more states of agonized longing and an acceleration of awareness of inner separation (an interior exclusion from the Master, or Source), creating within the participant a distress that bordered on extremity . . . and ultimately, in the oscillating nature of her experience, came bliss, the fullness of love, and the blessing of peace.

In the midst of this recurs continually her *leitmotif* of worry and fear for her future. If Bhai Sahib died, how would she live with her assets gone – with no home and no money? How would she complete her training and attain to Truth without him? Fortunately for Tweedie, her wish was granted. He did not die, and when he recovered sufficiently to speak, he asked after her (pp. 290–303).

The above situation occurred in early September, 1962, and Bhai Sahib's illness was at its most serious for almost a fortnight. Upon his eventual recovery, he made plain to Tweedie that he did not wish to speak to her nor to remain alone in her company, and this circumstance persisted until the end of October, when he suddenly communicated to her that his life had been spared in order to complete her training – to prepare her for her future work (p. 314).

Tweedie was intensely happy, and records the many states of bliss and peace she now experienced, and the "boundless love." Yet inexplicably, intermixed with these states were others that worried her, and which she mentioned to Bhai Sahib on November 9th. In these states everything seemed disagreeable, "even horrible." People appeared ugly and she literally hated them. When in this mood, her own condition became "barren and arid" and left her depressed (p. 324). The Guru assured her this would pass, that he too, had once hated everyone at the time he was with his own Guru. He explained the state as elementary, one that occurs when the heart is first focused upon the Teacher, and anything else becomes an intrusion. [I would stress that this was not my own experience, nor that of others known to me.]

On November 10th, without any forewarning, Bhai Sahib told Tweedie he was quickening the process of preparation – and that to facilitate this she must go back to England for "two or three years" and commence her work during his lifetime. She could then return to him for a while . . .

Tweedie was thunderstruck, her mind all but paralysed. She asked what she must do, and was reminded that she had formerly worked for the Theosophical Society. She could do this again – "lecturing, other work, whatever comes your way."

According to Tweedie, Bhai Sahib lived almost continually in *samadhi*, an inverted condition of consciousness in which he was unreachable by the world, and from which he permeated his ashramic environment with the qualities of his state. He entered *samadhi* now, when Tweedie tried to speak, and all queries had to be left for the following morning.

Her attitudes then were considered inappropriate, indeed very improper. In addition to the qualities of faithfulness and obedience, the Guru stressed the importance of respect to the Master, an area in which Tweedie had all too frequently fallen down heavily, as he made clear. Working on her own in England she would have to control herself, something she was unable to do when with Bhai Sahib, as she had demonstrated. She asked with trepidation when she must go. The reply was springtime, in March or April.

Having previously accepted that she would spend the rest of

201

her life in India, Tweedie was hurled into shock and despair. The thought of England minus her money, homeless and insecure, assailed her with horror. She wept bitterly. The Guru took pity on her, and with kindness made many explanations and alleviated her fear. Afterwards, as she records, she felt the first stirring of the brow *chakra* and a state of bliss and non-being, which she duly reported to Bhai Sahib. This, she felt, was an early phase of *Nirvana* – a "blissful dissolution," the closest she could yet attain to, which her Guru confirmed (pp. 332–333). Yet the worries persisted, depriving Tweedie of sleep. She described them as "terrible, slowly nagging and nagging, biting deeper and deeper."

Tweedie spoke to Bhai Sahib of the work that was required of her (she makes clear in several places that she had no knowledge of Sufism, nor of Bhai Sahib's "System") and learned that apart from lecturing and the writing of a book, people would "come and sit" with her. She realized then that she would act as a teacher in the Eastern tradition – would assist aspiring pupils with meditation and other practices. She told Bhai Sahib she had the suspicion that she had once chosen power, rather than love, and feared she might do so again. She had also noted her feeling of pride when she was singled out for special treatment, however harsh. Bhai Sahib made light of this and gave her much information and instruction. [It is noteworthy that all of this was given verbally. Her understanding of her work did not derive from interior knowledge or personal insight.] She had already produced symbolic dreams, most of them interpreted by the Guru. One dream he deciphered at this juncture was particularly significant. He said that it meant Tweedie would soon realize Absolute Truth, the ultimate achievement.

The blissful states continued, still interspersed with something quite other. The self or the mind, as Tweedie tells us; one or *both* apparently in rebellion. Lying in bed one night in late November, torn by fear and worry regarding her pending situation, her mind proceeded to attack the Guru viciously. The episode concluded with Tweedie cursing him repeatedly, and likewise "everything and everybody" within the entire Universe. She concluded by this that her mind feared annihilation and was putting up a desperate fight. There is no mention at all of attempting to control the extremity of her responses.

These dichotomies between spiritual experience and the self

202

running rampant did not stop here. More are recounted, the first a few nights later when she again attacked the Guru, this time because she felt he was not teaching her anything (p. 354). Some pages on she speaks of the hatred within her which does not abate; this, a few paragraphs from her expressed certitude that she will shortly experience God-realization (pp. 370–371). On 20th December Tweedie notes that the hatred "was much increased – a dark, killing hated" (p. 374), largely against those who consistently occupied Bhai Sahib's time to her own exclusion. For once, Bhai Sahib rebuked her and said that love could not exist in company with such thoughts. He further rebuked her for her continual focus upon money.

The hatred nevertheless continued to escalate – there was pain in her heart and "longing and longing" so terrible she cried non-stop – and "dark, deep" hatred against absolutely everybody. So acute was her experience on both spiritual and physical levels, that she thought she would die of it (p. 463). Full of misery and resentment, one evening in mid-March she happened to glimpse a mouse in her semi-dark room. Seized with sudden, uncontrollable rage, she chased it mercilessly with a broom, her hatred entirely fixated on the unfortunate creature. Beside herself now, she hit at it until it fell, and beat it furiously to death, hammering at it till nothing was left save a bloody pulp upon the floor.

Shocked by her own behaviour, she realized that with such an intensity of rage she could easily have killed a human being. When told of this incident, Bhai Sahib attributed Tweedie's action to "certain powers" in the human being which "bring out all the evils." He said it was not a bad thing – meaning, as Tweedie explains, that these propensities need to be released in some form or another. In reference to the hatred, she was advised that it was caused by pride; that she thought herself superior to those concerned, and hated them (pp. 464–466).

This all seems rather strange in view of Tweedie's imminent debut as a teacher, moreover a teacher who must, theoretically at least, take full responsibility for those who came to her, and whom she would train in the manner of an Eastern Guru.

On April 29th 1963, Irina Tweedie said good-bye to her teacher and began her journey back to England. It was a disastrous farewell. The Guru was downright rude to her. She had that morning spoken severely to his adult son, and women in India are considered inferior and may not rebuke such lordly beings, especially in front of other people. Bhai Sahib's last (shouted) words to her were "Go! I don't want to see your ugly face again! Go away!" She eventually remembered how he had once told her that he would endeavour to turn her against him, as part of a test, and several weeks later when in England she therefore wrote him the first of many letters. The *first* one was recriminative and reproachful, then she settled down to simply writing of her life and work.

Tweedie gives very few details of her time spent in London, which lasted for just over two and a half years. For several weeks she stayed with a friend, then found herself a first-floor flatlet (a small room, really, with basic services) at the junction of Ladbroke Grove and Holland Park. No other information is given, save that during this period she met a woman referred to as H., in whom she became interested, and who became her first pupil. [There were a number of them, but these are not mentioned until later (p. 721 and elsewhere in *Daughter of Fire*).] This woman was given a "definite" training, presumably similar to her own training, involving *asanas*, meditation, *zikrs*, *japa*, a few breathing exercises – and within four months H. was experiencing the state of *dhyana* by Tweedie's instrumentation and the "Grace" of Bhai Sahib. At the latter's request, H. was taken to meet him by Tweedie on her return to India in the December of 1965. There H. stayed for six weeks, but Tweedie resumed her former Indian lifestyle for a further seven months, until the death of her Guru, for Bhai Sahib died the following July. These seven months are covered by diary entries and make interesting reading.

For a start, we learn that H. had visited Tweedie daily at her London flatlet from 4 pm until 9 or 10 pm (p. 522), so her training must have been quite intensive. Tweedie, when discussing her pupil with Bhai Sahib, makes mention in particular of meditation. [The fact that H., as a consequence of prolonged meditation, was enabled to experience the introverted state of *dhyana* (defined on page 205 in *The Chasm of Fire* as "contemplation followed by complete abstraction of all outward impressions") does not automatically signify that Tweedie herself essentially understood the process, or what was entailed. She earlier makes plain that she had not at that time experienced it personally. In Part 1 of *Daughter of Fire* she mentions to Bhai Sahib that L. (Lilian Silburn), a French woman and his long-term disciple who also took pupils of her own, induced in them the same dhyanic condition. L. once told Tweedie that she had no idea what she (L.) was doing – "it just happens" (p. 500). The Guru's response was that if he gave the order, this could be done by anyone; the implication being that like *shaktipat* in Hindu gurus, some form of subtle energy was transmitted via his agency, and those trained to "merge" in him were conduits for that energy, and not necessarily conscious of what was operative through them. It is perhaps relevant to note that L. had practised Hatha Yoga before approaching Bhai Sahib and was known to have activated the force of *kundalini*, though whether before or after contact with the Guru is not on record.]

Yantras are again mentioned, and soon after their arrival, H. and Tweedie watched Bhai Sahib prepare a number of these for a family with smallpox. Tweedie observed that inscriptions were made on the *yantras* in Persian. Bhai Sahib told her that he was thinking of teaching her this skill for use with her students, for its effects were certain and "death cannot come near," whatever the disease, if one used the right *yantra*. Tweedie suggested she should learn the symbols by heart, as she did not know Persian, and it would be "a great service to humanity" to have the power of the *yantra*. Much more is disclosed on this subject by Bhai Sahib, but whether Tweedie was actually given this ability we are not told (pp. 511–512). [*Yantras* are an ingredient of Tantric magic, and have no discernible connection with Sufism, at least of the traditional kind.]

There is also the story of a young woman named Dolly, who was ten weeks pregnant and wanted a male child, requesting this boon of the Guru. After some preliminaries Bhai Sahib called Dolly into a private room, where his wife was seated, and Tweedie was thus unable to see what went on, much as she wished to do so. Dolly obligingly informed her afterwards that the Guru placed his personal towel over her navel and made some symbolic gestures above her recumbent body. He then told Dolly the child would be a boy. To Tweedie he reported that faith was necessary for this operation – if Dolly had no faith, the child would be female, but if her faith was strong (and he was sure that it was), her wish would be granted. He stressed that no charges should ever be made for these services, including the supplying of *yantras* (pp. 646–647).

Bhai Sahib provided Tweedie with much verbal information during her second phase of training, and she experienced states of happiness and bliss. The severity of former bodily sufferings had lessened considerably, and apart from occasional tremblings, and some infrequent heart activity, her greatest anxiety was the state of her Guru's health. Yet this did not preclude periods of boredom, or bouts of weeping and exhaustion, for reasons she could not always discern. The male disciples were, as before, a source of annoyance and distress to her, and the noise and smells of the more extrovert who regularly took time and attention from herself caused in her once more the familiar pangs of isolation. When Bhai Sahib on occasion resumed his former attitudes of indifference or left her excluded from what went on, she reproduced earlier syndromes. To her dismay, her mind again became resentful, and at these times she perceived her teacher as "evil," and the ashram as "a place of torture" (p. 560).

The foregoing concluded abruptly in mid-February 1966 when Bhai Sahib had a heart attack. She was left with an intensity of longing and a deep fear and desperation – that her Guru would die before her training was complete. So strong was this fear that in the night she cried out aloud repeatedly, and "such was the agony" that she "howled like a wounded dog" until she reduced herself to exhaustion, and fell asleep (p. 563).

Her problems now steadily increased. It soon became evident that far from surmounting past traits, there was still an abundance of anger and hatred within her, and that her mind, undisciplined as ever, remained charged with restlessness and confusion. To ease this latter, Bhai Sahib, when recovered, gave her the *zikr* practice of *La ilaha illa 'llah* ("There is no god, but God") to utter silently throughout her waking hours, whatever she might be doing (p. 566).

He advised her to make stronger efforts to control her mind, and warned her that her attitude towards him in a worldly sense was frequently intolerable. He also told her that although love and faith had been created in her (hence the heart experience), she had still not surrendered "physically and mentally," and that others would notice this; they would *feel* that her surrender was not total. Love was given by the guru, but control of the mind was the task of the disciple. She had yet to learn to curb it (p. 587).

Tweedie records her efforts in this direction, and her early belief that control was achieved. This was briefly upended by recurring situations which brought memories of past sufferings to the fore, and doubt and resentment rose with them (p. 602). But on page 622 she declares to Bhai Sahib that she thought she had now reached the last stages of her "Crucifixion," and the Guru appears to agree with this. Indeed, on several occasions he made clear to Tweedie that he was training her to succeed him – that she alone would be his successor in the lineage of Sufism he represented, i.e., the "Golden Sufis" of the purportedly Naqshband-iyya *silsila*.

This seems quite incredible, as Tweedie in fact knew nothing of Sufism, and says so more than once in her text. However, she thought she recognized similarities between Bhai Sahib's *modus operandi* with herself and the psychological theories of C. G. Jung (whose work she had read in London), and it was Jungian dreamwork she later utilized in her groups, and which, along with meditation, constituted the main body of her activity. [This must have bred confusion in the minds of her more serious students, for Jungian theories and authentic Sufi psychological methodology have only superficial likenesses and are fundamentally incompatible, despite attempts to amalgamate the two by some psychologists and self-professed "Sufis."]

At the end of her time with Bhai Sahib – on June 22nd, just one month before his death, Tweedie comments further on her hatred, still strongly manifest, and which she describes as representing "a great obstacle." On June 23rd she speaks to Bhai Sahib of the terrible longing for she knows not what, so intense it creates perpetual pain in her body, and causes her to cry almost ceaselessly in hopelessness and despair. She then refers to her state as pathological, and details her fear of the condition of "non-being" and the frightening sense of unreality which the Guru induced when in his presence. She tells him of her panic and confusion, and asks if the state of non-being is surrender? (pp. 709–711).

On July 1st Bhai Sahib once more reproached Tweedie for her "bad behaviour" and her lack of respect for him as a teacher. Surprisingly, instead of accepting the fact of her own faulty attitudes, Tweedie regarded this (as she had all similar rebukes) as a form of testing, an increase of pressure upon her designed to assess the extent of any residual hostility. It was perhaps this obdurate "blindness" in response to a reprimand intended as remedial, that caused Bhai Sahib when approached by Tweedie the next morning, to attack her verbally with much anger. He said emphatically that he did not wish to listen; that her mind was full of impurities, and that she would "NEVER, NEVER, NEVER" progress. To do what was necessary would take her years – the task of training her was quite beyond him. On the 6th he repeated firmly: "You will not progress," and this is the sum total of that day's entry.

Concurrent with the negative states that almost continually overwhelmed her, were states of deep happiness and peace, and yet others of mindlessness and unreality. On June 27th, for instance, Tweedie records that for three days her mind was a blank; she had no memory at all of events for that period.

This type of disorientation and the misconceptions that go with it have no place in traditional accounts of the heart experience, where insights are profound and the aspirant fully conversant with the inner realities of the situation. It is anomalies such as the above which evoke queries regarding the readiness of the pupil, in this case, Irina Tweedie, and the extent of the knowledge of the Guru who precipitated her into states for which she was clearly inadequately prepared.

Tweedie's lack of comprehension of certain vital issues is evident throughout her book, and nowhere more obviously than on the matter of surrender. On page 379 she expounds on "the inner realization of absolute oneness," and her belief that advanced processes of Sufi training are designed to prevent inflation of the ego when this ultimate stage (of surrender) is reached. This is nonsensical, for in authentic Sufism the ego is dealt with long before these processes commence. Tweedie also equates the tactics of the modern psychiatrist with the training of disciples, and thus betrays her total ignorance of the developmental processes in which she was so soon to be deemed proficient.

Bhai Sahib stressed that his work on Tweedie was a process of "infusion." This comes across very clearly in the text. His yogic power was daily and nightly infused into her system, and it was this that forced into wakefulness the latent energy of *kundalini*, prising open the *chakras* one by one (initially the heart *chakra*, we are told) and thereby invoking the incipient impetus of the heart experience. This yogic process automatically released the latent karmic impressions lodged in the lower *chakras*, and brought into play the syndromes that proved such an ordeal for the recipient, and which eventually pushed her to the brink of premeditated suicide (pp. 398–399).

The sheer volume of these impressions confirms the suspicion that Tweedie was activated prematurely. Her earlier life exhibited no indication of her future role as a guru, and until the death of her second husband was one entirely of frivolity. She was, as she says herself, a "worldly woman with no interests other than dresses . . . parties, excursions . . ." As an example, she used the three years she and her banker husband lived in an "elegant" hotel in Switzerland, addicted to social life, gourmet food and expensive restaurants – indeed, every kind of worldly enjoyment. Again, in her own words, she describes herself firmly as "intensely selfish, intensely greedy for life" (p. 554). And yet, after five years of contact with the scandal-ridden Theosophical Society, and little or no experience of even a psychic nature, far less mystical – Bhai Sahib told her that he would make her a *Wali*, a Sufi Saint, and provided her with nineteen months of intensive yogic training – at the end of which she was judged competent to train students of her own.

That Bhai Sahib was a versatile and powerful Yogi is beyond denial. He had various capacities but lightly touched upon in Tweedie's book. One of these was his practise of *"Ghat pranayam"* (*Ghatavastha*: the second stage of *pranayama* discussed in the *Siva Samhita*, a classical text book on Hatha yoga) described by Tweedie as "inward breathing," in which he was able to cease breathing at will for several hours, while his heart continued to beat as usual (p. 652). He asserted to Tweedie that Sufi Saints and Masters are like *dhobies* (washerwomen) – sweepers of the heart, who take into their (subtle) bodies the impurities of others (mainly of course disciples) which very often causes them illness, a capacity he inferred she in due time would inherit (p. 588 and elsewhere in *Daughter of Fire*).

Tweedie must certainly have realized how far she was from these possibilities, even assuming, as she believed (and as Bhai

209

Sahib confirmed) that she had been with him before, in a former incarnation. If this was so, whatever their connection, it had not extended to the nullification of past *karma*, or the "ancient evils" that bedevilled her would not have been there in such strength, indeed, would not have been there at all. She was nevertheless prepared to believe in her own potential, both as a *Wali* and a Sufi instructor – immediate and imminent as was the latter role – without any proof save obscure symbolic dreams and the intermittent assurance of her frequently peeved Guru.

Whatever the situation, the fact remains that Irina Tweedie, although instructed to teach, was left without *gnosis*, and throughout the two and a half decades of her activities was at all times obliged to meditate and request of the now-deceased Bhai Sahib what she should do at every turn. This may be sound discipleship but is wholly insufficient for an instructor. (An authentic mandate is not bestowed verbally; such a mandate is made operative in a higher dimension of consciousness and functions independently of yogic power and the use of techniques). A teacher without mandate is a danger to all students – bearing in mind that Tweedie acted the part of an Eastern Guru and distributed *mantras*, meditations, breathing practices and *asanas*, all exercises that evoke pronounced changes in the mindstream and the psyche.

The central core of *Daughter of Fire* is the little-known heart experience – that agonized phase of evolutionary development which precedes the first stage of mystical Union of the soul with its Source. This implies the prior completion of the necessary work on the human entity that is the vehicle of the soul. There is still more to accomplish beyond the culmination of this experience – a long way yet to go experientially, but without such prior completion, the evolutionary process is unfulfilled, and nothing further can be achieved until this is rectified.

Bhai Sahib himself said he used a "short cut" with Irina Tweedie, a much faster route to achieve the end result he envisaged. It is thus reasonable to conclude that the heart experience was induced by the use of yogic power, and in advance of the customary "hammering" (shaping) of the ego that normally follows a specific, and preparatory, type of intermediary development. Therefore, the stage by stage sequential growth upon which the maturation of certain qualities is dependent, and which are essential for the safe and intelligible reception of higher ranges of spiritual knowledge and experience, was by-passed entirely. This poses a serious question about Bhai Sahib.

The activations that were the result of the shortcut – the premature evocation of *kundalini* and the subsequent opening of the *chakras* – were consequently *too overt* (as Tweedie describes) – the trials too body-oriented. Physiological symptoms such as violent palpitations, heart pain, throat constriction, headache, giddiness, and a sense of almost pathological unreality, are not normally concomitant with *chakra* awakening. They certainly formed no part of my own experience, nor that of others known to me. Moreover, physical discomfort, heat, smells, noise, dirt, vomiting, are all incidental to the heart experience, which is entirely an interior phenomenon not in need of this form of accentuation.

Tweedie's book presents an enigma, for although it describes a "heart" episode of the most acute kind, it also describes an additional syndrome not found in any traditional material, nor in other contemporary accounts. I refer here to the extremity of fear and resentment, even hatred, of the teacher, which existed in juxtaposition to a similarly intense love. There is also the matter of the violent rage and black depression experienced by Tweedie. Along with disrespect and lack of reverence, these uncontrolled expressions have no place in such records.

A properly prepared aspirant traversing the "vale of the heart" is grievously aware of every blemish upon the soul, notwithstanding that these are rarefied blemishes, the last wisps of human origin that cling to the soul's substance. So fragile is their nature, they pass unperceived and unrecognized by the unawakened, and are far, far removed from the concretized accretions of gross hatred, violence, and lust.

Tweedie left no further writings, and did not enlarge upon her own later activities, at least in print. In her Foreword to *Daughter of Fire*, she tells us that the first draft of her manuscript was begun in September 1971, nearly ten years following her meeting with her teacher, and records that she could not bring herself to as much as reread the day to day entries before this date. So much suffering was involved that the mere thought of work on the diary filled her with panic. The text that eventually comprised her book must therefore have been rounded-out from memory, and the words in bold script ascribed to Bhai Sahib (which were certainly not verbatim, covering, as they do, entire conversations) may thus not always have been identical with his intention. In a much later taped interview with former feature writer on Indian spirituality, the American journalist Surya Green (referred to below), Tweedie acknowledged that because of her struggle "to find the right words," the aid of a dear friend (Jennine Miller) had to be enlisted to assist her editorially.

More specific information on the latter part of Tweedie's life is left to the discretion of her students, and Llewellyn Vaughan-Lee (her appointed successor) in his own autobiography inevitably has something to say of her as his teacher. Another person to mention Tweedie is her former student Sara Sviri, the scholarly author of *The Taste of Hidden Things: Images on the Sufi Path* (1997).

Sviri records that when Tweedie returned from India to London, and was wondering how to fulfil the task given her by Bhai Sahib, she discovered a book (which became her inspiration) about the 13th century Sufi mystic Jalaluddin Rumi (1207–1273). Sviri recounts the story of Tweedie's dilemma:

" 'What shall I do when I go back to the West?' she had asked him.

'Lecture,' Bhai Sahib answered.

'But on what shall I lecture?' she insisted.

'On Sufism.'

'How will I be able to do this? You have taught me nothing on Sufism; I don't know much about it,' Mrs Tweedie tried to argue.

'You'll find out.' " (p. 191).

What Tweedie had found (in the round reading room of the British Library) was a published dissertation, *The Metaphysics of Rumi*, written by Khalifa Abdul Hakim, a Pakistani scholar, on Rumi's "theory of evolution and spiritual transformation." Reading it, says Sviri, was to Tweedie like a revelation. The book in fact "confirmed to her the validity of her own experiences and destiny from the vantage point of the larger Sufi tradition." She felt she was "part of a chain (*silsila*) which had proceeded from time immemorial . . . [and] is transmitted from teacher to disciple" (*The Taste of Hidden Things*, pp. 191–192). A further source

212

is Surya Green's *Call of the Sun,* in which Green utilizes a whole chapter to incorporate a taped interview with Tweedie in December 1992.

It was an extraordinary act on Tweedie's part to permit publication of this interview, as the principal subject matter of *Call of the Sun* is Green's pupil-cum-personal relationship with the well-advertised and adulated Indian guru, HH Swami Purna (claimed by Green to be "Maitreya" of *Share International* magazine, the messianic publishing organ of the Benjamin Creme organization) – a charismatic yogi with the alleged ability, according to Green, to dematerialize his physical body and rematerialize it at will, whom she determinedly promotes as the much-prophesied World Teacher, or new Christ. (It is perhaps noteworthy that Green speaks of Swami Purna as a handsome "Prince Charming," and refers to the "instantaneous" mutual attraction between them when they met. See *Call of the Sun,* p. 114). The Swami also allegedly holds the status of current "Head of the immortal Himalayan Masters," a factor uncontested by Tweedie, along with the imputation by Green that, among others, Green and herself were members of his spiritual hierarchy. It is perhaps revealing that Surya Green received permission from Tweedie to write the latter's full biography (still pending at the time of writing).

[An example of Swami Purna's teaching (in this instance on the subject of *tantra yoga*) from a talk given in Amsterdam, is as follows: "The highest pleasures of spiritually transformed sex in tantra can be compared to the pleasure of the immortal soul" *(Call of the Sun,* p. 130). We thus can realistically conjecture what the new "Christ" is likely to promote.]

Green describes the events that led up to the interview, and notes that, despite Tweedie's receipt of "orders" from Bhai Sahib in meditation to retreat from the world and prepare for her death (she spent much of her time in meditation), she was persuaded by Green to agree to her visit – a circumstance which Green was convinced was connected with the hierarchical workings of Swami Purna, whom she promptly informed of the pending event. He also appears to have known of the meeting that came afterwards, on the following day, on which occasion Green announced "intuitively" to Irina Tweedie that she (Green), too, belonged to the Himalayan Hierarchy (Tweedie had already acknowledged her own place in the scheme of things). With a "Madam Blavatskyian sense of mission," Green added, "And we are here to do a work."

" 'Of course' responded Tweedie.

'And that is why I am brought before you.'

'That is very obvious,' said Tweedie . . . 'That is why I have time for you!' " (p. 319).

[It should perhaps be mentioned here that Bhai Sahib (in meditation) had purportedly instructed Irina Tweedie to appoint Llwellyn Vaughan-Lee as her successor and to direct him, and also most of her former students, to emigrate to America, where Vaughan-Lee would take over leadership of the so-called "Golden Sufis." Tweedie had therefore at this period withdrawn completely from all forms of groupwork.]

When asked by Green about additional points that should be included in "their" book (Tweedie's biography), the latter revealingly replied: "I act according to the moment . . . never premeditated. Just instantaneously, in response to the moment. That is Yoga." And when Green concluded the second interview, prior to arranging their next taped meeting some weeks later, such was the rapport between the two women that it seemed "perfectly natural" to Green to tell Tweedie that she loved her.

"I, too," Tweedie said warmly, and added the proviso: "but I must say, not on the human level. I can love only through the Beloved."

In this exalted atmosphere, it is less surprising to read a little further on that Bhai Sahib was "present" at one point in the conversation, as Tweedie imparted. This belief evoked Green's certitude that her proposed biography of Irina Tweedie was by divine intent, and that a Naqshbandi Sufi (Bhai Sahib) and his personally appointed successor had consolidated the validity of Swami Purna's hierarchical claims, and also her own (pp. 318–320).

The content of the interview makes evident that Tweedie did not "move on" through the years, but remained fixed in the psychological mould formed within her during her time with Bhai Sahib.

Green states in her book that Irina Tweedie "was the first Western woman trained within the ancient yogic lineage of Naqshbandi Sufism," a statement clearly approved by Irina Tweedie, who provided a mutually glowing testimony for Green's "mystical" experiences and work in the introductory paragraphs of *Call of the Sun*. It reads as follows: *"Surya Green's mystical experiences are the real stuff of the soul, and she has the power to express them in words. It is wonderful she has written this book. Whatever can increase faith in the world is precious, a gift of God. Her book will serve a lot of people."*

In view of the type and nature of Green's experiences (which include the inadvertant activation of *kundalini* as a result of overmuch unprescribed meditation and other disciplines), together with Tweedie's acknowledged role as a Naqshbandi Sufi, this makes perplexing reading to those nominal students studying Sufism as a whole. The findings of scholarship would strongly indicate that there was no "ancient yogic lineage" in the rather orthodox Naqshbandi order, and that any yogic feature was a late innovation of Indian locales.

Equally perplexing for students of genuine metaphysical studies is the information given in an annotated article written by Irina Tweedie's pupil, Sara Sviri, and entitled: *"Daughter of Fire* by Irina Tweedie: Documentation and experiences of a modern Naqshbandi Sufi" in E. Puttick and P. B. Clarke, eds., *Women as Teachers and Disciples in Traditional and New Religions*, 1993. The author accepts without question the belief that Tweedie was the appointed successor of a Sufi Master, and makes the following statement: "Bhai Sahib was a Hindu but received his *adhikara* (the authority to carry on the teaching; in Arabic: *ijaza*) from a Muslim teacher, and transmitted the *adhikara* to Irina Tweedie, an Orthodox Christian by birth. This statement implies an extension of the boundaries of Sufism" (pp. 77–89).

The article also implies that Irina Tweedie was herself a Sufi Master, and *ipso facto*, that her personally appointed successor, Llewellyn Vaughan-Lee, is likewise. In view of the total data, one may strongly doubt such implications.

To discern the validity of the currently ongoing system that stems directly from Bhai Sahib, who allegedly continues to function behind the scenes via directives received in meditation by his personal successors, it is necessary to turn to Llewellyn Vaughan-Lee (b. 1953), whose credentials for his high calling are worthy of consideration.

[It is *because* of Vaughan-Lee's claims to operate within the highest echelons of Sufism that I have given so much time and

215

attention to his books and his work. The Center he founded (The Golden Sufi Center, California) is "dedicated to making the teachings of the Naqshbandi Sufi Path available to all seekers," and is advertised in this manner in the latter pages of all his publications.]

Vaughan-Lee himself is happy to be known as a Naqshbandi Sufi, and is no doubt accepted as such by fellow contemporary Sufis like Pir Vilayat Inayat Khan (a "Chishti" Sufi), and the Californian-based International Association for Sufism, under whose aegis, according to Professor Carl W. Ernst, "dozens of Sufi groups of different origins gather for talks and *dhikr* performances" (*Shambhala Guide to Sufism*, 1997, p. 224) – events that ignore totally the Sufi requirement of *zaman, makan, ikhwan* (right time, right place, right people), and therefore "performance" is a very apt description for these activities. The word "Sufi" is currently devalued, and is sadly no longer of use as a yardstick of proficiency.

The extent of Vaughan-Lee's training, and what he disseminates as a consequence in the form of verbal tuition and methods of preparation towards higher ranges of spiritual growth, are contained in his autobiography. These details are of paramount importance to those who approach him as potential students, and who place their trust in a purportedly responsible lineage, i.e., the Naqshbandiyya. [Claims deriving sanction from venerable Orders are always suspect. Many things have been written about traditional Naqshbandis, some of whom were intolerant of anything other than Islam.] According to Louis Palmer, who during his travels in Afghanistan met many Sufis: "The Naqshbandis were dissolved by the Sufi leaders in the nineteenth century, but some imitators linger here and there" (L. Palmer, *Adventures in Afghanistan*, 1990, p. 142).

Many potential students of Sufism, particularly the youthful and enthusiastic stream within every university, will make the assumption that all present-day self-styled "Naqshbandi Sufis" are of the same authenticity as legendary patriarchs. Some may even believe that all "Sufis" are equally legitimate and equally knowledgeable. They are unlikely to be aware that even within traditional Sufi orders (of which there are a number of variations) the biased teachings of certain historically known Sheikhs (including those of the Naqshbandiyya) and their followers are

216

as sickening and as distorted as the doctrines perpetuated by many modern pseudo-spiritual organizations.

Vaughan-Lee's "spiritual journey" began when he was sixteen. Three years later he met Irina Tweedie, whom he accepted at once as his spiritual teacher. To quote from the cover of *The Face Before I Was Born: A Spiritual Autobiography* (1998): "The events that follow over the next twenty-two years tell of tremendous love, psychological breakdown, craziness, bliss, and the slow work of balancing the two worlds – the inner world of the spirit and the outer demands of everyday family life. This autobiography tells the ancient story of a spiritual transformation, one that took him into the terrifying depths and pushed him beyond every limit." Further down we learn that Llewellyn Vaughan-Lee, PhD, "writes and lectures about Sufism, dreamwork, and Jungian psychology." The book is published by The Golden Sufi Center, founded several years earlier by Vaughan-Lee himself on the verbal instruction of Irina Tweedie, thus the cover material was fully approved by the author (and may well even have been written by him).

Before commenting on Vaughan-Lee's autobiography, some space should be given to his earlier works, the first of which was published in 1990. These are, namely: *The Bond with the Beloved: The Mystical Relationship of the Lover and the Beloved*; *In the Company of Friends: Dreamwork within a Sufi Group*; *Travelling the Path of Love: Sayings of the Masters; Sufism: The Transformation of the Heart*; and *The Paradoxes of Love*, all of which are published by the Golden Sufi Center. These books are well-written and mystically oriented. Within their pages (according to the cover material) the author explores, among other subjects, "dreamwork," "psychological and spiritual processes" in spiritual groupings, and the "relationship between the Lover and the Beloved."

In the context of the latter, Vaughan-Lee details "the stages of this relationship as it unfolds in the heart of the seeker, from the pain of separation to the bliss of Union." He further explains "the tremendous importance of this mystical relationship not only to the lover but to the world," and suggests that by this means higher consciousness is brought into everyday life, and helps the world remember its origins.

All of this of course is true. What is less certain is the efficacy of his recommendations for unprepared individuals, i.e., his students, and his readership in general, and even upon himself. I refer in particular to the extensive use of silent *zikr* and meditation, and to the assumptions that the states of silence and emptiness, or nothingness, in the context in which they are described, and which he has personally experienced, are the actual achievements he considers them to be.

That these states are genuine is not questioned. They mark certain phases of the inner path. But darkness and emptiness is not the end of the journey, nor is Union with Silence and utter nothingness. To infer that they are is frightening and offputting to most seekers and aspirants, and incomprehensible to a wider audience.

A serious consideration is that Vaughan-Lee interprets developmental metaphysics through the media of Jungian theory, on which he lectures in various countries at great length, and which creates disastrous misconceptions. For instance, his books are filled with concepts of the "wounded feminine," "masculine and feminine aspects of the Self," the "collective shadow," the "anima and animus," "archetypal images," etc., all of which are construed according to Jung. This is hardly in keeping with Naqshbandi Sufism, and fails to hit the mark again and again in his delineation and analysis of spiritual growth.

What is queried here in the light of his formulations, is Vaughan-Lee's qualification to arrogate to himself the position of Sufi instructor, and to take into his charge in the name of Sufism the hundreds of students that make their way to the Golden Sufi Center and who throng his summer camps in the search for spiritual growth and understanding.

The Face Before I Was Born provides revealing and problematic documentation. The author tells us it was written from memory. Unlike Irina Tweedie he did not keep diary notes, and merely recorded "a few important dreams and visions" over the years. He therefore relies upon the "intensity" of spiritual experience for accurate recollection of surrounding life events, and notes the fact that many experiences "need time to reveal their real significance, to bring into consciousness the depth of their meaning" (p. xiii). This indicates that his reconstruction may be coloured by the assumed outcome of these experiences, and that the reality was not always as positive as he would like to think.

The reason for attempting the autobiography at all was due to the directive of Irina Tweedie, who told Vaughan-Lee in the summer of 1995 that he should "write and lecture more" about his personal spiritual experiences. The book is therefore the "direct result" of her instructions. Until that time, he tells us, he was reluctant to speak of these matters "fearing that the ego might get hold of them." By 1995 (the year of the directive) Vaughan-Lee was already the appointed successor, already running a "Sufi" Centre and training students. Such a statement therefore seems inappropriate.

The child of middle-class English parents, Vaughan-Lee was sent at an early age to Eton College as a boarder and was educated there until he was seventeen. In the background of his life loomed his mother, described by him as an alcoholic and a depressive, an unhappy combination which ultimately wrecked her marriage and undoubtedly affected her children (there were six) very adversely. The full extent of the family "shadow" did not communicate itself to Vaughan-Lee until his mid to late teens, during which time he entered into a relationship with a young artist named Beba, and lived with her under his mother's roof. Very little is said of Beba, and nothing at all of the nature of the relationship.

At the early age of sixteen, and just before leaving school, Vaughan-Lee discovered Zen meditation (*zazen*) and savoured for the first time in his present life the "deep peace of an empty mind" (p. 8). Continued use of the technique rapidly produced inner experiences which the meditator found "deeply satisfying." A year or so later he was introduced by friends to a macrobiotic diet (which he maintained for many years) and he also commenced the practice of Hatha Yoga. This led to the discipline of fasting and subsequent bodily weakness through lack of sufficient nourishment. In addition to this, Vaughan-Lee soon realized his self-imposed practises had inadvertantly awakened the energy of *kundalini*, an ongoing process that was to cause him problems over a period of years.

The effect of these amalgamated and unbalanced disciplines was an "energy build-up" which fuelled acute feelings of nervousness, along with "a neurosis about food and continual stomach problems that were both physical and psychological" (pp. 10–14).

Despite the above, Vaughan-Lee continued with his Hatha Yoga although he had already learned by experience that *asanas* and breathing exercises increased the physiological effects of *kundalini*. A brief contact with the nihilistic former Theosophist, Krishnamurti, at the latter's annual summer school, further increased his difficulties, for Krishnamurti, apart from denying the existence of a spiritual Path, or the need of a teacher, said "realization could happen" – and that to attain to such a state one must go beyond ideas and concepts and likewise beyond all "doing."

Vaughan-Lee thus attempted to put these directives into practice, and when spending a two week holiday on his own the following spring in his father's country residence, he sat for hours at a time, letting his mind become empty, or staring at a wall while watching his thoughts come and go. Not very surprisingly, he became both physically and emotionally yet more highly sensitized, and when people came to visit him, he "could not cope with their presence" and locked himself in the bathroom.

Further (major) problems confronted Vaughan-Lee in his life with his mother. Her acute alcoholism and depression created a "psychic darkness" and "treacherous, twisted chaos" impossible to live with, the net result being that he and Beba ceased to speak to her, and departed from the maternal home while the owner was away on holiday.

Vaughan-Lee now commenced to seek a meditation method other than Zen, as this had ceased to serve his need. He also consciously sought a spiritual teacher and tried several avenues with this in mind, without success. He felt isolated and resentful of life, his nervous system overstrung with his continued macrobiotic diet and the negative effects of various "spiritual" disciplines. In the midst of this psychic upheaval, Irina Tweedie entered his life, and Vaughan-Lee found what he was seeking, or so he assumed.

He was nineteen at the time, and "very arrogant" and proud of his "spiritual learning." He says that he had read many books and "practiced yoga." Yet on meeting Tweedie, all this "crashed to the floor" and he knew himself as nothing, and nowhere.

He felt overwhelmed, "not by love or devotion, but by the power of annihilation, the destruction of the ego" (p. 27). Restrospectively, he was convinced that he had been thrown into *fana* (the state of annihilation), and had become "dust on the floor" at the feet of his teacher.

Yet, as he makes clear, he did not know that Tweedie was a Sufi at the time he was introduced to her. He knew only that his earlier meeting with the two artist friends who introduced him had precipitated an "explosion" of *kundalini* in his back, and that the meeting with Tweedie generated an immediate experience which he (much later) related to the Sufi state of *fana*. These incidents (in retrospect) he viewed as highly significant. They are not so auspicious, however, if one is aware that the energy of *kundalini*, once awakened (if yogically induced), transmits to others with the same syndromes – like calls to like.

Irina Tweedie's group at that period was kept secret, and no-one could join it save with the invisible permission of Bhai Sahib, which was individually sought by Tweedie in meditation. One of the young artists, aware of Vaughan-Lee's intensity of aspiration, requested that he might be included, and he was swiftly invited to the meditation group and took Beba along with him (p. 30).

Strangely enough, despite the "explosion" of *kundalini* and the alleged state of *fana*, Vaughan-Lee discloses that he had no thoughts at the time of how the group would be, nor did he mention it to Beba, who was merely aware that they were visiting an old lady for tea. Only retrospectively, many years later, did he recollect and think about these experiences in the light of the stated significance.

The first meeting gave him the sense of "coming home." For once in his life he "belonged," and Tweedie's small room in north London henceforth became his "home," and the group he found there became his "family." There were twelve or so members who met twice weekly for meditation and tea and biscuits, and who animatedly shared their dreams and aspirations and received interpretations and guidance in return.

Even this beneficient situation, however, had its problems. Although Vaughan-Lee lived "from meeting to meeting" and made the group the focal point of his life, spending much of his spare time in between meetings with the members (they would "talk, drink tea, listen to music, and meditate"), he quickly ran into the difficulties created by excessive yoga, too much fasting, and "the pressure of psychological problems." The heightened intensity of group meditations made things worse, the build-up of energy was too great, "the longing desperate." Vaughan-Lee found his body, with its hyper-acute nervous system, an obstacle and a hindrance (p. 32).

According to Vaughan-Lee, the urgent desire to urinate is one of the effects of *kundalini*, and as soon as the group commenced to meditate, this energy would surge within him and produce urinary need to such an extent that he could hardly sit still.

Irina Tweedie talked to the group about Bhai Sahib and her personal experience in India, and at times gave individuals the messages she had received for them from the deceased Bhai Sahib in meditation. It seems quite extraordinary that she did not caution her new pupil against his extremes of behaviour. Instead, he was immersed in yet more meditation. It transpired that the discarnate Bhai Sahib had informed her (as she in turn informed Vaughan-Lee some fifteen years later) that the new pupil should be left alone for *him* (Bhai Sahib) to deal with. *He* would train Vaughan-Lee personally (p. 40). Thus this intelligent and intense young man received no overt guidance, and hurtled headlong into the shattering crisis that awaited him two years hence, a crisis that, with help, could have been avoided.

We are told that Irina Tweedie would not permit any form of personal relationship between herself and her students – that the teacher is always "without a face and without a name," which is directly in contradistinction to her own experience. This doubtless protected her from the acceptance of too much responsibility, yet Vaughan-Lee was convinced that her knowledge and authority was that of the ultimate Reality, and to this assumption, and to Irina Tweedie, he surrendered unreservedly (p. 34).

He writes of the fear that arose with his surrender, a fear of the teacher, confirmed as valid by Tweedie from her own trials with Bhai Sahib. This fear related to the power of the teacher to annihilate the ego, and Vaughan-Lee experienced it over a number of years as he trod the path to his teacher's door. [It is worth considering, however, that his fear may have been through the "blindness" of his own submission, and an innate and suppressed awareness that something was wrong.]

Vaughan-Lee's autobiography is very poetically worded and often devoid of basic descriptive material in terms of psychological experience and more mundane sequences and events. It is also devoid of discrimination, as he makes many assertions *for which at the time* he had no means of confirmation, stating in several places in his text that his observations "bypassed the mind and any judgement," the inference being that he *inwardly* (and unconsciously) recognized the truth of what he later posited.

But was it all truth, or was much of it distortion? A close link with an authentic teacher, in my personal experience, brings the very antithesis of fear. Fear does not enter into the relationship (unless due to the disciple's conscience over some undeclared wrongdoing). And to unconditionally surrender to a teacher and at the same time have fear of that same individual is a contradiction in terms. Egos are not annihilated in the unready, nor in persons in the state of instability and psychological stress of the type that assailed Vaughan-Lee.

An immediate effect of Tweedie's meetings was that Vaughan-Lee gave up reading and dispersed all his books, feeling he no longer had need of them. [Books were to reappear in his life many years later, but at that time he "no longer" sought knowledge in them, only quotations to assist in his literary work. Hence the very large number of selective quotes from traditional Sufi literature which seemingly give strength to his viewpoint.] He accepted Tweedie's dictum that all guidance comes from within, and thus followed in future what came from his "Higher Self."

On his own initiative he gave up his career prospects in architecture and found a job in a café. Yet his abnormal stress levels and digestive troubles meant he could only eat little and as a consequence did not have much energy, so he soon left for something less tiring. He also tried alternative methods of healing, to no effect. His psychological problems were such that at length in despair he requested spiritual advice of his teacher. To his great surprise she suggested he take valium, and said that she herself had frequently found this substance helpful. This he did, and it certainly calmed his nerves and relaxed his body. He felt he was learning the necessity to live a "balanced, everyday life," something he found incredibly difficult.

Valium unfortunately did not assist his recently acquired pattern of insomnia, a condition he describes as a "torture," and for two years he slept no more than two or three hours each night. Sleeping pills did not help either. The active *kundalini* generated an inner energy entirely unmatched to his physical lethargy. One morning Vaughan-Lee suddenly "knew" what was happening. He

223

was being "ground down," was being shown that his life "was no longer" his own. Like an unbroken horse he needed training to attune to the spiritual path and the condition of surrender. At the conclusion of this long drawn-out period, he was quite certain (at least retrospectively) that Bhai Sahib held the reins of his life (pp. 37–40).

This begs the question of the over-indulged disciplines and the formidable *kundalini*. Did Bhai Sahib (who was dead) really require of Vaughan-Lee this particular route? The latter had initially stumbled into this tragic syndrome in youthful ignorance, a syndrome which had effectively ruined his young life. It is hard to believe that any responsible teacher, living or dead, would use these methods for the purposes described. Rather would they require the pupil to cease all disciplines and diets and live normally. There are problems enough arising through the legitimate course of teaching operations to more than adequately serve the requirements of attunement and surrender.

Vaughan-Lee faced yet further devastation. Finding himself "afloat" in the world after leaving architectural college, that world proceeded to fall apart. Continually exhausted and suffering severely with his errant digestive system, all he had aimed for seemed suddenly without meaning. To complete his desolation, his long-term girlfriend, Beba, now deserted him, and not long afterwards she ceased to attend the meditation meetings altogether. Vaughan-Lee dreamt of her return, and found in this longed-for reunion, "tremendous, unbelievable love." He took this dream literally, and when it did not manifest, he was much later convinced that it connected with Bhai Sahib, and was his first intimation of spiritual bliss and of the Beloved. Yet the fact remains that a quite overwhelming love affair awaited him in the future, one leading to his marriage, and thus the dream was conceivably a comforting and precognitive glimpse of that event. Vaughan-Lee, however, comments quite categorically in his autobiography: "Dreamwork, which was to become central to my life's work, began with this first dream of union which took me over ten years to understand" (pp. 42–43).

Following the loss of Beba, Vaughan-Lee suffered an inner "chaos and confusion," an inability to relate to others, a terrifying sense of aloneness, and the psychic awareness of a growing depth of darkness and fear. This latter threatened to swamp him completely, and again in despair he approached his teacher and asked her advice. She told him "not to do anything" – that the fear in time would dissolve through meditation, and he had to learn patience. Thus *more* meditation was unwisely prescribed, not less, and Vaughan-Lee was obliged to endure the consequences.

Perhaps Irina Tweedie assessed this anguished pupil by the limited standard of her own experience, yet the two, as individuals, were entirely different, as any close study of their autobiographical work affirms. He was a striving, highly sensitive aspirant virtually from childhood, and what he manifested is common to many male students of a certain type. In my view Tweedie, who had suffered countless problems herself through the overuse of meditation, failed him disastrously at this crucial juncture.

Sometime during this period, and following several unsatisfying modes of employment, Vaughan-Lee grasped that his life was going nowhere, that his past was in ruins and his future uncertain. All he had left was a love of English literature, and he utilized this by applying for a degree course at a north London college. His application was accepted, and his life soon improved significantly, at first as a student and, much later, as a teacher. But despite this positive change, it manifested largely on the surface, and his interior situation continued as before.

On page 53, Vaughan-Lee expounds upon his personal knowledge and experience of *kundalini*, and corroborates that this energy was awakened in him three years formerly by the practice of Hatha Yoga. He then relates how this and other "energy imbalances" in his body were unexpectedly healed. In the telling he reveals a certain gullibility, the extent of which is conjectural. It seems that for a short while he and other members of Irina Tweedie's Sufi meditation group attended an unaffiliated meditation group "related to the cosmic Christ energy" (this was possibly during the long summer holiday recess when his own grouping closed down). He tells us that the person leading this group "had an inner contact with certain masters who were helping with the evolution of the world." To one of these masters was ascribed the power of healing, and names were brought to the group of those needing help – much in the manner of a Spiritualist absent healing session. Vaughan-Lee mentioned his own problems, and "to his wonder and delight," within two weeks these problems had disappeared (p. 54).

225

This encouraged him to confront his psychological condition (never fully divulged). His diagnosis was that "the dark side of the feminine" was the root cause of the deep feelings of anger and resentment he had always carried within him. These, as he now believed, linked with his maternal situation and were pre-existent to his birth when, from "a world of light" he had fallen into the darkness of the womb and the limitations of his own body. He writes: "The instinctual feminine had imprisoned me in her darkness. I had deep anger at being conceived and born into a world of forgetfulness, into a physical dimension governed by instinct and not spirit" (p. 56). But hand in hand with these lofty assertions was the recognition of his own "inborn arrogance," which stemmed from an "ancient shadow" left over from previous life-times, and was entirely his own.

It is at this point in his autobiography that Vaughan-Lee launches into the complex terminology of Jungian therapy, translating all his trials and symptoms according to the theories of Carl Jung, and leaving Sufism by the wayside. It is quite clear from here onwards that the author's understanding of the process of inner development in relation to the ego and the soul is severely constrained by the limitations of personal ignorance and the total acceptance of all things Jungian. Vaughan-Lee eventually embraces the concepts of Christian mysticism, but as these are all thrown into the same pot, i.e., Jung's conception of psychological individuation as opposed to authentic Sufi insight, it does not take him very far. He was doubtless handicapped by his teacher's use of Jung's work when interpreting dreams, and her astonishing conviction that the *modus operandi* of Sufism equated with Jung's psychological theories, and Kundalini yoga.

Vaughan-Lee had attended college for two years when his psychological problems caught up with him. During the summer recess he agreed to flat-sit for neighbours in their absence, feeling the need "to be totally alone." At first he worked at some outdoor craftwork, enjoying the sunshine in the flower-filled garden and the release from academic studies. As he worked, he became aware of an intense introversion of energy – his attention was drawn more and more deeply inward. He noted also that "energies" began to stream through his body, and that his consciousness was fixed upon their circulation. As he made these obser-

226

vations, the energy commenced to encounter "psychological blocks and hidden pain."

Feeling the driving necessity to stay with this experience, Vaughan-Lee focused fully on what was happening to him, and the process itself led him into what he describes as a "maze of agony." The craftwork was abandoned, and as the days passed, he entered ever more deeply into an exhausting and demanding *via crucis*, during which he remained indoors upon his bed for hours on end.

The pain, according to Vaughan-Lee, belonged to "the very nerves" of his psyche, and constituted an essence of suffering such as he had never before experienced. After ten days or so this reached an apogee, although the participant was unable to describe why, or what it was for. He felt it to be a cleansing process, that the impurities of the *nafs*, or lower self, were being scourged "by pain and inner fire."

The entire description, which runs to several pages, is unsatisfactory, in that whatever the author desires to communicate is unclear. He did not recollect any sense of presence, or any form of reassurance. All he was aware of was his own "ruthless desire" and the unceasing drive that kept him riveted to the task in hand. There was no warmth, no love, no bliss, just an "agony of purification." Out of it all came the consciousness that he was a soul who belonged elsewhere than this planet, to which he had come for a purpose, "to do a certain work." He felt he had been reborn.

At the conclusion of his flat-sitting, which coincided with the culmination of his experience, he wished urgently to see his teacher and share with her the "miracle" of his rebirth. He had not seen her for some time, as the group was closed for the summer recess. Vaughan-Lee anticipated that she would *know* what he had undergone, not recognizing, as he now states, that "she only knew" what was necessary for her work. He had projected a total knowledge onto his teacher, but realized now, by her response, that on the spiritual path one is alone, and must be "empty, merged into emptiness" (pp. 59–64). [This is not my own experience of authentic teachers. They definitely *do* know what is happening to those in their charge.]

It seems quite incredible that Tweedie did not register the state he was in, which must have been quite readily perceptible. He was but a few hours away from attempting to take his own life while under various delusions, and if she detected a trauma, she would surely have sought to take steps for his safety. And if she *did not* detect it, where were her faculties, the supposed tools of her profession? Did she in fact possess such faculties? Or did she rely entirely on "messages" received in meditation?

After his visit to Irina Tweedie, Vaughan-Lee visited his father, and here his experience reached its true climax. He had not grasped that he was in a disoriented state of consciousness and thus "very open" (as he tells us) to what he called the inner prompting of the Self. He began to behave very oddly, to talk in a manner not akin to his normal characteristics. He could not afterwards recall the details, save that he shortly commenced to remove his clothes. He was aware of the shock his father was experiencing, but he "could not stop" either words or actions, which he "knew to be crazy." (He nevertheless attempts to rationalize this event as some form of statement, or expression, of an inner dynamic that was wholly positive).

Vaughan-Lee was bewildered by his dichotomy of experience. His father sent for relatives, all of whom were concerned and perplexed. After they left, he was alone with his father and his sister. The night that followed was "the most terrible" of his life. It was filled with an accusatory voice that grew louder and louder and continually reiterated that he had failed. He now speaks of "inner voices" in the plural, and interjects a past-life memory of his own misuse of spiritual power, and of having to pay a "terrible price." He brought into this life a fear of failure, and the voices now accused him of affecting, not simply himself, but everyone else – that he had flooded the whole world, indeed the entire solar system, with appalling darkness. The petrified Vaughan-Lee was aware that the only way to redeem this failure was by a sacrifice, that of himself. His father's home was a flat on the sixteenth floor of a multi-storied building. During the night, Vaughan-Lee opened a window and prepared to cast himself out. His sister, disturbed perhaps by his presence in her room, "awoke in shock."

The following day, Vaughan-Lee was accompanied to see a psychiatrist, and within hours found himself in a south London nursing home. Whether through sedation, electro-convulsive therapy, or some other factor, he has no memory of the ensuing week, or even longer. It took a while after this to regain his normality, and throughout this period he remained in the nursing home.

His comments on this situation cover several pages. In them he tries to explain what had happened to him, not always very convincingly. Later he was told (by whom he does not say – whether terrestrial or otherwise) that his psychological problems "were being cleansed of their poison."

His account implies that his consciousness fluctuated between states both positive and negative. There were powerful elements of delusion. He speaks several times of rushes of energy in his body, and of exploding energies that created oscillations of experience. This sounds very much like the hyper-activity of an uncontrolled *kundalini* activation, yet Vaughan-Lee does not mention this, perhaps because he really believed that this problem had been "healed." Again, for the second time, he speaks of what he was "told," and on this occasion it is clearly a non-physical communication (p. 71). He "knows" at this juncture that he has been released from all the shackles of this physical world; that he could now die and return unfettered to his "spiritual home." What held him back, he tells us, was the need of his soul to serve humanity. The experience made him "so high" he could scarcely remain on his feet. This entire episode leaves a big question mark. Vaughan-Lee's assertions, on which his current status relies, do not altogether ring true.

Twice when in the nursing home, Vaughan-Lee received electro-convulsive treatment, which is some measure of his condition at the time. He worried about this as he knew it could have damaging after-effects. But he also felt that his Sheikh (Bhai Sahib) would protect him. Since receiving this treatment, however, his memory is sometimes dysfunctional, and he still finds it difficult to recollect past incidents, particularly those that occurred prior to this period. Yet he posits that this blanking of memory could derive from other reasons – spiritual reasons connected with his preparatory development for the task ahead. Even after his return from the nursing home he would "sit for hours without thoughts." All his teacher's talks on "non-being" and "emptiness" had clearly taken root.

This was not a temporary condition. Upon his discharge from the home he went to live at his mother's house, she being the only member of his family available to look after him, and was obliged to take a year off from his college course as his mind "was still on the borders of the beyond." Some people no doubt considered he had undergone a complete mental breakdown. Even his attendance of the Sufi group was very infrequent, a fact in itself surprising.

Once more Vaughan-Lee diligently fasted and spent many nights in meditation and prayer. He was "not altogether present" in the mundane world at all. Mostly, he sat in the "emptiness," unthinking, silent, and alone.

Some months later he began to experience bliss, and would lay on his bed in a state of bliss and emptiness all day long. This continued for a further five months, and his mind then began to resume function. When not in meditation, he read — not "spiritual" books this time, but the entire works of Charles Dickens. Earlier on, in January, Vaughan-Lee dreamt that he would be given his heart's desire, and as he awoke (most curiously, in view of all the foregoing), he knew that his heart's desire was a (formerly unmentioned) woman in Tweedie's group, whom he loved.

In the summer he took voluntary work in a London hospital assisting with menial tasks, and went back to college at the end of September to resume his degree course (p. 74). He also returned to the meditation group and fell deeply in love with his "heart's desire."

Vaughan-Lee describes, in typical Jungian terms interspersed here and there with elements of Sufism, his personal view of what he had undergone; of the healing of his "wounded" relationship with his mother, and the healing of his own psyche. He perceived symbolically in sleep that he needed now to ground himself, to live in the world and not apart from it in isolation of mind and spirit. He notes that many of his problems were bred from arrogance and a sense of superiority; an "egoistic pride" which had now been broken — or so he believed. His love for an earthly form was a tangible expression of this grounding, and one he most readily embraced.

"Falling in love" for Vaughan-Lee was a very complex business. Steeped in Jungian concepts, he speaks of the world of the Goddess; the instinctual round (Ouroborus, the serpent eating its tail); feminine mysteries; the projection of the *anima*; individuation; "shadow" patterns; the Great Mother – and expands upon the difficulties of a physical relationship conjointly operative with a spiritual one (pp. 89–91). There is, of course, no conflict when the mind is functioning normally and interior processes are correctly aligned. Of his wife (whom he adored) he expected an almost impossible perfection, and found it inordinately difficult to reconcile the "Goddess" with the living woman. Passion, too, (to which he makes brief reference), reminded him of more cerebral ecstasies and the need to give *the whole of oneself* to God. This he likened to the mores of mystic love poetry, expressing his view that "there is real reason" why such poetry contains an abundance of erotic imagery (p. 96). Here he exhibits a consistently misplaced eroticism – the transference of one mode into another, to which it does not, and has never belonged, despite the assumed "erotic imagery" of numerous texts – save in the case of those written by tantrists.

He still does not recognize that the "agony of isolation, the desolation of loneliness" can spring from aspirationally-based origins other than the heart experience, which latter arises from a form of spiritual growth he neither describes nor refers to, and presumably, did not undergo. It is *utterly impossible* to equate the stages of this growth with Jungian theory, which in essence circles around personality integration, and even here yields only a partial truth.

The abundance of traditional Sufi anecdotes and quotes in Vaughan-Lee's autobiography is another aspect of his work in need of comment, for these carefully selected extracts relate only to hagiologized accounts of Sufi expertise; the essential core of real interior function is missing, as is any reference to such function.

Much of this chapter, aptly titled "Romantic Love," is incomprehensible to anyone unversed in Jungian terminology or the nomenclature of some relatively obscure contemplative Christian mystics, and conceals as much as it reveals of the author's psychological traumas when living close to another person. The "wounded feminine" is much in evidence.

The dynamic within this archetypal relationship, or marriage, lasted in the form described for seven years. By then Vaughan-Lee knew he "could never be in love again." This phase of his life was over. Once again, he "felt separate from the normal

231

patterns of human life," experiencing instead the "inner loneliness of the mystic." Since that time, he tells us, he has found a greater love (the Divine Beloved), one without "psychological problems" and disparate characteristics (p. 111). From this one could justifiably conclude that his marriage was at an end, but this was not so. Much more was to come, including the upbringing of two children.

In his next chapter Vaughan-Lee describes his advent as a schoolteacher, the birth of his son, Emmanuel, and the eventual purchase of a house in north London with monies disbursed from a family trust. The house was actually two flats, having been altered in the 1960s, and at the suggestion of Vaughan-Lee's wife, the ground floor flat was offered to Irina Tweedie, who at the time lived in rather distressing circumstances (she had even been subject to assault, and was "almost strangled" by a thief who made off with her pension). They were all to live under the same roof for eleven years, a situation which strongly strengthened their relationships (p. 119).

According to Vaughan-Lee, the "energy of the path" and the power of his teacher's presence "permeated" the entire house, and for a time affected the possibilities of an "ordinary" life for the upstairs inhabitants. The atmosphere generated by Irina Tweedie's pronounced proclivity for meditation stilled Vaughan-Lee's mind and rendered it thought-less, which was not very useful for a schoolteacher preparing literary work for senior pupils. Moreover, all the group meetings were held in Tweedie's flat and the climate of meditation greatly accelerated. But having lived for two years in very cramped accommodation, the roomy upstairs abode was both satisfying and fulfilling, and the new owner enjoyed immensely the life of a householder.

He did not rest for long on his laurels, for bitter lessons were to be learned as he duly discovered, some of which he describes in considerable detail. One of the trials of parenthood was the repressed anger Vaughan-Lee discovered within himself, and which was aroused in great measure by his small son, whose strong will "raged" against his own. Soon, with a part-time teaching position and a new baby daughter, Vaughan-Lee found himself for four days each week assisting in all matters domestic, and often taking charge of the older child, Emmanuel. This continually brought forth the angry "shadow" (delineated in depth in

Jungian terms) that caused him to shout explosively "against this small child." The whole episode illuminates Vaughan-Lee's unconfronted psychological difficulties and his as yet inadequate ability to establish control of his own emotions (pp. 127–128).

These problems point to a lack of personality integration that is utterly at variance with the mystical states the author describes. The significations he refers to all indicate inner attempts by the psyche to draw together these fragmented parts and release the impacted energies lodged within them – rather than any form of training for his future role as instructor.

There were shortly to be changes in the meditation groups. Irina Tweedie now kept "open house" for six hours on four days of each week, and held the "closed" group meeting on the fifth. Her work was no longer conducted in private. For two to three years, ten to twelve people had regularly attended, but with the publication of her book *The Chasm of Fire*, numbers began to increase, and anyone was welcome. In later years, Vaughan-Lee records, almost one hundred people at a time would crowd into her flat.

Initially, Vaughan-Lee and his wife took turns to attend on the days he did not teach, as the children had to be cared for. Whereas Anat (his wife) was happy meditating with the group, her husband preferred to meditate in solitude, considering the social trappings of group life unnecessary. He tells us that his meditation was proceeding well and that he had regular daily experience of *dhyana*, "when the mind merges somewhere and one is left in a state of unconsciousness which can seem similar to sleep" (p. 129). He then makes the comment that for "an hour or so" in the afternoon, he would shut himself in his room and "leave the world behind." (This was presumably when he was not in charge of his children).

Dhyana, it seems, and the experience this brought of excluding the world, became utterly essential to him – "a necessary intoxicant" which he likened to a drug. This "precious" time carried him through each day and gave him sustenance.

Family life had drawbacks for Vaughan-Lee, for it drew him out of the meditative state in which he wished to live. He records various incidents from their communal life, yet notes that even in the midst of hectic activities, he frequently felt himself an onlooker, and that although much of his life was closely inter-

233

twined with that of his children, he found having a family "slightly strange," and his focus of attention remained elsewhere (not a surprising statement in view of his continual experiences of *dhyana*). His daughter particularly felt his "inner absence" and lack of involvement, years later dubbing him an "absent parent."

An interesting factor throughout his autobiography is Vaughan-Lee's absorption in his inner life and guidance to the extent of reducing the validity of everyday life and the people living it, and his acceptance of this as natural to a mystic, which he clearly considered himself to be. This remoteness extended even to his teacher, for he records of Irina Tweedie that he was "tremendously in awe of her" and could not relate to her "in any normal human way."

Soon after his marriage, Tweedie gave him a *zikr* for silent inner repetition, a practice which after three weeks became an habitual part of his interior life – such was the intensity of his focus. Whereas *zikrs* had been parsimoniously dispensed at the earlier meetings (and according to Vaughan-Lee, solely upon the instruction of the deceased Bhai Sahib), they were now given to *everyone* entering the group. No reason is offered for this anomaly.

In the following pages, Vaughan-Lee describes the awakening of his inner guidance and the way in which "blocks" and "shadows" were removed from his psyche. It is relevant to note the unusual form in which the guidance was presented, for the *modus operandi* stemmed from the flows of energy in his body and head. He refers once again to the pressures of *kundalini*, and implies that his guidance was the derivative of a process of attunement to this energy. It is also significant that he did not always follow what was indicated, as any desire or "psychological block" could get in the way. In the same section he records the "states and stages" of his heart experience, which went hand in hand with his deepening practises. These, too, seldom follow the traditional pattern as exemplified by Sufi and Christian mystics, nor that of more contemporary writings where gnosis was an accompanying attribute.

A noteworthy point is that psychological blocks and "shadows" pertain to the ego, and the heart experience belongs to the purified psyche in the final phases of the path, long past the stage where such troublesome nuclei find resolution. That Vaughan-Lee experienced certain aspects of the heart experience might be credited, but whether he experienced them out-of-sequence, with all that this implies, is seriously open to consideration.

Living so close to his teacher meant that Vaughan-Lee had opportunities for insight into her personal characteristics, and parallel with his conviction of her total "emptiness" and surrender was his awareness of her essential human-ness and fallibility. He very soon learned that she was not immune from human error, and could be irritated and angry "like anyone else."

When not teaching, Vaughan-Lee began attending the afternoon meetings, and later in the day while their children slept, he and his wife would rejoin the current grouping for the closing hour. As numbers increased, their involvement grew, covering all practical aspects like finding accommodation for visitors, and cleaning Tweedie's burnt cooker and pans when she left something on the stove and forgot it, having lost herself in meditation. This apparently occurred with frequency, and does not say a great deal for her own practicality, particularly as these oversights constituted a fire risk for all concerned (pp. 129–146).

Three years after acquiring his house, Vaughan-Lee had a dream in which he was told to read the works of the psychologist Carl Jung. He accepted this as a genuine instruction and did as he was asked. This directed reading, as he states, formed the basis of his understanding of "spiritual psychology," and became an "integral" part of his future work (p. 149).

On the same page he reveals to the reader the nub of "Naqshbandi" Sufism as taught by Irina Tweedie, recounting how she had studied Jung when she worked as librarian for the Theosophical Society in London, long before she met Bhai Sahib. He describes how Tweedie observed the resemblance between Bhai Sahib's work and Jung's expositions on the process of individuation, and here he quotes certain elements of Jungian psychology – the rejected shadow, for example, and the danger of inflation, all of which Tweedie believed she discerned in Bhai Sahib's training of herself. When, following his death, she started her group in London, she combined Jungian theory and practice with Sufi teachings (the latter no doubt gleaned principally from the book she found on Jalaluddin Rumi), centring her work on meditation and the language of dreams.

As a consequence, Vaughan-Lee through the years absorbed the essence of Jung's formulations, and interpreted his experiences

235

accordingly, e.g., in the light of such concepts as *anima* projection, and the "shadow." Until now, however, he had read none of Jung's books, having put aside all "spiritual" literature on entering the group. And it is at this juncture that his lack of gnosis, or direct knowledge, becomes glaringly apparent.

Vaughan-Lee wholeheartedly accepted Jung's theories as valid truths. He considered Jung spoke with authority and had already made the "inner journey." For ten years, says Vaughan-Lee, he (personally) had immersed himself in inner processes, "confronting the shadow" and much else. Yet he had little consciousness of what was happening to him. Only retrospectively (through reading Jung) did he comprehend (pp. 150–151).

Earlier, when *The Chasm of Fire* was published, in his sixth year with Irina Tweedie, he read the book avidly and fully accepted everything she had written. He queried nothing, neither her level of understanding nor her interpretation of events. The work of Tweedie and Jung formed the basis of his knowledge, which he was later to present to the world as Sufism.

From this point onwards in *The Face Before I was Born*, Jungian terminology holds pride of place. Dreams and events are meaningfully translated in the light of that terminology as the author analyses his own psychological processes and the emergence of his "inner Self." When later, in the midst of various circumstances, Vaughan-Lee decided to utilize his time by taking his PhD, the vehicle he chose for this endeavour was Jungian psychology.

Several months after commencing to research his thesis, and whilst in the reading room of the British Library, Vaughan-Lee ran into a stumbling-block. His mind suddenly blanked, and he ceased to absorb what he read. He returned to his home, lay down on his bed, and sank into the depths of the unconscious. So began a "strange and transformative" phase of his life, when for over a year he daily submerged himself into the deep and primordial "collective unconscious" of mankind, and worked for "an hour or more" with the archetypal images he found there, "healing and transforming" them.

And here one must either mentally part company with Vaughan-Lee, or concede that all that he records as inner guidance and his soul's purpose is as he affirms it to be. It is moreover

236

unclear how the work he mentions is conducted, whether through the "inner journey" type of loose imagery so common to New Age workshops, or something quite other. Vaughan-Lee uses the term "active imagination" coined by Jung, and states that by this means he was able to make a connection with the archetypal dimension. He refers to his Higher Self as the operative agency for the work done, and points out the dangers of entering this archetypal domain unless under the protective guidance of the Self.

The surrealistic quality of the episodes detailed again bear kinship to early phases of *kundalini* activation, particularly when the human system suffers exhaustion from the stresses involved. Vaughan-Lee links these episodes with the work of shamans, which may be so when aided by hallucinogens, but is otherwise unlikely. It is relevant to point out that the acquisition of a higher range of faculties would have rendered this excursion into the Jungian realm of active imagination an unnecessary enterprise.

Vaughan-Lee's academic thesis provided the groundwork for his future role as a teacher. He would rely upon, and employ, Jungian theory in all his dealings with prospective students – those who came to his door in search of spiritual growth. The methods offered, however, (as I must stress) were presented under the name of Sufism, not of Jung, on whose work they were actually based.

It is at this juncture that we learn a little of Irina Tweedie's methods as a teacher, how she would close the group and disappear for unspecified periods, leaving her pupils suspended in states of uncertainty. This was apparently to destroy their expectations and dependence, either upon herself, or upon the group as a regular activity. No notification was given of this – people turned up at her flat to find the door locked, which would cause "quite a shock," particularly if they had travelled long distances to be with her (p. 202). A companion procedure was to ruthlessly eject from the group any student unfortunate enough to become attached to her. To a sensitive aspirant, this harsh "shock" treatment must have been devastating and destructive, and cannot be equated with the treatment sometimes received in metaphysical groupings by individuals with a wholly different type of focus and orientation to that described, and for very specific purposes. These same vulnerable rejects had already been given *zikrs*, too much meditation, and/or were plunged into *dhyana* at each meeting. (Unlike certain other Sufi groupings, which have a time

237

limit and specific aims, Tweedie's groups spread over decades with no evidence of either).

Tweedie allowed the extraordinary practice of her pupils laying on the floor to meditate and, as their numbers grew, so the entire flat and its hall and garden (when fine) became crammed with recumbent bodies. A two-week summer camp in Germany drew six hundred people, and Tweedie's lecturing work in Europe markedly increased as her book became known.

In the June of 1987 came a lecture tour of the USA, officially for the promotion of *Daughter of Fire*, and leading to later tours which were conducted by Vaughan-Lee, as Tweedie now felt too restricted by age for the exhausting demands of such schedules. Two such tours followed yearly, spring and autumn, for the next three years. All were intended to boost *Daughter of Fire* and Tweedie's work. On the first of these, she insisted that Vaughan-Lee's name must appear on the lecture fliers as her successor. The year was 1989, and he was thirty-six years old (p. 241).

His first talk was given at the Esalen Institute, a controversial New Age Centre in California, where he spoke in Jungian terms of the mystic marriage and the realm of the archetypes. His second lecture was held in a New Age "market-place" in San Francisco, where he afterwards presented his first fee-charging workshop on Jungian dreamwork. (Tweedie had said one could charge for anything studied with the intellect, and that he should earn a living from his work).

From San Francisco, Vaughan-Lee and the male friend travelling with him moved on to Georgia and a Christian Jungian Conference. Through his doctoral work on Jungian Archetypal Psychology, he was invited to give talks all over the country on dreamwork. These talks were addressed to audiences of Jungian enthusiasts, despite his promotion as a "Naqshbandi Sufi."

These lecture tours gave him an unrivalled opportunity to put his concepts into practice, namely, the amalgamation of Jungian Psychology, the "heart" aspect of Sufism, and "spiritual" dreamwork. In between tours he wrote on the same subjects, and quite rapidly produced two books, both of which achieved publication.

Throughout his autobiography, Vaughan-Lee speaks in glowing terms of Irina Tweedie: of the love she generated and the powerful energies that flowed through her. It is therefore disconcerting to find on page 216 that she openly says to a friend, in his presence, that he had "hated" her for years. Vaughan-Lee declares that he had not recognized this hidden hatred "until that moment," when he suddenly realized that his ego had resented Tweedie because of her "power and authority," and, most revealingly, because *she was a woman*. The depersonalizing use of the term "ego" is also interesting, as it detaches the human self from the destructive and jealous emotion it had generated, thus making this seem of less significance. This incident aparently occurred about three years after being named as Tweedie's successor.

Vaughan-Lee's descriptions of his spiritual experiences invite some analysis. Most are too amorphous to be impressive, but others indicate a movement within him towards greater insight. There is a dichotomy in these experiences, in that some are recognizable in all genuine aspirants, whereas others apply uniquely to himself, or to a type of experience unknown to the present writer. For example, his delight in a total abstraction of the senses akin to unconsciousness (*dhyana*), and his resentment of his own mental faculties when this daily condition eventually gave place to what he calls a "dual consciousness," a being present in everyday life, and at the same time abiding in some inner space of emptiness. The result was that he was neither completely present in body or in spirit – he frequently hovered in the space in between, unable to speak or move as much as a finger – trapped, as he says, in a meditational state outside his control.

Sometimes this state impinged upon his everyday life, when talking to others. He would pause in mid-speech and merge into a different form of awareness – his mind a total blank or imbued with some form of mediumistic message. He regarded these states as steps towards something more positive – such as the overwhelming love with which he was at times flooded. Nevertheless, another viewpoint is possible. States that proceed from an incorrectly formed basis can on occasion give rise to the (pronounced) dichotomies Vaughan-Lee describes. He speaks of the conscious experience of leaving his ego with all its attributes and expanding into a higher dimension – "the inner emptiness of the Self." Yet upon his return, the ego encloses him just as before, with all its flaws and psychological problems intact (pp. 218–224). The change is not radical or transformative, merely the result of saturation in imaginal exercises and an excess of yogic *dhyana*.

In 1991, Vaughan-Lee took his family to live in America, his intention being to found a "Golden Sufi" Center in California. This event arose unexpectedly and seemingly before time. He had thought to remain in London with Irina Tweedie throughout her lifetime, and to initiate the Center (which they had discussed together) when his succession to her work became operative. Suddenly, while standing one day in their kitchen with his wife, he was "hit by a blast of energy" of such voltage that he all but fell to the floor. At the same moment he registered that it was time for his planned exodus to begin, not at some future date, but now. His wife had seen him stagger, and when he informed her of his new directive, she accepted it. Irina Tweedie, however, was outwardly shocked, though she too accepted the decision, and within two months the Vaughan-Lees had gone.

A notable factor is that the money for this new venture was already in process of donation by large numbers of group members, who were appealed to by Irina Tweedie some months earlier. The previous autumn she had suggested to Vaughan-Lee that he investigate various spiritual centers in America to see how they were run, and in the spring, when his next lecture tour took place, he and those with him found an ideal property for their needs, one identical to the Center Vaughan-Lee had seen in a dream. Despite this augury, the intended purchase unfortunately fell through for some reason just one week prior to his strange experience.

A "blast of energy" seems an extraordinary way to introduce an interior directive, though this is what is claimed. Powerful insights do not normally require such means as being knocked sideways to introduce a shift in consciousness, though random *kundalini* episodes have been known to produce similar effects. The fact remains that the donated money was available and Vaughan-Lee was ready to go; indeed, he *wished* to go, and his inner directive clearly supported this (pp. 261–264).

Eventually a Center was found, and a small publishing business inaugurated. Vaughan-Lee's work expanded – there were meditation meetings, lectures, retreats and group dreamwork, also the writing of books. Yet, curiously, he describes an "essential absence" – that wherever he was, and in whatever he did, his real self was not present, was not "integrating with people and events." Within human relationships he felt an impostor – he could not relate fully to another human being. He likened his condition to that of an empty shell, and also to the Sufi state of *baqa* ("abiding" after the passing away known as *fana*, of which there are various degrees of intensification; for an unusually graphic version, see Meher Baba, *God Speaks: The Theme of Creation and Its Purpose*, second edition 1973, pp. 134ff.). *Baqa* is a state which applies to different levels of development, and fundamentally means the reverse of Vaughan-Lee's predicament – basically involving a complex physicalizing process of integrating and stabilizing the introverted, intensified state of consciousness with normal consciousness, principally achieved by grounding oneself fully in everyday life.

There are lengthy descriptions of his psychological states, all centred on emptiness and lack of involvement, and of the much desired attainment in meditation, in which his whole being is totally dissolved into the emptiness that is his goal.

Much of this he related to an earlier dream which in essence had puzzled him (*The Face Before I Was Born*, p. 255). This was a dream in which the outcome was an effacement, a total annihilation – in which the dreamer was left as a hermit, a mindless "shell" of his former self who becomes just an onlooker on life. He is utterly lost and desolate.

With Jungian fervour Vaughan-Lee dissects this dream and subjects it to analysis, describing at the same time the way it externalized into his consciousness and daily life. The ego still functioned, but there was – sometimes terrifyingly – no sense of personal identity. [He had found, in fact, an empty room in which nothing existed – not even himself.] Yet Vaughan-Lee makes of this condition a mystical statement of some form of Union, and clearly indicates in many passages in his book his conviction of total mergence with his Sheikh, and the use of every aspect of his life and being in service to a greater reality.

Six months after the Vaughan-Lees left London, Irina Tweedie brought to an end her work as a spiritual teacher and closed her meditation group, leaving only a few remnant members with whom she concerned herself. She made known to all participants that her work was continuing through Vaughan-Lee's activities in America. Thus, from this time onwards, he was acknowledged

241

increasingly as a Sufi teacher. In accepting this functional status, he made note of his greatest strengths, or qualities, one being his absolute commitment to Truth, which included a "quality of cruelty" that, "like a knife," would cut quite ruthlessly through any obstruction to his commitment. He compared this "cold, hard, unchanging" quality to "the stamp of the divine executioner" (p. 275). A formidable aspect indeed.

Throughout these latter pages runs the thread of his love for his Sheikh, Bhai Sahib (whom he had never encountered in the flesh), and the mystical states of love and intimacy he experienced. In these he takes the stance that the soul is feminine before God, or when in the presence of the Beloved. Some of his statements here are dubious, equating as they do the erotic with the transcendental. For instance: "The body arches in ecstasy as bliss explodes, bliss upon bliss. . . . every cell seems a woman penetrated by her lover. . . . everything is ravished" (p. 279).

At the end of the book is an account of Vaughan-Lee's dramatic severance from Irina Tweedie, his former teacher. He records in some detail how this came about, and the extremity of Tweedie's anger against himself over certain vexed issues she regarded as vital, and the effects of her accusations upon numerous disciples. At the point of climax of this situation, on a visit to London when Vaughan-Lee and Tweedie were alone, the room in which they were seated became suddenly charged with "tremendous intensity" – and in that moment, which the author transposes into a number of paragraphs, the relationship between himself and Irina Tweedie no longer had consequence – the outer teacher was "totally demolished" and he retreated inwardly to his Sheikh.

He later considered that though Tweedie was not consciously aware of what she was doing, she had played a "masterly part" in releasing him from all outer limitations, having been used as an instrument to take him yet closer to Bhai Sahib (pp. 292–294).

It is, of course, traditional Sufi practice to occasionally blacken a successor before disciples, for reasons not presently under discussion, but of which both parties (teacher and successor) are inwardly fully cognizant. However, if neither Tweedie nor her successor were actually operative on a functional level, and thus not wholly conscious of what was being done (and Vaughan-Lee makes plain his view that Tweedie's responses were instinctual, not *conscious*), then this whole episode takes on a different complexion to that postulated by Vaughan-Lee.

Whether Vaughan-Lee and Tweedie ever met again is not recorded, nor is there mention of a renewal of friendship. Despite the book's copyright date of 1998, Vaughan-Lee re-uses an adapted Foreword written by Tweedie in happier days for his first published book, when she eulogized him as her successor. The date given for this is 1989.

*   *   *   *   *

There is no indication in the writings of Irina Tweedie or Llewellyn Vaughan-Lee that either teacher experienced an overall view of spiritual evolution. Nor do they convey even a basic knowledge of the mechanics of completion of the human entity. Had they attained to such knowledge, it is feasible to assume that they would not have administered technical exercises to all-comers, including raw recruits. They would instead have been fully aware of the dangers of faulty development.

Rather than penetrating primary matters, Vaughan-Lee expressed admiration for the scholarly work of the Islamicist Henry Corbin; this is undoubtedly because Corbin was an admirer of Jung, "and showed how Jung's understanding of the archetypal world of the collective unconscious is mirrored in Sufism." He adds that Corbin's work "has been very influential in certain schools of Jungian psychology, in particular the work of James Hillman and his school of Archetypal Psychology" (*Sufism: The Transformation of the Heart*, p. 27).

Unfortunately, in the view of those with insights at variance to the theories of Corbin, Hillman, and Vaughan-Lee, Jung's understanding of interior development is wholly inadequate, and his methods and conclusions are in no way mirrored in the mysticism of authentic Sufism, or in any other legitimate form of evolutionary metaphysics.

The body of Jung's work is very much a haphazard affair, which he himself changed as new findings and theories were introduced. His methodology does not originate "from above to below" with a comprehensive other-dimensional view of human evolution (as does authentic Sufism) but proceeds from the imaginal recesses of his own subliminal processes, and from the "astral" strata of influences penetrated by trance mediums and occultists.

Jung stumbled into the imaginal realm in his youth. He was himself a classic example of lopsided development, a man who "forced the door" of the interior world by means of trance techniques, hypnosis, automatic writing, and the continuous use of a highly controversial type of psychoanalysis. According to the sources utilized by Richard Noll, the clinical psychologist who authored *The Aryan Christ: The Secret Life of Carl Gustav Jung* (1997), these processes produced in Jung the overwhelming, often terrifying, dreams and visions that for a lengthy period threatened his sanity and brought him close to suicide. Noll records how Jung "kept a loaded pistol next to his bed and vowed to blow his brains out if he ever felt he had entirely lost his sanity" (p. 151).

These experiences contained what Jung accepted as evidence of his own self-deification, information he eventually released to his disciples. In Noll's view, it was the *"highly dissociative"* technique of trance induction that enabled Jung *"to travel to the realm of the gods and talk to entities such as Philemon, the spiritual guru who functioned as his spirit control . . . He had also established an ongoing dialogue with an inner feminine voice that he later called the anima. At times he would allow this female entity to take over his own vocal chords and would spend entire evenings in his study asking questions in his own voice and then answering himself in the falsetto of this entity whom he originally thought was one of the ancient female gods of matriarchal prehistory."* (*The Aryan Christ*, pp. 148–150).

Jung entered his "archetypal" world with his ego and sensual appetite unredeemed and unregenerate, a condition in which distortion and delusion are inevitable, and any truths glimpsed can only at best be partial aspects of the whole. Moreover, he based his researches on data acquired from mentally sick persons undergoing the above-mentioned form of psychoanalysis, most of whom were already institutionalized; or from colleagues in process of that same psycho-analysis, or, more significantly, from his own "mystical" experiences induced in the imbalanced manner above-described.

The life of Jung has been more thoroughly researched than in the selective information made available in his (highly edited) autobiography, *Memories, Dreams, Reflections*. Prominent among the most recent, seriously investigative, publications on Jung, as a man, as a psychiatrist, and as a guru, and essential reading for anyone engaged in utilizing the potentially dangerous dissociative Jungian techniques beloved by therapists and New Age exponents alike, are R. Noll, *The Jung Cult: The Origins of a Charismatic Movement* (1996); R. Noll, *The Aryan Christ* (cited above); and F. McLynn, *Carl Gustav Jung* (1996).

These books elucidate Jung's theories and also his historical background and personal activities in detail, including long-term adulterous relationships; distortions of truth in clinical letters to eminent colleagues; outright advocation of polygamy for personal sexual satisfactions; and (according to well-informed sources) a pronounced, though covert, anti-Semitism. Other important inclusions cover his well-authenticated period of psychosis, and his subsequent creation of a "spiritual cult" of admirers who believed that the collective results of their individual, long-term psychoanalyses could save the world. The foregoing, and much else besides, does not indicate the presence of either spirituality or knowledge.

The introduction of Jungian theory into Sufism is a significant phenomenon: a misplacement of magnitude, and a measure of the deficient knowledge of those who introduced it. Irina Tweedie encouraged Jungian concepts among her pupils whilst at the same time laying great stress on "the way of the heart." She also taught that a teacher, though useful, is not essential; they are simply way-pointers to the methods required to gain contact with the Higher Self.

Another prime mover in the incorporation of Jung's work into areas in which it is inappropriate is Llewellyn Vaughan-Lee, whose disparate writings on the mystical "heart" experience have given him a voice he may not otherwise have had. His placing of this experience in tandem with Jungian analysis and dreamwork has proven entirely acceptable to some Western Sufis. His book, *Sufism: The Transformation of the Heart*, was ecstatically reviewed on the cover by Pir Vilayat Khan in the following words: "In this wonderful book Llewellyn Vaughan-Lee has extracted the quintessence of the emotional springheads motivating Sufi dervishes." He has also extracted the novelty of Jungian theory within the same pages, but the reviewer does not refer to this.

Pir Vilayat is accepted in New Age circles as Head of the Sufi Order in the West, which is how he has presented himself. He is well known for his generosity in dispensing *zikrs*, *chakra* meditations, and other technical practices to anyone attending his lectures and summer camps. Surya Green recalls in *Call of the Sun* how she attended one such camp in the French Alps, and what she experienced:

"Every morning he led us through sunrise and light practices, breathing and purification exercises, mantras and contemplation. . . . Repeatedly we executed together with him a *zikr*, the invocation to remember God by reciting mystical Arabic words while breathing in a certain way and circling the head. One day this lasted five solid hours, Pir's enthusiasm carrying us through 3,000 repetitions of the sacred phrase. When he got up to leave, he was reeling" (*Call of the Sun*, p. 269).

How the others fared is not described. The participants had already been taught a series of exercises "designed 'to force the consciousness into relation with higher planes' . . . and to recite a certain mantra while walking."

Green records that during one session they were told by the Pir, "My main purpose is to give you a cosmic experience, to transport you beyond yourself . . . I will help you force the door." She continues: "Showering us with practices of Sufi background and teachings of various traditions, he aimed to get us into a state in which 'you won't know who you are or where you are'" (p. 270). This type of teaching can best be described as irresponsible, and a proof of incompetence, whatever institutional claims are invoked.

All attempts to "force the door," particularly those associated with breathwork and deliberately induced trance states, are capable of producing flashes of experience from other areas of the self. These may be positive in nature and create lasting faith in other-dimensional existence and the continuity of consciousness outside the frame of human life, and it is these positive attributes which persuade researchers and seekers to persevere in mistaken procedures. But it must always be remembered that these same techniques can also induce alarmingly negative experience which is incomprehensible and traumatic to the individual concerned, the effects of which can be similarly long-lasting. To ignore this fact is the height of folly.

The "heart experience" is subject to equally serious modifications. If induced out of sequence by yogic techniques or other potent practices, the resultant half-fledged experience can negate all possibility of further development. The unprepared ego is only partially burned out, leaving a nucleus of crystallized impressions that bring the experiencer back into unredeemed life in the body but *psychically trapped* between two planes or levels of being.

Bibliography

Albery, N. *How to Feel Reborn?: Varieties of Rebirthing Experience—An Exploration of Rebirthing and Associated
Primal Therapies, the Benefits and Dangers, the Facts
and Fictions*. London: Regeneration Press, 1985.

Anand, M. *The Art of Sexual Ecstasy*. London: Aquarian Press,
1992.

Anderson, S. R. and Hopkins, P. *The Feminine Face of God: The
Unfolding of the Sacred in Women*. Dublin: Gill &
Macmillan, 1991.

Anderson, W. T. *The Upstart Spring: Esalen and the American
Awakening*. Menlo Park, CA: Addison-Wesley Publishing Co., 1983.

Anthony, D., Ecker, B., and Wilber, K. *Spiritual Choices: The
Problem of Recognizing Authentic Paths to Inner Transformation*. New York: Paragon House, 1987.

Avalon, A. (Sir John Woodroffe). *The Serpent Power*. New York:
Dover Publications, Inc., 1974.

Barker, A. T. (ed.). *Mahatma Letters to Mr. Sinnett from the
Mahatmas M. and K. H.* London: T. Fisher Unwin,
1924.

Bhattacharyya, N. N. *History of the Tantric Religion: A Historical, Ritualistic and Philosophical Study*. New Delhi:
Manohar Publications, 1992.

Bohm, W. *Chakras, Roots of Power*. York Beach, ME: Samuel
Weiser, Inc., 1991.

Breaux, C. *Journey into Consciousness: The Chakras, Tantra and
Jungian Psychology*. York Beach, ME: Nicolas-Hays,
Inc., 1989.

Campbell, B. F. *Ancient Wisdom Revived: A History of the Theosophical Movement*. Berkeley, CA: University of Cali-

fornia Press, 1980.

Carter, L. F. *Charisma and Control in Rajneeshpuram: The Role of Shared Values in the Creation of a Community.* Cambridge: Cambridge University Press, 1990.

Castro, S. *Hypocrisy and Dissent within the Findhorn Foundation: Towards a Sociology of a New Age Community.* Forres: New Media Books, 1996.

Chinmoy, Sri. *Kundalini: The Mother Power.* New York: Aum Publications, 1974.

Cohen, A. *An Unconditional Relationship to Life: The Odyssey of a Young American Spiritual Teacher.* Larkspur, CA: Moksha Press, 1995.

Cohen, A. *Autobiography of An Awakening.* Corte Madera, CA: Moksha Foundation, 1992.

Cohen, A. *My Master Is My Self: The Birth of a Spiritual Teacher.* Larkspur, CA: Moksha Press, repr. 1995.

Coney, J. *Sahaja Yoga: Socializing Processes in a South Asian New Religious Movement.* Richmond: Curzon Press, 1999.

Darrel, I. *Serpent of Fire: A Modern View of Kundalini.* York Beach, ME: Samuel Weiser, Inc., 1995.

Donkin, W. *The Wayfarers: Meher Baba with the God-Intoxicated.* Myrtle Beach, SC: Sheriar Press, 1988.

Dunaway, D. K. *Huxley in Hollywood.* London: Bloomsbury, 1990.

Eliade, M. *Shamanism: Archaic techniques of ecstasy.* Princeton University Press, 1974.

Engel, Klaus. *Meditation: Vol. 1 History and Present Time.* Frankfurt: Peter Lang, 1997.

Engel, Klaus. *Meditation: Vol. 2 Empirical Research and Theory.* Frankfurt: Peter Lang, 1997.

Ernst, C. W. *The Shambhala Guide to Sufism.* Boston, MA: Shambhala Publications, Inc., 1997.

Evola, J. *The Yoga of Power: Tantra, Shakti, and the Secret Way.* Rochester, Vermont: Inner Traditions, 1992.

Feuerstein, G. *Encyclopedic Dictionary of Yoga.* London: Unwin Hyman Ltd., 1990.

Feuerstein, G. *Holy Madness: The shock tactics and radical teachings of crazy-wise adepts, holy fools, and rascal gurus.* London: Arkana, 1992.

Franklin, S. *The Promise of Paradise: A Woman's Intimate Story of the Perils of Life with Rajneesh.* New York: Station

250

Hill Press, 1992.

Frost, G & Y. *Tantric Yoga: The Royal Path to Raising Kundalini Power*. York Beach, ME: Samuel Weiser, Inc., 1989.

Gordon, J. S. *The Golden Guru: The Strange Journey of Bhagwan Shree Rajneesh*. Lexington, MA: Stephen Greene Press, 1988.

Green. S. *The Call of the Sun: A Woman's Journey to the Heart of Wisdom*. Shaftsbury, Dorset: Element Books, 1997.

Grof, S. & Grof, C. (eds.). *Spiritual Emergency: When Personal Transformation Becomes a Crisis*. Los Angeles: Jeremy P. Tarcher, Inc., 1989.

Grof, S. *Beyond the Brain: Birth, Death and Transcendence in Psychotherapy*. Albany, NY: State University of New York Press, 1985.

Grof, S. *Realms of the Human Unconscious: Observations from LSD Research*. London: Souvenir Press, 1979.

Grof, S. *The Adventure of Self-Discovery: Dimensions of Consciousness and New Perspectives in Psychotherapy and Inner Exploration*. Albany, NY: State University of New York Press, 1988.

Gyatso, Geshe, K. *Clear Light of Bliss*. London: Tharpa Publications, 1995.

Gyatso, Geshe, K. *Tantric Grounds and Paths*. London: Tharpa Publications, 1995.

Harner, M. *The Way of the Shaman*. San Fransisco: Harper Collins, 1990.

Jong-Keesing, E. *Inayat Khan: A Biography*. The Hague: East-West Publications, 1974.

Karagulla, S. & Kunz, D. *The Chakras and the Human Energy Fields*. Wheaton, Ill: Quest Books, 1989.

Krishna, G. *Kundalini: The Evolutionary Energy in Man*. Boston, MA: Shambhala Publications, Inc., 1985.

Krishna, G. *Kundalini—The Secret of Yoga*. New Delhi: UBS Publishers' Distributors Ltd., 1996.

Krishna, G. *Living with Kundalini: The Autobiography of Gopi Krishna*. Boston, MA: Shambhala Publications, Inc., 1993.

Luhrmann, T. M. *Persuasions of the Witch's Craft: Ritual Magic in Contemporary England*. Oxford: Blackwell, 1992.

M. (trans. Swami Nikhilananda). *The Gospel of Sri Ramakrishna*.

Mylapore, Madras: Sri Ramakrishna Math, 1969.

Malik, A. D. *Kundalini and Meditation*. New Delhi: Manohar Publications, 1994.

Mann, W. E. *The Quest for Total Bliss: A psycho-sociological perspective on the Rajneesh Movement*. Toronto, Ontario: Canadian Scholars' Press, 1991.

Manné, J. *Soul Therapy*. Berkeley, CA: North Atlantic Books, 1997.

Masson, J. *My Father's Guru: A Journey through Spirituality and Disillusion*. London: Harper Collins, 1993.

McLyn, F. *Carl Gustav Jung*. London: Black Swan, 1997.

Meher Baba. *Beams from Meher Baba on the Spiritual Panorama*. Walnut Creek, CA. Sufism Reoriented, repr. 1968.

Meher Baba. *Discourses*. Myrtle Beach, SC: Sheriar Press, 1987.

Meher Baba. *God Speaks: The Theme of Creation and Its Purpose*. New York: Dodd, Mead & Co., repr. 1973.

Melton, J., Clark, J., and Kelly, A. *New Age Almanac*. Detroit, MI: Visible Ink Press, 1991.

Milne, H. *Bhagwan: The God that Failed*. London: Caliban Books, 1986.

Minett, G. *Breath & Spirit: Rebirthing as a Healing Technique*. London: Aquarian Press, 1994.

Mookerjee, A. *Kundalini: The Arousal of the Inner Energy*. Rochester, Vermont: Destiny Books, 1986.

Motoyama, H. *Karma & Reincarnation: The Key to Spiritual Evolution & Enlightenment*. London: Piatkus, 1992.

Motoyama, H. *Theories of the Chakras: Bridge to Higher Consciousness*. Wheaton, Ill: Quest Books, 1995.

Muktananda, Swami. *Play of Consciousness: A Spiritual Autobiography*. New York: SYDA Foundation, 1994.

Mumford, J. *A Chakra & Kundalini Workbook*. St. Paul, MN: Llewellyn Publications, 1995.

Nicholson, S. (ed.). *Shamanism: An Expanded View of Reality*. Wheaton, Ill: Quest Books, 1990.

Noll, R. *The Aryan Christ: The Secret Life of Carl Gustav Jung*. London: Macmillan, 1997.

Noll, R. *The Jung Cult: Origins of a Charismatic Movement*. London: Fontana Press, 1996.

Oppenheim, J. *The Other World: Spiritualism and Psychical Research in England, 1850–1914*. Cambridge: Cambridge University Press, 1985.

Palmer, Louis. *Adventures in Afghanistan*. London: The Octagon Press, 1990.

Paulson, G. L. *Kundalini and the Chakras: A Practical Manual—Evolution in this Lifetime*. St. Paul, MN: Llewellyn Publications, 1977.

Peterson, A. J. *Approach to Reality*. Cambridge: Roseking Publications, 1983.

Powers, John. *Introduction to Tibetan Buddhism*. New York: Snow Lion Publications, 1995.

Puttick, E. and Clarke, P. B. (eds.). *Women as Teachers and Disciples in Traditional and New Religions*. Lampeter and New York: The Edwin Mellen Press, 1993.

Radha, S. *Kundalini Yoga for the West*. Spokane, WA: Timeless Books, 1993.

Radha, S. *Radha: Diary of a Woman's Search*. Porthill, ID: Timeless Books, 1981.

Rajneesh, Osho. *In Search of the Miraculous: Chakras, Kundalini & the Seven Bodies*. Saffron Waldon: C. W. Daniel, 1996.

Rajneesh, Osho. *Tantra Spirituality & Sex*. Rajneeshpuram, Oregon: Rajneesh Foundation International, 1983.

Ramjoo, Abdulla. *Ramjoo's Diaries 1922–1929: A Personal Account of Meher Baba's Early Work*. Walnut Creek, CA: Sufism Reoriented, 1979.

Rawlinson, Andrew. *The Book of Enlightened Masters: Western Teachers in Eastern Traditions*. Chicago: Open Court, 1997.

Ritchie, J. *The Secret World of Cults*. London: Angus & Robertson, 1991.

Rowan, J. and Dryden, W. *Innovative Therapy in Britain*. Milton Keynes: Open University Press, 1988.

Sannella, L. *The Kundalini Experience: Psychosis or Transcendence?* Lower Lake, CA: Integral Publishing, 1987.

Scott, M. *Kundalini in the Physical World*. London: Arkana, 1989.

Shamdasani, S. (ed.). *The Psychology of Kundalini Yoga: Notes of the Seminar Given in 1932 by C. G. Jung*. Princeton, New Jersey: Princeton University Press, 1996.

Shepherd, K. *Meher Baba, an Iranian Liberal*. Cambridge: Anthropographia Publications, 1988.

Shepherd, K. *Minds and Sociocultures: An Analysis of Religious and Dissenting Movements. Volume One: Zoroastrianism and the Indian Religions*. Cambridge: Philosophical Press, 1995.

Silburn, L. *Kundalini: Energy of the Depths*. Albany, New York: State University of New York Press, 1988.

Sivananda, Swami. *Kundalini Yoga*. Rishikesh, India: The Divine Life Society, 1991.

Sloss, R. R. *Lives in the Shadow with J. Krishnamurti*. London: Bloomsbury, 1991.

Storr, A. *Feet of Clay: A Study of Gurus*. London: Harper Collins, 1996.

St. Romain, Philip. *Kundalini Energy and Christian Spirituality*. New York: Crossroad Publishing Co., 1995.

Sviri, S. *The Taste of Hidden Things: Images on the Sufi Path*. Inverness, CA: Golden Sufi Center, 1997.

Tarlo, L. *The Mother of God*. Brooklyn, NY: Plover Press, 1997.

Tart, C. (ed.). *Altered States of Consciousness*. San Francisco: Harper Collins, 1990.

Tart, C. *States of Consciousness*. El Cerrito, CA: Psychological Processes, Inc., 1983.

Thomas, K. *Beloved Executioner. An account of training for seership*. Cambridge: Roseking Publications, 1986.

Thomas, K. *Signals from Eternity: The autobiography of a 20th century mystic*. Cambridge: Roseking Publications, 1984.

Thomas, K. *The Destiny Challenge: A record of spiritual experience and observation*. Forres: New Frequency Press, 1992.

Tweedie, I. *Daughter of Fire: A Diary of a Spiritual Training with a Sufi Master*. Nevada City, CA: Blue Dolphin Publishing, 1986.

Tweedie, I. *The Chasm of Fire: A Woman's Experience of Liberation through the Teaching of a Sufi Master*. Longmead, Shaftsbury: Element Books, 1985.

Vaughan-Lee, L. *In the Company of Friends: Dreamwork within a Sufi Group*. Inverness, CA: Golden Sufi Center, 1994.

Vaughan-Lee, L. *Sufism: The Transformation of the Heart*. Inverness, CA: Golden Sufi Center, 1995.

Vaughan-Lee, L. *The Bond with the Beloved: The Mystical Relationship of the Lover and the Beloved*. Inverness, CA:

Golden Sufi Center, 1994.

Vaughan-Lee, L. *The Face Before I Was Born: A Spiritual Autobiography*. Inverness, CA: Golden Sufi Center, 1998.

Wade, J. *Changes of Mind: A Holonomic Theory of the Evolution of Consciousness*. Albany, NY: State University of New York Press, 1996.

Walsh, R. *The Spirit of Shamanism*. London: Mandala, 1990.

Werner, K. *Yoga and Indian Philosophy*. Delhi: Motilal Barnarsidass, 1989.

Whinfield, E. H. (trans.). *Teachings of Rumi (Masnavi i Ma'navi: The Spiritual Couplets of Maulana Jalalu-d-in Muhammad i Rumi)*. London: The Octagon Press, 1979.

White, J. (ed.). *Kundalini, Evolution and Enlightenment*. New York: Paragon House, repr. 1990.

White, R. *Working With Your Chakras*. London: Piatkus, 1993.

Wolfe, W. T. *And the Sun is Up: Kundalini Rises in the West*. Santa Fe, NM: Sun Books, 1987.

Woodham, A. *HEA guide to Complementary Medicine and Therapies*. London: Health Education Authority, 1994.

Index